Amazon.com®
Mashups

Francis Shanahan

Wiley Publishing, Inc.

Amazon.com® Mashups

Published by
Wiley Publishing, Inc.
10475 Crosspoint Boulevard
Indianapolis, IN 46256
www.wiley.com

Copyright © 2007 by Wiley Publishing, Inc., Indianapolis, Indiana

Published simultaneously in Canada

ISBN-13: 978-0-470-09777-9

ISBN-10: 0-470-09777-9

Manufactured in the United States of America

10 9 8 7 6 5 4 3 2 1

1B/RU/RS/QW/IN

Library of Congress Cataloging-in-Publication Data is available from the Publisher.

For Karen, Sydney, and Ethan, without whom none of this would mean anything.

About the Author

Francis Shanahan

Francis Shanahan is a senior software architect with more than ten years of industry experience. He bought his first computer when he was 12 years old (an Atari 130XE) with money saved from a summer job. Within a month, he had written his first game. He specializes in new and emerging technologies in the areas of Web services, the user interface, and digital identity. Most recent examples are the Windows Communication Foundation (WCF), Windows Presentation Foundation (WPF), and CardSpace. He has led several multimillion dollar engagements for Fortune 50 companies through the full project life cycle. He has published numerous articles in both paper and online media, including Microsoft's MSDN Web site. When he's not building prototypes and messing around aimlessly on the computer, he enjoys cutting dove tails, the pentatonic scale, crystal oscillators, breaking 100 with his Callaway, and spending time with his family. You can contact Francis or read his blog at http://www.FrancisShanahan.com.

Credits

Executive Editor
Chris Webb

Development Editor
Kevin Shafer

Technical Editor
Darrel E. Herbst, Jr.

Production Editor
Felicia Robinson

Copy Editor
Kim Cofer

Editorial Manager
Mary Beth Wakefield

Production Manager
Tim Tate

Vice President and Executive Group Publisher
Richard Swadley

Vice President and Executive Publisher
Joseph B. Wikert

Project Coordinator
Erin Smith

Graphics and Production Specialists
Carrie A. Foster
Brooke Graczyk
Denny Hager
Barry Offringa
Alicia B. South

Quality Control Technician
David Faust

Proofreading and Indexing
Richard T. Evans
Techbooks

Acknowledgments

George Orwell once said, "Writing a book is a horrible, exhausting struggle, like a long bout of some painful illness. One would never undertake such a thing if one were not driven on by some demon whom one can neither resist nor understand". Like Orwell, I was driven to write this book by a force I cannot understand. Indeed, I am driven to do many things by that same force. Unlike Orwell, I had a lot of help to keep me going.

Above all the other people I need to thank I wish to acknowledge my wife Karen's sacrifice. Thanks for all the ways you covered for me so that I could work on this book; for taking the kids to the park so that I could finish up that chapter; for taking them to the toy store so I could write that last line of code. Most of all, thanks for understanding this personal goal of mine, for sharing in it, and for encouraging me when I realized I was in over my head.

Thanks to Sydney and Ethan, who send me to work each day with a smile on my face and welcome me home with hugs and kisses. I'm done guys. Let's roughhouse!!!

Thanks must go to Chris Webb who started me on this path. Thanks, Chris, for pioneering mashups at Wiley. Now, what about that second edition?

Many thanks to Kevin Shafer, my editor, who took my rambling stream of consciousness and provided the guidance that turned it into a legible text.

Sincere thanks to Darrel Herbst, my technical editor, who had the unenviable task of testing all the code associated with this book, ensuring it all worked and that all the technical references made herein are accurate. I could not have trusted it to another.

Thanks to Amazon's evangelist par excellence, Jeff Barr, who despite an enormous workload of his own, always manages to be supportive of the various initiatives I come up with. It was really Jeff and people like him that attracted me to the Amazon Web services platform, more than the services themselves.

And finally, thanks to John Musser of the ProgrammableWeb.com for providing the community with an excellent reference for all things mashup related.

Winston Churchill once remarked, "Writing a book is an adventure. To begin with, it is a toy and an amusement; then it becomes a mistress, and then it becomes a master, and then a tyrant."

I hope you will enjoy reading this book. It spent a short while as an amusement and then jumped straight to being a tyrant. And now finally, in the words of Churchill, I am killing the monster and flinging it out to the public.

Contents

Contents

Contents

Contents

Contents

Contents

Introduction

This book is all about how to take data from disparate sources on the Web and combine that data to make new and innovative applications (affectionately called *mashups*). The Internet is at an inflection point, and all across the Web, more and more sites are exposing their data through Web services and eXtensible Markup Language (XML).

This is great news, because it means *you* as the developer can now build much more sophisticated applications that previously either would not have been possible, or would have required hundreds of developers to create.

This book shows you how to take advantage of these data sources, and combine them to form new and never-before imagined applications. Think I'm kidding? Here are just a few examples of applications that have already been built, most of them by a sole developer:

❑ Craig's List + Google Maps = Interactive maps showing you where apartments are for sale.

❑ Google Maps + 911 call information = Visual representation of where crime is happening in real-time!

❑ Amazon + RSS = Feeds of product reviews that allow you to monitor your favorite products and find out when someone's submitted a review, or when a product goes on sale.

There are two factors influencing mashups as a viable development approach: presentation capabilities and Web service offerings.

Certain techniques such as Asynchronous JavaScript and XML (Ajax) have re-kindled developers' imaginations in terms of what's possible within a browser. Another influencing factor is broadband connectivity. With the advent of faster Internet connections and ubiquitous network access through WiFi, the landscape of possibilities available in the browser has expanded.

Web services and their availability greatly influence the direction of mashups as a development approach because, after all, without the Web service, there is nothing to mash.

At this point, I would say that mashups are in their infancy, but the future of mashups is bright. There are still just a handful of companies offering Web services to the eager developer.

Service-oriented architectures are slowly being adopted by major corporations, and once this happens, new services will begin to appear. With the proliferation of Web services comes the opportunity to combine these services in new and interesting ways.

Microsoft is steadily working on ways to enhance the online experience. These include new platforms and products such as Avalon, eXtensible Application Markup Language (XAML), and Windows Vista. This will open up yet more possibilities in terms of the user experience.

Watch for new developments. As mentioned, the future of mashups is ever-evolving. Mashups are as much a cultural-driven phenomenon as they are a technical one. To stay up to speed requires that you are plugged into the "mashup community." There are countless resources available on the Internet, and I encourage you to go forth and find the ones that appeal to you.

Review new mashups and try to figure out how they're built. If you want to know how something's done, *view the source code*! Every good developer is a good detective, and you should never dismiss your investigative talents.

Mashups were born out of creativity and a need for new forms of information. This book was born out of a need to explain those same mashups. This book should start you on the path to new and exciting adventures with Web services and XML. If you are already on this path, then this book should provide a fresh perspective as to how to apply these tools. In some respects, this is a time of rebirth for the Internet. This book should serve as a useful companion on that journey.

Who This Book Is For

This book is aimed at programmers. Not just server-side gals or user interface guys, I'm talking about the soup-to-nuts programmer. As you'll see, between messaging, presentation, server-side scripting, and so on, there are a lot of moving parts with any given mashup.

Some basic understanding of Web and server technologies is expected. If you're up to speed on XML, Web services, Dynamic Hypertext Markup Language (DHTML), JavaScript, and ASP.NET, then you should have no problems. If not, don't worry. Everything in the book is explained in detail, and because source code is supplied, you should be able to leverage this text regardless of your experience level.

How This Book Is Structured

I am a software architect by trade, and a programmer at heart. I really don't enjoy reading manuals. This book is an easy read, I promise. Each chapter builds upon the previous one, if that's how you prefer to work. Alternatively, I've tried to structure the book so that you can crack it open at any chapter and start slinging code. Sidebars and callouts will provide handy tips and tricks as you go.

This book consists of 16 chapters divided into three parts.

Part I, "A Brave New Web," consists of the following chapters:

❑   *Chapter 1, "Web 2.0"*—This chapter sets the stage by introducing the user to the current state of the Internet from a programmer's perspective.

❑   *Chapter 2, "The Amazon Web Service Platform"*—This chapter continues the theme by exploring the in-roads Amazon has made into Web 2.0 as a concept. This chapter covers not only the eCommerce APIs (which will be the primary focus of the book), but also the other APIs such as the Mechanical Turk and S3 platforms.

❑   *Chapter 3, "Other Mashable Services"*—This chapter widens the developer's perspective by describing some of the more popular Web services that are freely available to the developer. The emphasis is on free technology to lower the barrier for entry. (No one wants to pay just to be able to experiment.)

Part II, "Get Ready to Mash," consists of the following chapters:

❑ *Chapter 4, "Development Tools"*—This chapter sets the stage by describing the recommended programming tools and development environment. The emphasis again is on free tools.

❑ *Chapter 5, "The Technology"*—This chapter describes the various technologies pertinent to the Web 2.0 world. These technologies and their associated acronyms are mentioned throughout the remainder of the book.

❑ *Chapter 6, "Mashup Techniques"*—This chapter provides an overview of the various techniques and theories available for constructing Web-based mashups.

❑ *Chapter 7, "Creating Your First Remix"*—This chapter gets down and dirty by walking you through creation of your first "remix." The example here, while relatively simple, illustrates core concepts such as SOAP API calls, and XML consumption.

Part III, "The Mashups," consists of the following chapters:

❑ *Chapter 8, "Building Your First Mashup"*—In this chapter, you build a search application that consolidates results from Yahoo and Amazon. The results are combined on the server, as opposed to the browser.

❑ *Chapter 9, "Putting the Browser to Work"*—This chapter builds on Chapter 8 by pushing processing down to the user's browser. You'll learn some fundamental JavaScript techniques and build an application that can retrieve data from Amazon or YouTube using REST-style APIs.

❑ *Chapter 10, "An Ajax-Powered Wish List"*—This chapter explains Ajax from soup to nuts. The sample in this chapter queries Amazon for Customer Wish List information, and combines that with live running auctions on eBay.

❑ *Chapter 11, "Let's Eat!"*—This chapter builds on the Yahoo Maps platform to implement a simple mapping utility that plots restaurants in your area. The restaurant data is all supplied by Amazon's Web services.

❑ *Chapter 12, "A Customer Brower Using JSON"*—This chapter illustrates how to use the JSON notation and Dynamic JavaScript to retrieve data from Amazon without the use of a proxy.

❑ *Chapter 13, "Improving Performance"*—This chapter deals with the all-important topic of performance. In this chapter, you'll learn how to execute multiple calls in parallel to perform more work in less time.

❑ *Chapter 14, "Amazon Mobile"*—This chapter shows you how to take what you've learned on the desktop and apply it to mobile devices. You'll build an interface into Amazon accessible from a cell phone or BlackBerry device.

❑ *Chapter 15, "A Generic Storage Solution Using Amazon S3"*—This chapter covers the relatively new storage service from Amazon. You'll learn how to authenticate against this service and store files of up to 5GB in size on Amazon's servers.

❑ *Chapter 16, "Further Ideas"*—This chapter wraps up by walking you through some existing applications built by the author. These all use the techniques taught within this book. This chapter will fuel your creative fire with plenty of examples of what can be done with a little lateral thinking.

The book concludes with the following two appendixes:

❑   *Appendix A, "The E-Commerce Service FAQ"*—Here you'll find a useful reference to some of the more commonly asked questions pertaining to the Amazon Associates program and the Developers community.

❑   *Appendix B, "Exercise Answers"*—Here you'll find answers to the exercises at the end of each chapter.

What You Need to Use This Book

To limit the scope of this book, I have used the Microsoft stack of technologies for most samples. However, the concepts explained here are, in most cases, generic, and can easily be translated into an alternative technology such as J2EE, Python, Ruby, and so on.

C#, .NET 2.0, and ASP.NET 2.0 are the order of the day. Luckily, Microsoft has chosen to make these development tools available free of charge.

I've used Visual Web Developer 2005 Express Edition, which you can download from the following location:

```
http://msdn.microsoft.com/vstudio/express/default.aspx
```

Of course, any version of Visual Studio that supports Web services can be used (for example, Visual Studio 2003). The sample code associated with this book is targeted at Visual Studio 2005.

Example code in this book is all provided in Visual C#. The companion code is comprehensively commented and explained throughout the book. I have purposefully avoided including comprehensive error checking and exception handling in order to illustrate each technique as clearly as possible. The companion code is really just a starting point, and I encourage you to take this code and build upon it as you see fit.

The Visual Basic .NET (VB .NET) developer should not feel left out, because tools are available to convert C# into VB.NET. Consider freely available Open Source tools such as Fidalgo that offer automated conversion of C# into VB.NET.

The companion code does not require an enormous amount of computing power to execute efficiently. A typical development machine with 512MB of RAM will suffice. An Internet connection is essential, however, and, as always, the faster the better, in this case.

Some samples rely on the ability to make files such as XML or eXtensible Stylesheet Language (XSL) files available via the public Internet. A good hosting provider will prove useful in these cases. Hosting is a commodity resource, and you should be able to find a comprehensive Web hosting provider for a very competitive price.

Conventions

To help you get the most from the text and keep track of what's happening, we've used a number of conventions throughout the book.

Try It Out

The "Try It Out" is an exercise you should work through, following the text in the book.

1. They usually consist of a set of steps.

2. Each step has a number.

3. Follow the steps through with your copy of the database.

How It Works

After most "Try It Out" sections, the code you've typed will be explained in detail.

> **Boxes like this one hold important, not-to-be forgotten information that is directly relevant to the surrounding text.**

Tips, hints, tricks, and asides to the current discussion are offset and placed in italics like this.

As for styles in the text:

❑ We *highlight* important words when we introduce them.

❑ We show keyboard strokes like this: Ctrl+A.

❑ We show file names, URLs, and code within the text like so: `persistence.properties`.

❑ We present code in two different ways:

```
In code examples we highlight new and important code with a gray background.
```

```
The gray highlighting is not used for code that's less important in the present
context, or has been shown before.
```

Source Code

As you work through the examples in this book, you may choose either to type in all the code manually or to use the source code files that accompany the book. All of the source code used in this book is available for download at `http://www.wrox.com`. Once at the site, simply locate the book's title (either by using the Search box or by using one of the title lists) and click the Download Code link on the book's detail page to obtain all the source code for the book.

Because many books have similar titles, you may find it easiest to search by ISBN; for this book the ISBN is 978-0-470-09777-9.

Once you download the code, just decompress it with your favorite compression tool. Alternatively, you can go to the main Wrox code download page at `http://www.wrox.com/dynamic/books/download .aspx` to see the code available for this book and all other Wrox books.

Errata

We make every effort to ensure that there are no errors in the text or in the code. However, no one is perfect, and mistakes do occur. If you find an error in one of our books, like a spelling mistake or faulty piece of code, we would be very grateful for your feedback. By sending in errata you may save another reader hours of frustration and, at the same time, you will be helping us provide even higher quality information.

To find the errata page for this book, go to `http://www.wrox.com` and locate the title using the Search box or one of the title lists. Then, on the book details page, click the Book Errata link. On this page, you can view all errata that has been submitted for this book and posted by Wrox editors. A complete book list including links to each book's errata is also available at `www.wrox.com/misc-pages/booklist.shtml`.

If you don't spot "your" error on the Book Errata page, go to `www.wrox.com/contact/techsupport .shtml` and complete the form there to send us the error you have found. We'll check the information and, if appropriate, post a message to the book's errata page and fix the problem in subsequent editions of the book.

p2p.wrox.com

For author and peer discussion, join the P2P forums at `p2p.wrox.com`. The forums are a Web-based system for you to post messages relating to Wrox books and related technologies and to interact with other readers and technology users. The forums offer a subscription feature to email you topics of interest of your choosing when new posts are made to the forums. Wrox authors, editors, other industry experts, and your fellow readers are present on these forums.

At `http://p2p.wrox.com`, you will find a number of different forums that will help you not only as you read this book, but also as you develop your own applications. To join the forums, just follow these steps:

1. Go to `p2p.wrox.com` and click the Register link.
2. Read the terms of use and click Agree.
3. Complete the required information to join, as well as any optional information you wish to provide, and click Submit.
4. You will receive an email with information describing how to verify your account and complete the joining process.

You can read messages in the forums without joining P2P, but to post your own messages, you must join.

Once you join, you can post new messages and respond to messages other users post. You can read messages at any time on the Web. If you would like to have new messages from a particular forum emailed to you, click the Subscribe to this Forum icon by the forum name in the forum listing.

For more information about how to use the Wrox P2P, be sure to read the P2P FAQs for answers to questions about how the forum software works, as well as many common questions specific to P2P and Wrox books. To read the FAQs, click the FAQ link on any P2P page.

Part I
A Brave New Web

In This Part:

Web 2.0

This book deals with Web 2.0 topics. But then again, maybe it doesn't. You see, the problem is that no one really knows what Web 2.0 is. In this chapter, I'll present some thoughts on the matter and then you can decide what it really means to be Web 2.0. Being Web 2.0 or not might not really matter in the end. What you will learn from this book are some cool techniques to take the Web to the next level.

What Is Web 2.0?

Web 2.0 as a term was first coined during a brainstorming session at a conference on Internet technology. The breakout session was the easy part. Web 2.0 as a tangible entity has taken quite a while longer to manifest itself.

In the old days, six years ago (back in Web 1.0), Web sites were well-insulated entities that executed entirely within the browser and well within their own sphere of influence. If you wanted to build a Web site, you thought only of yourself. Users were important, but no one would dare venture so far as to suggest that you let the users tell you what they wanted, or worse still, write the requirements.

Web 2.0 challenges this line of thinking on just about every level. Web 2.0, like art, has no real definition, but you'll know it when you see it. Web 2.0 companies take a different approach to almost every aspect of their business.

Traditional Thinking

A typical approach to starting a business circa 2000 would dictate that you figure out the business you want to be in, conduct a series of brainstorming sessions, document requirements, get some funding, build out your site, and sit back and wait for the money to roll in.

This "forklift" approach demanded a huge investment up front and, of course, venture capitalists were quite happy to oblige. There was also a large amount of effort before the product ever hit the market.

Many companies got their start this way, and huge amounts of venture capital were blown through before dollar one was ever earned. This continued for a number of years (the "salad days," as they say), and then the roof caved in.

For a time, investment ceased, and the general opinion was that the Internet held no more promise as a business platform. This opinion is slowly being changed.

In recent years, the entrepreneurial spirit of the Internet has been rekindled, and smart companies are taking small, gradual steps into new and unconventional business directions. The result is what's commonly referred to as Web 2.0.

There are many elements that contribute to this phenomenon. The remainder of this chapter describes these elements, many of which are explained in detail in subsequent chapters.

Folksonomies

What are folksonomies? The term *folksonomy* refers to the process whereby a group of people collaborate to organize information using an impromptu vocabulary. This can happen anywhere, and it can be either implicit or explicit.

A common example in the corporate world is team-building exercises, whereby a group of individuals rearrange flash cards on the floor or stickies on a white-board. By getting a large group of people's input, you have a higher probability of getting an appropriate classification of the information in question.

How Do Folksonomies Apply to Web 2.0?

In the Web 2.0 world, there is a huge amount of information and it's updated constantly. It would be naive to think that any one company could categorize that information so accurately that the classification would make sense to everyone. Rather, a collaborative approach makes more sense in this instance.

Who better to categorize data than the people closest to it? You've probably participated in folksonomies already without even realizing it.

Amazon now allows users to tag products with keywords. These are words of the customer's choosing and can be completely arbitrary. Over time, this will evolve into its own folksonomy whereby the *users* are adding value for other users simply by using the Amazon site.

This is essentially a self-defining taxonomy, as illustrated in Figure 1-1.

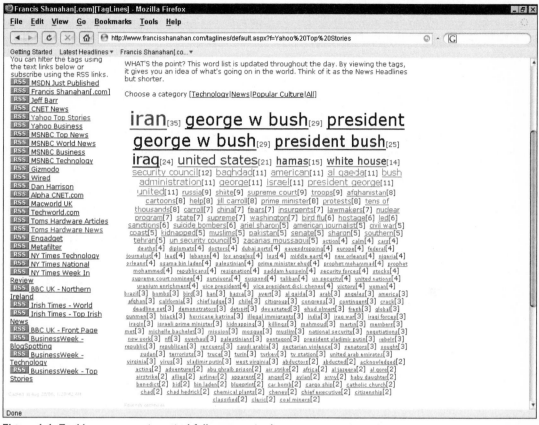

Figure 1-1: TagLines — an automated folksonomy tool

Software as a Service

The Web 1.0 paradigm consisted of a human sitting behind a browser. Sites were not meant to be machine-readable or manipulated. Web 2.0 is about exposing a rich functionality set and much more data. The data is generally accessible to both humans and machines, leading to more automation and derived applications than ever before.

In the "old days," a company would create a service and then package it up in a Web site and publish it out on the Internet. The only way to access that functionality was through the pre-packaged mechanism implemented by the company, usually its Web site.

In the Web 2.0 world, companies are seeing more and more value in offering functionality in reusable and interoperable channels such as Web services. These channels are then handed over to the user for them to do with as they see fit. In essence, a Web 2.0 approach puts more trust in the user than ever before.

Data Is King

The mantra "content is king" has been rewritten as "data is king." Allowing the users to consume data makes it possible to define an entirely new business model and functionality other than those that were originally intended.

Independent developers are now capable of delivering applications that would be impossible without a large team of resources. For example, developers have combined Google Maps with numerous other sources of information to build new and useful applications. It would be very difficult for an individual developer to gather satellite images of the world, or a street map of the entire United States. Yet, Google gives this data away for free.

By making the data available, the *idea* of how to apply this data is what becomes important. This is as it should be. The developer is no longer concerned with basic plumbing and is freed up to think in broader terms of overall application features.

Convergence

At present, applications are diverging from the desktop and being accessed from various devices. The next logical step will be a convergence whereby these various access channels become integrated. My personal guess is that this convergence will be centered around the television.

A *personal media center* is basically a television hooked up to a computer. You can view and record television without the use of tapes. You can view an enhanced programming guide with links out to Internet content. You can view RSS and news headlines on this PC viewing them as television, and so on and so on.

By integrating additional devices into the media center, new usage scenarios are enabled. For example, imagine taking a phone call by pausing live television and broadcasting the audio over your 5.1 stereo system. The television display might show caller ID, combined with a photo of the caller. Finally, the entire call could be recorded for your records, synched with your MP3 player, and published to a personal blog using RSS.

That's just one scenario, and there will be many others. In this book, you learn the techniques necessary to implement such scenarios.

Iterative Development

Rather than use a "forklift" approach to getting functionality out the door, Web 2.0 companies tend to operate in very short cycles of design, develop, launch, get feedback, repeat. This means time-to-market is reduced. Companies purposefully leave features out to achieve shorter cycle times. Rather than guess at what the users want, it's better to launch a small subset of functionality and then take real-world users' feedback. The feedback is then used to drive feature definition in subsequent cycles.

This constant loop of development and product releases is commonly referred to as *perpetual beta*. Rather than delivering a finished product, the application is never complete. It's constantly being iterated on and refined.

By shipping functionality early and more often, a company's projections and estimates become more accurate. The gap between users' needs and a project's requirements is lessened. The value to the users is that they get an application that doesn't attempt to solve *all* their problems, but just some (one or two) of their problems extremely well.

Rich Browser Experience

The browser is the traditional interface to the Internet. Dealing with an application in a browser (versus a rich client installed on the desktop) has typically meant reduced functionality and/or reduced productivity. Pages need time to load. Data is static in the browser until it is refreshed. Advanced controls such as "draggable" grids are not available, and so on and so on.

The arrival of faster Internet access, improved JavaScript support, and the proliferation of Web services have made a rich browser experience possible.

Asynchronous JavaScript and XML (Ajax) is usually top-of-mind whenever anyone mentions Web 2.0 or rich browser experiences. Ajax provides the ability to communicate asynchronously with a Web server while a page is being viewed in a browser. Using Ajax, you can perform partial page updates so that data is kept fresh, even if the user doesn't refresh the page.

You will implement an Ajax powered application in Chapter 10. Ajax is not the only game in town, however, when it comes to enabling a rich experience in the browser.

JavaScript Object Notation (JSON), when combined with some clever JavaScript, can also be used to dynamically update a page's content. Chapter 12 describes how this works and walks you through building a JSON-powered application.

Regardless of what rich Internet application (RIA) features a site might implement, the experience is ultimately more important than the technology.

Multiple Delivery Channels

Most applications start out as Web application–accessible via a standard browser on a desktop or laptop. With the advent of broadly available Internet access via WiFi (and, to some degree, Bluetooth) application functionality is now being delivered more and more through cellular telephones and wireless devices such as the Pocket PC or Palm.

In Chapter 14, you'll build a mobile interface into Amazon's database accessible from a BlackBerry device or a cell phone.

Social Networking

We've all been to dinner parties where you attend despite knowing only a single other person. Through that person, you get introduced to someone else, and, before you know it, you're leaving the party with a series of new business contacts.

The same thing is happening on the Web, except on the Internet, you really don't need to know anyone. Sites such as MySpace, YouTube, and Flickr (Figure 1-2) allow users to create their own personalized areas free of charge and publish content to the same. This was possible in the Web 1.0, too, but not to the same level of sophistication. Interfaces have become far more accessible, and having a personal Web site is no longer the domain of the programmer or advanced user. Literally everyone can enjoy the experience of having an online persona.

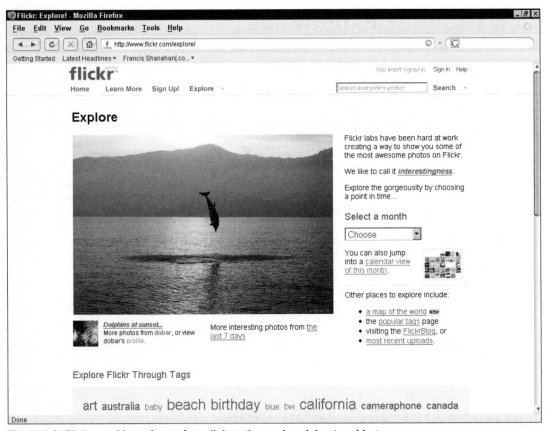

Figure 1-2: Flickr provides a forum for collaboration and social networking

Cross-pollination is also a factor. There is something fundamentally liberating about reviewing or critiquing published content. The psychological effect of publishing one's thoughts in a blog is heightened when a reader comments or links back to that blog.

Bloggers link to other bloggers, and reputations are born. Slowly, a community of real people forms around a given topic. In this manner, the leap is made from a set of technologies such as Hypertext Markup Language (HTML), Hypertext Transfer Protocol (HTTP), eXtensible Markup Language (XML), and so on, to a living, breathing community that enhances people's lives through a sense of belonging.

The Rise of the Individual Developer

Conventional thinking would indicate that to build an application of any great significance, you need a lot of people. Web 2.0 thinking exposes this as incorrect.

Web 2.0 affirms that you can develop a better application, faster, with a handful of developers who know what they are doing. Conversely, nine mothers cannot make a baby in one month.

For example, in the gaming industry, some of the most sophisticated three-dimensional games ever produced have been written soup-to-nuts by just a handful of developers. Doom started the three-dimensional first-person shooter genre, essentially launching an industry, yet it was coded by a small handful of developers.

The most popular mashups and remixes follow a similar pattern. For example, Google Maps (which kick-started the rich browser application movement) was developed by a very small company in approximately two weeks. Productivity and, consequently, business impact is so high because developers have the tools they need on hand, and because, at the end of the day, the developers know what they're doing.

All of the samples in this book have been developed by a single developer, yours truly. These applications are purposefully kept simple so that you can take them and run with them without having to understand a lot of code.

Chapter 16 provides explanations of some more complex applications. These, too, were developed by a single developer, but these applications really try to push the boundaries of what's possible in a Web 2.0 mode of thinking.

Amazon and Web 2.0

Amazon as a company has adopted the Web 2.0 line of thinking with open arms. Having weathered the dot-com bubble, it has its sights fixed firmly on the future, and is making great strides toward defining the direction of its company and, to some degree, the Internet itself.

Amazon and the Consumer

The Amazon consumer Web site offers a wide range of individual features to the customer that, when combined, provide a highly interactive experience. For this reason, Amazon customers tend to be repeat customers, even when prices are cheaper on competitor sites.

Amazon allows customers to review products, tag and categorize them, rate products, and even rate product reviews by other customers.

Over time, a customer can build a reputation as a reviewer. This promotes a sense of ownership on the site. Customers can even publish photos they've taken of products they've bought. This all serves the buyers by providing additional data points that factor into their purchasing decisions.

It doesn't stop there. An Amazon customer can build arbitrary lists of items that they recommend as a group. For example, you could define an "Xbox essential accessories" list that might include all the miscellaneous items such as game controllers, games, cables, and so on, a buyer would need in addition to the core Xbox console.

This is all explicit content contribution. But Amazon also watches its customers' actions and garners information from their patterns. If a customer looks at one product but ends up purchasing another, that's a data point that can potentially influence a buying decision for the next customer. Amazon gathers this data and builds a product ranking, along with auxiliary information that ultimately gets published along with the core product details.

Amazon and the Developer

For the developer, the Web 2.0 thinking is self-evident. Amazon has maintained a Web developers program for a number of years. Amazon provides comprehensive access to its repository of functionality and data. This access is provided free of charge, so developers have a very low barrier of entry. This attitude of embracing developers rather than restricting access is typical of the forward-thinking Web 2.0 culture.

Probably the biggest contributing factor to the success of Amazon's developer program is its ability to build a community around the services. The best services in the world would not be widely adopted were it not for a supporting community, both internal and external to Amazon. Tools are provided such as online documentation and an active developer's forum that encourages developers (both new and seasoned alike) to get their hands dirty. Amazon has recognized that the community around any Web service platform is just as important, if not more so, than the platform itself (Figure 1-3).

With the recent additions of Amazon's Mechanical Turk, Simple Storage Solution, and Elastic Computing Cloud, Amazon has widened its offering far beyond the scope of the original product database. Rather than stick to the core business model of online e-tailor, Amazon is reacting to a need and redefining its business model and business environment as it goes. Again, this adaptability is indicative of the level to which Amazon's leadership has adopted the spirit of Web 2.0.

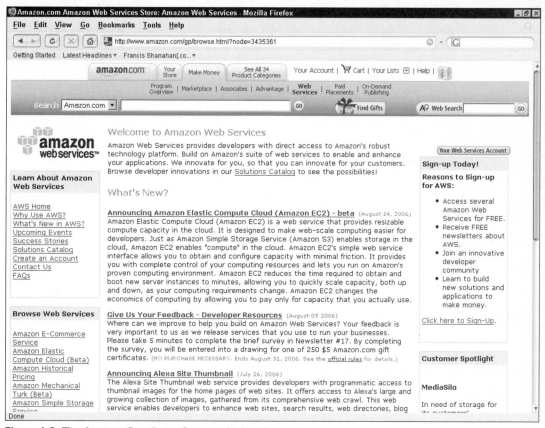

Figure 1-3: The Amazon Developer Community landing page

Summary

The Web is alive and well and more compelling than ever. I once sat in a conference room where one CEO likened the creation of the Internet to the discovery of fire. Now, even with my best propeller hat firmly in place, I think fire was a little more significant. Nevertheless, there is a wealth of opportunity on the Web for developers and business people alike.

This book teaches you everything you need to know to begin leveraging that opportunity with minimal investment.

In the upcoming chapters, you learn about the Amazon Web service platform in detail, along with other offerings from a cast of supporting characters. You learn ways to recombine these offerings into new applications.

In Chapter 2, you learn some fundamentals about how to work with the Amazon E-Commerce Service (ECS), as well as the other services available through the Amazon Developer's Platform.

The Amazon Web Service Platform

Amazon is no longer just one of the leading retailers on the Internet. Amazon has rolled out a comprehensive Web Services platform that pushes it to the front of the technology providers in the world today.

This chapter outlines the major components that make up the Amazon Web Services platform. You learn what types of information and functionality are available, as well as how to go about accessing those services. Subsequent chapters leverage this information in sample applications.

The Amazon Web site is built on a database of literally hundreds of thousands of products. Amazon as a company has had the vision to allow customers to contribute to and enrich this content through reviews and ratings.

When it comes to Web services, Amazon was one of the first to expose its data to the general public. As a result, it has one of the richest suites of Web interfaces available. It offers both free and pay-per-use services for you to play with!

The Amazon Developers Program

To make method calls into Amazon's Web Services platform, it's necessary to participate in the Amazon Developers program. Each API invoked passes a number of parameters, one of which is the developer ID known as the AWSAccessKeyId.

The sample code has a placeholder that you will need to replace with your own AWSAccessKeyId. Whenever you see the words "[YOUR KEY HERE]", replace this in the code with your own AWSAccessKeyId. Failure to do this will mean the application will not work.

Registration is free and you can sign up here:

```
https://aws-portal.amazon.com/gp/aws/developer/registration/index.html
```

You will find that almost all Web platforms (whether it is Amazon, Yahoo, Google, and so on) have developer programs that require registration before you can use the APIs. The good news is almost all of these are free to the non-commercial user.

The E-Commerce Service

The Amazon E-Commerce Service (ECS) exposes Amazon's vast product database. This includes access to customer-contributed content, as well as detailed product information. Not only that, the ECS exposes comprehensive e-commerce functionality for you to build on. An example is the remote shopping cart features that are illustrated in Chapter 10.

The ECS Developer Web site, including reference documentation, sample code, and developer forums is available as a link off of the Amazon Web Services main site located here:

```
http://aws.amazon.com
```

Core Data Types

The main types of data available through ECS are detailed in the following table.

Data Type	Description
Product Data	All things product related. The product database is a world unto itself, and even includes restaurant information.
Customer Content	Any content that a customer might have contributed and marked as public is available through the ECS. This includes Wish Lists, List Mania lists, Wedding Registries, and product reviews.
Seller Information	Amazon also sells products for third parties. You can access ratings and general information about those sellers.
Third-Party Product Information	Products not sold directly by Amazon, but through a third-party seller.
Shopping Cart Contents	Carts are stored on Amazon and accessed remotely. Chapter 10 illustrates how to implement the remote shopping cart.

Interface Types

The Amazon ECS supports both Simple Object Access Protocol (SOAP) and Representational State Transfer (REST) style interactions.

Amazon's implementation of the REST architectural style uses HTTP to transmit all necessary information to execute a query into the ECS. Method calls, parameters, and values are all specified using a simple URL and query string approach. This means you can use a simple Web browser to test your ECS interactions before plugging them into your code.

Try pasting the following URL into the address bar of your browser:

```
http://webservices.amazon.com/onca/xml?Service=AWSECommerceService&AWSAccessKeyId=
[YOUR KEY HERE]&Operation=ItemSearch&SearchIndex=Books&Keywords=Amazon Mashups
```

The result is an XML document containing, in this case, a list of search results. This is how you get data from ECS using REST. SOAP uses a more sophisticated approach, but achieves the same result. You learn more about SOAP and REST in subsequent chapters.

Locales

The Amazon Web site is split into various locales to best serve various parts of the world. It would not be much use for an Irish customer to view product prices in U.S. dollars. Similarly, you can query the ECS for one of the following specific locales:

❑ United States (US)

❑ France (FR)

❑ Canada (CA)

❑ United Kingdom (UK)

❑ Japan (JP)

❑ Germany (DE)

US is the default locale.

The URL in the previous paragraph queried items in the US locale. To change to Japanese, for example, simply modify the root of the URL as follows:

```
http://webservices.amazon.co.jp/onca/xml?Service=AWSECommerceService&AWSAccessKeyId
=[YOUR KEY HERE]&Operation=ItemSearch&SearchIndex=Books&Keywords=Amazon Mashups
```

Note the change from .com to .co.jp. This returns Japanese products. The root URLs for all locales are listed in Chapter 7.

Core Operations on the ECS

Whether you're using the REST or SOAP interfaces, the operations you'll request against the ECS are consistent. The following sections examine the operations available in the ECS, and present a high-level description of each.

Product Operations

Although, strictly speaking, there are only three operations directly related to products, they are deceptively powerful:

- ❑ ItemSearch — Probably the most commonly used operation. This performs a search for a specific item, typically using a set of keywords. Capable of executing advanced queries to narrow results and accurately target searches.

- ❑ SimilarityLookup — Given an Amazon Standard Identification Number (ASIN), this returns a list of similar products based on product specifications and features.

- ❑ ItemLookup — Provides access to all manner of data related to a specific product. Typically used to build detail pages.

Remote Shopping Cart Operations

The following are operations related to the management of remote shopping carts. The cart resides on Amazon's servers; hence, it is remote to your site.

- ❑ CartCreate — Creates a remote shopping cart.
- ❑ CartAdd — Adds an item to the shopping cart.
- ❑ CartGet — Obtains the contents of an existing cart.
- ❑ CartModify — Removes an item from an existing cart.
- ❑ CartClear — Removes all items from an existing cart.

List Operations

These methods let you access things such as Wish Lists, Baby Registries, or other customer-defined lists:

- ❑ ListLookup — Lets you look up the detailed contents of a given list. This operation requires a List ID.

- ❑ ListSearch — Provides a keyword search across lists created by customers.

Customer Content Operations

These operations enable access to content contributed by Amazon's active customer base. This includes reviews, ratings, and Wish Lists:

- ❑ CustomerContentLookup — Used in combination with a CustomerId to retrieve any information contributed by that customer.

- ❑ CustomerContentSearch — Provides a keyword search across customer content, such as reviews or even the "about you" information a customer might have marked as public.

Third-Party Listing-Related

Amazon also provides an avenue for third-party merchants (merchants other than Amazon) to sell items. In many cases, a merchant or seller might have an item that Amazon itself does not stock. In other cases, a seller might have a used or refurbished item. The possibility even exists than a seller will have the same item as Amazon, but for a different price. These operations provide access to that information:

- ❑ SellerListingSearch — Searches for products among third-party merchants selling goods through the Amazon platform.

- ❑ SellerListingLookup — Allows you to look up product details for a given seller.

- ❑ SellerLookup — Retrieves the details of a seller, including an average customer satisfaction rating, location of the seller, and so on.

Miscellaneous Operations

These are operations that don't necessarily fall neatly into one of the previous categories. Nevertheless these operations supply useful information and, thus, have their place in the ECS platform:

- ❑ TransactionLookup — Provides access to a subset of information pertaining to transactions made by an Amazon customer. The data is limited to order totals and sundry information for reasons of confidentiality.

- ❑ BrowseNodeLookup — This operation facilitates navigating the Amazon product hierarchy. See the BrowseNodes overview later in this chapter.

- ❑ Help — Used primarily as a development aid. This operation supplies additional documentation to supplement the developer E-Commerce Service Documentation.

The ASIN

All products in Amazon are identified by the Amazon Standard Identification Number (ASIN). Every product has an ASIN, and every ASIN is unique. ASINs are used all over the place, and once assigned to a product, they rarely change. In fact, you've probably already seen ASINs in action through regular use of Amazon.

The following URI provides the detail page for the movie *Casino* (Figure 2-1).

```
http://www.amazon.com/gp/product/B0007VZ9DK
```

The ASIN in this case is B0007VZ9DK. ASINs are consistent across locales, so, while the previous URI is specific to the US locale, the following URL locates the same product in the UK locale:

```
http://www.amazon.co.uk/exec/obidos/ASIN/B0007VZ9DK
```

If you have the ASIN for a product, you can query the ECS for the product details using the ItemLookup operation.

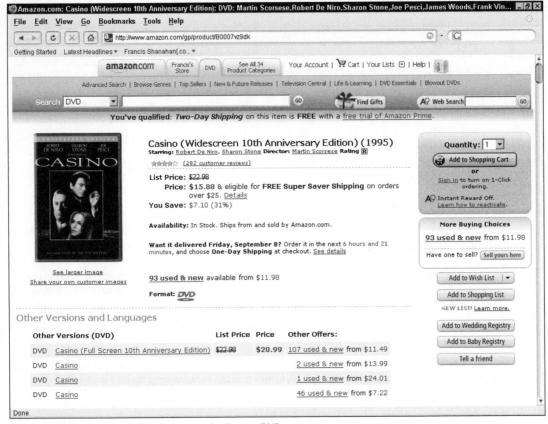

Figure 2-1: The U.S. page for the movie *Casino* on DVD

BrowseNodes

Amazon has a countless number of products. To keep things organized, the products are arranged into categories in a hierarchical structure. You can visualize this structure as an upside-down tree.

The categories in the hierarchy are known as `BrowseNodes`. A `BrowseNode` might contain further `BrowseNodes` underneath it, or it might just contain actual products. For example, the `BrowseNode` "Video Games" might contain "PC Games" and "Xbox 360 Games" as child nodes. Each of these nodes, in turn, might contain further classifications. The further down the tree you go, the more specific the classification.

Products can belong to more than one `BrowseNode` and, thus, be classified in more than one category.

A `BrowseNode` entity typically contains the following properties:

❑   `BrowseNodeID` — The unique identifier for this `BrowseNode` (for "Video Games," the node ID is 468642).

❑   `Name` — The friendly name for the `BrowseNode` (for example, "Video Games").

❑   *Ancestor nodes* — Nodes that are further up the classification. You can navigate to these nodes to broaden the classification (for example, from DVD or Video moving up to "Movies").

❑   *Child nodes* — The next level down in the hierarchy.

Things to Do with BrowseNodes

`BrowseNodes` are a useful tool in your arsenal. Take search as an example. Imagine you are searching for the song "Screwdriver" by the White Stripes.

If you are executing a blanket search across all products for the term "screwdriver," the results returned might include items related to Tools and Equipment, or even how to mix a Screwdriver cocktail!

However, if you know the `BrowseNode` for CDs, you could specify this in the parameters of the search. This limits the search to that product group or its children. Limiting the search with the `BrowseNode` in this manner will be more likely to yield results for the White Stripes than for a hand-tool.

By specifying the `BrowseNode` in an operation, you can more accurately target the execution of that operation.

Required Parameters

You will find that with almost all Web APIs (including Amazon's), certain parameters are required to be passed into each and every method call. This is to enable a stateless implementation on the server side. If the server doesn't maintain state, it can scale more effectively.

Every REST call requires the `Service` parameter to tell Amazon the request is for the ECS service. For ECS, `Service` should be set to `AWSECommerceService`.

Basic ECS request parameters such as the `AWSAccessKeyId` never change and are present in all requests. If you are also an Associate then you should pass in your `AssociateId` to enable tracking and payout of any commissions earned by your application.

Of course, all methods require the name of the desired operation. This is passed in through the `Operation` parameter.

Here's an example REST URL that executes the `ItemSearch` operation for Radiohead-related Music:

```
http://webservices.amazon.com/onca/xml?Service=AWSECommerceService&AWSAccessKeyId=
[YOUR KEY HERE]&Operation=ItemSearch&SearchIndex=Music&Keywords=Radiohead
```

By adding your `AWSAccessKeyId` where specified, you can paste this URL directly into a browser to obtain the XML response.

Listing 2-1 shows the resulting XML response. You'll become intimately familiar with this in subsequent chapters.

Listing 2-1: An Example `ItemSearch` XML Response

```
<?xml version="1.0" encoding="UTF-8"?>
<ItemSearchResponse
xmlns="http://webservices.amazon.com/AWSECommerceService/2005-10-05">
  <OperationRequest>
    <HTTPHeaders>
      <Header Name="UserAgent" Value="Mozilla/5.0 (Windows; U; Windows NT 5.1; en-
US; rv:1.8.0.6) Gecko/20060728 Firefox/1.5.0.6"></Header>
    </HTTPHeaders>
    <RequestId>01DT4VM33K6R7R6R22EW</RequestId>
    <Arguments>
      <Argument Name="Service" Value="AWSECommerceService"></Argument>
      <Argument Name="SearchIndex" Value="Music"></Argument>
      ...
      <Argument Name="Keywords" Value="Radiohead"></Argument>
      <Argument Name="Operation" Value="ItemSearch"></Argument>
    </Arguments>
    <RequestProcessingTime>0.0907800197601318</RequestProcessingTime>
  </OperationRequest>
  <Items>
    <Request>
      <IsValid>True</IsValid>
      <ItemSearchRequest>
        <Keywords>Radiohead</Keywords>
        <SearchIndex>Music</SearchIndex>
      </ItemSearchRequest>
    </Request>
    <TotalResults>340</TotalResults>
    <TotalPages>34</TotalPages>
    <Item>
      <ASIN>B000002UJQ</ASIN>

<DetailPageURL>http://www.amazon.com/gp/redirect.html%3FASIN=B000002UJQ%26tag=ws%26
lcode=xm2%26cID=2025%26ccmID=165953%26location=/o/ASIN/B000002UJQ%253FAWSAccessKeyI
d=[YOUR KEY HERE]</DetailPageURL>
      <ItemAttributes>
        <Artist>Radiohead</Artist>
        <Manufacturer>Capitol</Manufacturer>
        <ProductGroup>Music</ProductGroup>
        <Title>OK Computer</Title>
      </ItemAttributes>
    </Item>
    ...
... Abridged ...
    ...
    <Item>
      <ASIN>B00000735Z</ASIN>

<DetailPageURL>http://www.amazon.com/gp/redirect.html%3FASIN=B00000735Z%26tag=ws%26
```

```
lcode=xm2%26cID=2025%26ccmID=165953%26location=/o/ASIN/B00000735Z%253FAWSAccessKeyI
d=[YOUR KEY HERE]</DetailPageURL>
      <ItemAttributes>
        <Artist>Radiohead</Artist>
        <Manufacturer>EMI</Manufacturer>
        <ProductGroup>Music</ProductGroup>
        <Title>Itch</Title>
      </ItemAttributes>
    </Item>
  </Items>
</ItemSearchResponse>
```

ResponseGroups

When you're building a product details page, you may need to obtain as much information as possible. In your listing screens, however, you might want just the bare minimum. When you make a query to Amazon's ECS, you can tell the platform how much information to send back by specifying a ResponseGroup.

The following table describes a subset of the available ResponseGroups.

Not all ResponseGroups apply to all operations.

ResponseGroup	Description
CartNewReleases	Displays the top five New Releases related to the first product in the cart. So, if the first product in a user's cart is a DVD, you might obtain the top five new releases in DVDs.
CartSimilarities	Provides items similar to the items in the cart. You might have seen these on Amazon listed under the heading "Customers who purchased this item also purchased the following."
CustomerFull	Displays data created by a customer. Typically, this includes customer information such as location, nickname, email address, along with reviews or ratings provided by that customer.
EditorialReview	Supplies Amazon's internal review of a given product if one has been written.
Images	Limits the response to images for a specific product. You might use this ResponseGroup to construct a list page of product thumbnails, for example.
ListMinimum	Returns a minimum amount of product data that can be used to build a lightweight list of search results.
New Releases	Returns the newly released products for a given product category (BrowseNode).
Request	A special ResponseGroup, this provides all parameters that were sent into the original request. You can combine this with other ResponseGroups, for example, to enable pagination of results.
TopSellers	Provides the best-selling products for a given BrowseNode.

Of course, many more `ResponseGroups` are available than listed here. For more information, refer to the Amazon ECS product documentation or Appendix A later in this book.

Becoming an Amazon Associate

To gain access to the Web Services platform, you must sign up as an Amazon developer and obtain an `AWSAccessKeyId`. To actually make money, however, you must sign up as an Amazon associate and obtain an Associate ID. This identifier is then included in every operation made against the ECS.

If users execute a search against Amazon from your site, they can obtain a list of results. Each result points to a detail page for that product. The detail page links will include your `AssociateId`. If a user clicks one of those links and ends up buying the product, you'll earn a commission on the sale.

Here's an example link including my own `AssociateId` (francshanacom-20):

```
http://www.amazon.com/exec/obidos/ASIN/0470097779/francshanacom-
20?creative=327641&camp=14573&adid=12ZZ2PAKY4ZY32Q1B7Q2&link_code=as1
```

Over time, the commissions earned in this manner add up. As an associate, you can choose to be paid in cash, or in the form of an Amazon gift certificate.

Scenarios Enabled by the ECS

The ECS opens a number of business opportunities for both developers and non-developers alike.

The obvious choice for developers is to build a shopping Web site on top of the ECS. Although obvious, this is an approach that has proven very successful. Using the ECS, you can create a specialized store providing enhanced product recommendations centered on a given topic. Following are some examples:

- ❑ *Home audio* — Provide guidance to home audio novices. What products do you need to set up Dolby 7.1 in your living room?

- ❑ *Having a baby* — For prospective parents, what to expect, what products can ease a pregnancy, and what do you really need to bring home a baby?

- ❑ *Movie enthusiasts* — Create a community to review, rate, and recommend hard-to-find DVDs or VHS movies.

By building an enthusiastic community around a topic, cross-selling and product placement become far more effective.

Here are some other ideas:

- ❑ *Novelty store* — Provide a unique shopping experience with enhanced features such as Live Search or Flash. You can drive traffic with a little imagination, or a shopping experience that differs from the norm.

- ❑ *Product image compilation* — The ECS exposes literally millions of product images for almost all of Amazon's products. These can be used as part of a typical shopping experience, or re-purposed to modern art as highlighted in the Zollage project explained in Chapter 16.

❑ *Use the ECS as a data mining tool* — The data contained in the ECS is a really useful resource. You can use it to determine what types of products are selling and where they are selling. You can track product sales rankings over time. You could even aggregate the data into larger sets to derive key performance indicators at the product group level. This type of approach can yield useful and interesting results. For example, you could analyze the seasonal popularity of certain products and target which products your sales model pushes.

The Amazon Developer Web Site

The ECS is not the only Web service offered by the Amazon Web service program. The main Amazon Web Service landing page (Figure 2-2) includes links to a variety of innovative and useful services.

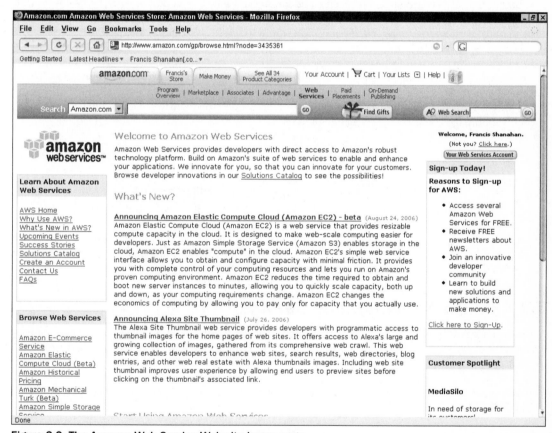

Figure 2-2: The Amazon Web Service Web site home page

The following sections describe the various other services that the Web platform includes.

The Amazon Mechanical Turk

The Amazon Mechanical Turk is a Web service that allows you to submit an operation to be executed, not by a computer, but by the thousands of human beings behind the service. Amazon calls this *artificial artificial intelligence*. That's not a typo. If *artificial intelligence* is computers thinking like humans, *artificial artificial intelligence* is humans performing tasks and supplying the results to a computer.

The name Mechanical Turk comes from a Hungarian named Wolfgang von Kempelen, who, in 1769, invented a mannequin that could play chess. This was quite a feat using 1769 technology. Not only could the automaton play chess, but it beat the majority of its opponents. The secret to the mannequin's prowess, however, was that inside the cabinet on which it sat was a human being directing its every move.

The same technique is used to great effect by the Amazon Mechanical Turk Web service. Employers can submit a task to be completed and specify a dollar amount they are willing to pay. The task is typically a small atomic task that can easily be completed by a human. An example task might be discerning the contents of a photo or writing a text paragraph summarizing the content of a video file.

Workers can then review the tasks available, accept them, complete them, and receive payment. The Web service works by allowing tasks to be submitted programmatically from within an application. That same application can then retrieve the results of the completed tasks as they are finished. To the user of the application, it appears just as if the application had coded the logic to complete the task, when in reality a human is performing the actual logic.

Amazon calls this "Artificial Artificial Intelligence."

Imagine the time and skill it would take to write an application that could reliably tell you what a video file contained? Would it be worth writing such an application? There are many such tasks that require such a high-order of intelligence that it makes more sense for humans to perform them.

The Mechanical Turk can also distribute a huge task among many workers. The results can be tracked and processed as the overall objective approaches completion. In this manner, the Mechanical Turk can provide distributed computing power to the artificial intelligence field.

The Amazon Simple Queue Service

Queues have been used for many years to provide reliable message communication between applications. "Reliable" in this context means that whether or not the recipient of the message is running, the message will be kept safe until such time as the recipient is ready to accept it.

If you place a message in a queue, it's going to sit there until something pulls it off. That's a queue at the 50,000-foot level.

A queuing infrastructure is usually set up internal to a company's network to allow systems and applications to communicate with one another. The Amazon Simple Queue Service (Amazon SQS) takes this concept and brings it to the Internet in a simple-to-use Web service form factor.

By using the Amazon SQS, developers can develop distributed applications and communicate between them in a secure, scalable, and reliable manner. Any machine with Internet access can read from or post to an Amazon queue. The intended recipient can then start up at a different location, at a different time, and read the data sitting on the queue.

Queues can be named and assigned permissions to restrict who has access to reading and writing to them. The Amazon SQS also provides built-in support to avoid deadlock situations, or race conditions where two subscribers attempt to access the same message at the same time.

Any messages posted to a queue are stored redundantly across servers and data centers within Amazon's infrastructure to ensure no data loss. Companies can struggle for years to achieve reliable redundant data storage, so this capability alone is a huge boon to the independent developer.

The Amazon SQS is another pay-as-you-go service, but the incremental charges are incredibly small and are only incurred based on usage of the platform.

The Amazon Elastic Compute Cloud

The Amazon Elastic Compute Cloud (EC2) provides scalable computing power to developers on an as-needed basis. This service lets you build an application and then execute it on Amazon's servers. It's like having your own personal grid computing environment.

The notion of as-needed computing power is best explained with an example. Imagine you have a tough mathematical problem or large amount of data to process. Naturally, the first step to tackle this task might be to create an application to process the data. To run the program you need hardware. That might mean procuring an environment, wiring it, deploying it, and so on. This brings its own challenges in terms of time frames, scheduling, management, people, and so on.

The Amazon Elastic Compute Cloud lets you build an application and run it on Amazon's managed environment. Should your business grow and you need more hardware to process more data, the computing environment can be grown without going back through a procurement cycle. That cuts your time to market from weeks or months to literally hours.

Entire operating systems images, containing the code to execute, can be uploaded and stored on the Amazon Simple Storage Service (S3) and then executed by the EC2.

The EC2 is a pay service, but you are only charged for the CPU time you actually use. The net effect is to lower the barrier of entry to high-end computing power.

Amazon Historical Pricing

The Amazon Historical Pricing Web service is another great data mining service made possible by Amazon's history as a retailer.

Developers can gain access to sales data for books, DVDs, and music for the last three years. By analyzing the price of a given product over a given time period, you can more accurately determine when to push certain products in your store. For example, slippers might tend to sell better around Father's day.

Amazon Simple Storage Service

The Amazon Simple Storage Service (S3) is a way to store files securely on Amazon's infrastructure. The Amazon S3 is accessible via the Internet, so you can access your data from anywhere through an Internet connection.

With this type of scalable storage solution, a number of possibilities are open to the independent developer. These opportunities would have previously required huge amounts of up-front investment (both dollars and time). Possibilities include the following:

- ❏   Build the next YouTube and store the videos on the S3.
- ❏   Grow the next Flickr organically by storing the photos on the S3.
- ❏   Share files with your team members.
- ❏   Reduce your email content by linking to files stored on the S3.
- ❏   Back up your data by storing it on the S3.

Naturally, the interface into the S3 uses Web services and, hence, it's easy to build applications that use the S3 as their data storage repository.

File objects can be up to 5GB in size and, as with the other pay-per-use services, you only pay for the storage and bandwidth used by your application.

As with other Amazon services such as the Mechanical Turk or SQS, comprehensive authentication is layered on top of the S3 service. Files can be stored publicly, or restricted by assigning permissions to individual users or groups of users. All objects stored are accessible via HTTP, which makes for a highly interoperable platform.

Chapter 15 walks you through how to access the S3 and leverage it to build a generic file store that you can then customize or tailor to your own specific application needs.

Alexa

Alexa is an Amazon company that provides Web site and traffic analytics based on data gathered through its Alexa Toolbar. Users download an install the Alexa Browser Toolbar, and data gets fed back to Alexa while the users are browsing. This provides a more accurate gauge of what users are actually doing than traditional Web log analysis.

You can find more information on Alexa at the following URL:

```
http://www.Alexa.com
```

Alexa Web Search Platform

Over the past ten years, Alexa has been crawling the Web and building its repository of Web site data. The Alexa Web Search Platform is a set of Web services (in beta) that provides access to this repository. Developers can use this platform to build their own search engines directly on the massive Alexa data store, or abstract and re-aggregate the data to apply their own data analysis algorithms.

If you are in the market to build a new search engine, but are not interested in the up-front task of crawling the Web, the Alexa Web Search Platform can provide you with a huge jump-start toward your goal.

You can learn more about the Alexa Web Search Platform at the following URL:

```
http://websearch.alexa.com
```

Alexa Top Sites

Alexa Top Sites is a Web service that provides developers access to Web sites ranked according to popularity and traffic. Using this service, you can quickly determine which sites matter for a given topic. Data can be narrowed by individual country to determine where (geographically) traffic is coming from.

Alexa Site Thumbnail

Alexa not only crawls and indexes Internet sites in a traditional Web spidering fashion, but it also takes screenshots of the actual Web sites as they appear in the browser. These screenshots are then stored along with the data gathered about that site. Site screenshots are re-sized to provide convenient thumbnail images of a given Web site.

The Alexa Site Thumbnail Web service allows you to access those screenshots through Web services. This information can be used in concert with the other Alexa Web service offerings to provide enhanced search results for a given set of criteria. Being able to see the Web site in question before clicking a link to visit it gives users a better sense that they have found the site they are looking for (Figure 2-3).

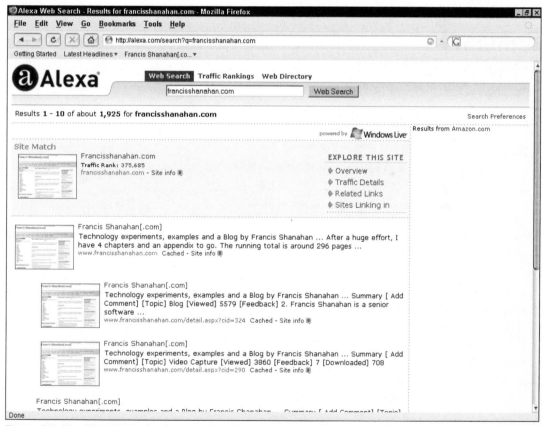

Figure 2-3: The Alexa Web site displaying a list of site thumbnails

The service is constantly being improved, and if you request an image that doesn't exist, Alexa promises to make that thumbnail available within 24 hours.

Alexa Web Information Service

The Alexa Web Information Service provides comprehensive Web site information in a ready-to-use form factor. The Web Information Service can supply your application with everything you would expect in a search engine, such as the following:

❑   *Search engine functionality* — Obtain a list of pertinent sites based on a set of search criteria.

❑   *Browse functionality* — Navigate Alexa's pre-compiled hierarchical directory of Web sites.

❑   *Metadata* — Obtain Web site metadata such as contact information, related links, and so on.

> *The Alexa Web Search Platform provides a lower level of access than the Alexa Web Information Service. If you simply need programmatic access to Web search information, the Web Information Service will better suit your needs.*

Summary

This chapter has laid out the 50,000-foot view of the Web services available through the Amazon Developer Platform, including the services provided by Alexa.

In this chapter you learned the following:

❑   What the ECS is and how to access it

❑   What the main data entities available through the ECS platform are such as Product Details, Search results, Customer Reviews, and so on

❑   What additional services Amazon has to offer

By now, you've gained a broad sense as to the possibilities available in the current Web service environment. Amazon has clearly established itself as a leading technology provider on the Web. This represents a brave move for a company traditionally known as a book store.

In the upcoming chapters, you learn about service offerings being made available by similar forward-thinking companies such as Yahoo, Google, and eBay. You learn more about the ECS, and begin using it to build new and interesting applications. In doing so, you'll implement a variety of mashup techniques and learn how to combine these emerging data sources together.

Chapter 3 describes some of the most popular Web services available today. These services are then used in later chapters to build mashups.

Other Mashable Services

Chapter 2 brought you up to speed on Amazon's Web service offerings. This chapter continues that trend with an overview of platforms from some other companies.

You're priming the pump here. The more services you're aware of, the better. You need this awareness to create mashups. If you're only familiar with a few APIs, you will run out of ideas quickly. If you are familiar with many different Web services from many different providers (at least at a high level), then you can start to imagine new and interesting applications to build out of them.

There are literally hundreds of companies now exposing their data and services through Web services in the hope that developers will take these and create new businesses from them. This chapter covers a few of the more popular services, and also points you in the right direction so that you can find these services yourself.

Yahoo

Yahoo (`http://www.Yahoo.com`) has been fostering the developer community around mashups and Web services for some time now. It has launched a number of useful and innovative offerings beyond its core Web Search API.

Yahoo has a wide array of services available, including Answers, Finance, Search, and Marketing. The main Yahoo services are described in the following sections.

Yahoo Maps

Google first brought the notion of an interactive map to the browser. This was quickly followed by Yahoo's implementation. Now that same concept is mashable by virtue of the Web services built on top of the platform. Using Yahoo Maps, developers can create interactive geographical map applications. Both an Ajax-powered user interface and a Flash interface are supported, and can easily be customized.

Satellite photos, vector-based maps, or hybrid views are available. In Chapters 11 and 12, you'll implement two different mashups involving Yahoo Maps and Amazon. Each application illustrates a different data integration technique (Figure 3-1).

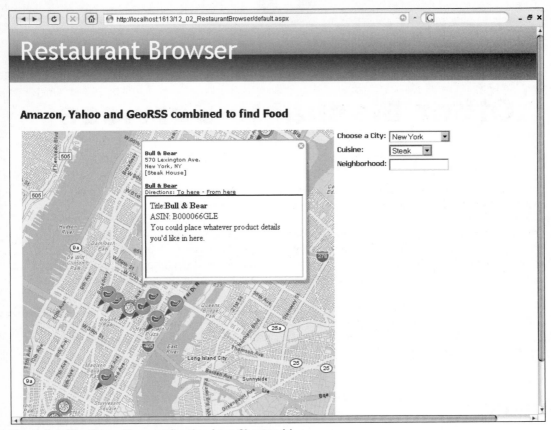

Figure 3-1: The Yahoo Maps application from Chapter 11

Yahoo Search

The Search API is perhaps the core Web service from the Yahoo offering. Yahoo Search provides comprehensive search capabilities that extend beyond the typical text-based search results.

Yahoo Search includes a number of features, with each one, in turn, offering a great deal of functionality. The next few sections list some of the more salient services available.

Audio Search

If you're building an online music store or audio file aggregator, Yahoo Audio Search can help you out. Audio Search provides access to the artist, album, and song information in a structured manner. Once you've found the song you're interested in, the Audio Search service can also provide a list of download locations or online providers for that media.

News Search

News differs from typical Web content in that a news item is typically published in a feed format such as Really Simple Syndication (RSS) or Atom and news stories are updated much more frequently than standard Web content. The Yahoo News service searches registered news publishers to retrieve actual news stories made public by providers such as the Associated Press or the British Broadcasting Corporation (BBC).

Video Search

Video Search provides search results that comprise links to independently hosted video clips. The clips are categorized and indexed just like regular Web content. You can obtain a link to the movie clip, along with a thumbnail of the video generated by Yahoo's servers.

Image Search

Yahoo provides a dedicated search interface into its image catalog. Just as you can search through `Yahoo.com` for image results only, the Image Search interface provides programmatic access to the same data source.

Web Search

As you would expect, the Web Search APIs let you tap into Yahoo's own ready-made search index. Web Search provides you the same result set as the `Yahoo.com` site itself. In this manner, you can incorporate Yahoo search results directly into your application. To further customize the experience, you can gain access to localized search results through the Local Search API.

Local Search provides search results tailored by geography. This can enable a higher degree of relevancy to the user.

Content Analysis

The Yahoo Content Analysis service is extremely useful. It allows you to take a piece of content (such as a paragraph or a blog entry) and submit that content for analysis. The service returns the relevant keywords based on the context of the content. This is a high-order analysis function that is not trivial to implement. By exposing this as a service, Yahoo has provided users with a sophisticated analysis tool for use in construction of its own data categorization algorithms.

Yahoo Traffic Alerts

Traffic Alerts provide real-time access to traffic information. If there's a pile-up on Route 66, or construction on Highway 44, you can find out in advance. This innovative service is available as either a REST-based API or an RSS feed. A link to Yahoo Maps is supplied, complete with map markers for any relevant traffic hot-spots.

In addition to services built on REST- and SOAP-based Web protocols, Yahoo also provides access to a wide range of data through various feed formats such as RSS. Chapter 7 describes RSS in more detail and walks you through implementing your own RSS feed using Amazon data.

Yahoo Shopping

Yahoo aggregates product information from a wide variety of retailers and exposes these results through its main Web site www.Yahoo.com. The same information is available through the Yahoo Shopping services via the Product Web methods. Chapter 8 walks you through using the Yahoo Product Search service to comparison shop with Amazon.

> It's worth noting that Yahoo does not charge for access to any of its Web services. You read that correctly — all Yahoo Web services are free to use. Yahoo takes the approach of limiting the number of calls you can make to any of its services within a specific time frame. This limit, known as a *rate limit*, varies per service and, if exceeded, API calls will be suspended until such time as the rate limit has been renewed.
>
> You sign up for access to the Yahoo Developer Network and learn more about the Yahoo Web services at the following URL:
>
> ```
> http://developer.yahoo.net/
> ```

Del.icio.us

Del.icio.us (http://del.icio.us) is a community-driven site that lets you store links (bookmarks) to your favorite sites online. Links can be categorized, tagged, and classified at will. Because everything's online, you can access your bookmarks from any computer. Over time, your repository builds, and you slowly arrive at a critical mass of sites for a given topic (Figure 3-2).

The genius of del.icio.us is that you can share your favorites with other members of the community. Just like blogging, it's a great way to reach out and make a connection with others. It's also a great way to discover new things and stay up to speed on what's going on in the Internet.

The del.icio.us API is relatively straightforward and to the point. It provides the following functionality:

- ❏ Programmatically retrieve new bookmarks posted by other users
- ❏ Restrict your search by tag or category
- ❏ Add a link to del.icio.us
- ❏ Tag and reclassify existing bookmarks

The del.icio.us developer API is available at the following URL:

```
http://del.icio.us/help/api/
```

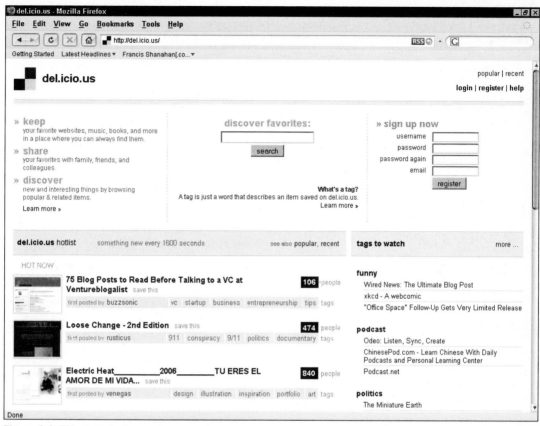

Figure 3-2: The `del.icio.us` **home page**

Technorati

Technorati (http://www.technorati.com) is a blog monitor and aggregator. That means that it tracks individual blogs and provides feed aggregation services on top of the content people are publishing. Technorati currently tracks around 50 million individual blogs. That is a lot of content.

Blogging is all about getting your opinion out there. As such, bloggers often link to and comment on other people's blogs. Technorati takes note of this kind of relationship, and uses it to formulate a ranking of blogs relative to one another. More frequently linked-to blogs are assigned a higher ranking.

Technorati can also be used to aggregate and view content from multiple blogs. As a Technorati user, you can create a list of blogs (commonly known as a *blog-roll*) and be notified when any content on the list is updated.

The Technorati API provides access to this content repository. As a developer, you can use the Technorati API (which is a typical REST-style API) to search and display content in real time as it's published on the Web.

Technorati breaks down into areas of functionality as shown in the following table.

Functionality	Description
Search	You can search blogs by keyword or phrase. You can also query blogs based on the tags associated with them. Lastly, you can search for blogs that link to a given URL, to allow you to build your own relevancy for a given Web site.
Browse	Blogs can be tagged with a given word depending on their content. My blog, for example, might be tagged with the words "mashup," "ajax," "amazon," and so on. Using the Technorati Browse API, you can supply a tag such as "amazon" and view how many blogs are tagged with that keyword.
Blog Information	Comprehensive metadata is available for a given blog, including its ranking and the number of sites linking into it.
User Information	You can query Technorati for information on a given blogger. The information returned includes what blogs that user has authored.

You can register for access to the Technorati Developer program, as well as obtain additional information about its APIs, from the following URL:

```
http://www.technorati.com/developers/
```

Flickr

Flickr (`http://www.flickr.com`) is a community-driven Web site focused around publishing and sharing photos (Figure 3-3). Flickr as a company is owned by Yahoo and, hence, has a rich Web service capability.

The Flickr Web services provide access to photos and related information hosted on the Flicker site. Specifically, you can do the following:

- ❑ Search for photos based on a given keyword or attribute
- ❑ Submit photos as part of Web service call
- ❑ Search for Flickr users and obtain photos posted by those users
- ❑ Obtain a listing of photos tagged with a specific keyword or tag

Flickr supports REST, XML-RPC, and SOAP-based method calls. In addition, it also provides a number of regularly updated XML-based feeds. Unlike the services, Flickr feeds do not require registration. Feeds supply information around recent photos submitted, discussions, and even Flickr News.

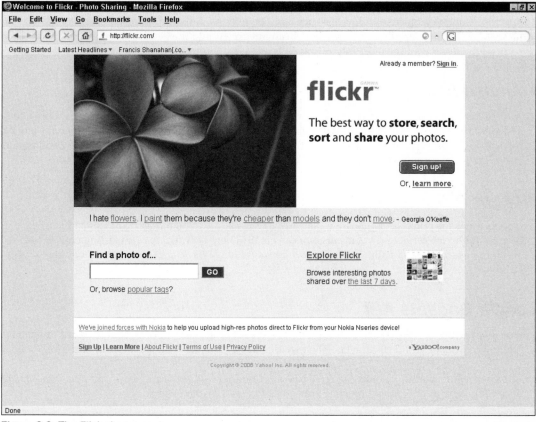

Figure 3-3: The Flickr home page

Here's an example URL that generates an RSS 2.0 format feed of photos tagged with the word "red":

```
http://api.flickr.com/services/feeds/photos_public.gne?tags=red&format=rss_200
```

Flickr users are a talented and passionate community. The ability to incorporate regularly updated photos into your application allows a richer experience for content- and media-driven sites.

You can learn more about the Flickr Web service platform at the following URL:

```
http://www.flickr.com/services/
```

Google

Google (`http://www.Google.com`) is a forward-thinking company. It has taken action to put the tools in the hands of developers to allow them to build on top of its revolutionary platform. Just as Amazon branched out from its original retailer roots, Google has branched out from its core search offering to provide a suite of targeted applications such as Google Maps, AdSense, Google Earth, Google Mail, and so on. Many of these applications have now been integrated into the Google suite of APIs. The following sections detail a few of the more interesting APIs available through Google.

AdSense API

AdSense is Google's advertisement platform and the source of the majority of its revenue. Publishers and subscribers to the AdSense program can now access many of the ad management features (such as reporting), modify ads, and view earnings through the AdSense APIs. This data can then be integrated into third-party applications.

Blogger API

Google owns the popular blog hosting platform `Blogger.com`. The Blogger API lets you manage your blog through Web services. That means you can create a new posting, update existing entries, and so on, and integrate this functionality into your own presentation layer so that users aren't required to visit `Blogger.com` directly.

Google Gadgets API

Google provides a "personalize-able" home page as part of its core offering. That page is available by logging in to Google and clicking "personalize this page" from `www.Google.com` (Figure 3-4).

The Google Personalized Home Page consists of individual Gadgets arranged based on a user's preferences. A gadget might display sports scores, stock quotes, weather, and so on.

Using the Google Gadgets API, you can easily create your own gadgets that can be deployed and registered on the Google homepage. Other users can then leverage these on their personalized Google page.

Google Maps API

Google Maps was hacked soon after launch by an independent developer. Rather than discourage such activity, the community embraced it and mashups were born. At least that's how the story goes. The Google Maps API lets you build your own interactive map applications and display all manner of geographic information within the browser.

Volumes have been written on the Google Maps API as it pertains to mashups. Rather than re-hash existing content, this book illustrates the lesser lauded-over Yahoo Maps API.

Google Toolbar API

The Google Toolbar is a thick client browser plug-in that users install on their machines. The Toolbar API lets you customize this plug-in to add buttons and functionality to the toolbar.

Figure 3-4: The Google Personalized Home Page

Google Web Search API

Google exposes comprehensive search capability to third-party developers through its immensely popular search API. This API provides access to the same repository that powers Google's main site, so you are assured of relevant results every time.

> Google provides sample code in a variety of technologies for most of its Web services. These sample implementations include Perl, Python, Java, PHP, and C#.
>
> The Google APIs are experimental and subsequently free to use. Developers are limited in the number of calls they can execute per day.
>
> Sign up at the following URL to obtain your Google developer keys:
>
> ```
> http://www.google.com/apis/
> ```

eBay

eBay (http://www.Ebay.com) is currently the undisputed leader when it comes to online auctions. You can often find the same item available on eBay as you'd buy in a store for a fraction of the price. eBay has created its own developers' program to allow secure access to the auctions currently being held (Figure 3-5).

Figure 3-5: The eBay developers' Web site

As with Amazon, the eBay Web services supply a comprehensive set of operations to the independent developer. Developers can use these Web services to perform the following actions:

❑ Search active listings by keyword or phrase

❑ Submit a new item for sale on eBay

❑ Re-list an item whose auction did not result in a sale

❑ Obtain the transactions related to a given item listing

❑ Obtain information about a given seller, buyer, or bidder

eBay provides a number of development toolkits in a variety of technologies to suit your individual needs, including Java, .NET, SOAP, XML, and REST.

eBay also supplies a sandbox environment that contains a set of sample data. This sandbox environment can be used to test your application before pointing it against actual live auctions. The ability to unit-test the application in this manner is a boon, and leads to a more predictable rollout with no surprises once in production.

You can register for access to the eBay development platform at the following URL:

```
http://developer.ebay.com/DevProgram/developer/api.asp
```

Chapter 10 shows you how to use the eBay API in concert with Amazon to comparison-shop for the best price.

MSN Search

Perhaps one of the lesser-known Web services, MSN (`http://www.MSN.com`) now provides access to its search catalog via SOAP over HTTP. The service is free to use, although sample code is limited to mostly Microsoft technologies.

Like Google and Yahoo, usage of the service is free and results are comprehensive and useful. One distinguishing feature of this service is the high rate limit on usage. MSN offers up to 10,000 queries per day before throttling comes into effect.

You can access the MSN Search service along with developer forums and usage guidelines through the following URL.

```
http://search.msn.com/developer/
```

411Sync

411Sync (`http://www.411Sync.com`) is a small company with a compelling offering. If you are out and about without access to a computer, you can use your cell phone to search for content through 411Sync.

Developers can register their search applications with the company. 411Sync then acts as a search aggregator or conduit through which users can access these results. 411Sync itself provides the infrastructure to deliver the search results to the mobile device.

411Sync also works with Wireless Access Protocol (WAP) capable devices and standard desktop browsers.

In Chapter 14, you learn how to build a mobile search application of your own using Wireless Markup Language (WML), Amazon, and XML/XSLT.

You can learn more about 411Sync, as well as register your search application, at the following URL:

```
http://411sync.com/
```

The BBC

The British Broadcasting Corporation (`http://www.BBC.co.uk`) now makes programming available via its BBC Web API (beta). Programming and channel information is available, including the programming schedule.

You can use the service to plan your weekly viewing, or just check what's on now. Data is returned in one of two XML formats, the "simple" format or TV-Anytime.

The BBC's Web services are available here:

```
http://www0.rdthdo.bbc.co.uk/services/
```

TV-Anytime is a global association aimed at better leveraging local persistent storage in consumer electronics. The TV-Anytime forum has developed a specification around delivery of programming-related media.

You can learn more about TV-Anytime at the following URL:

```
http://www.tv-anytime.org
```

YouTube

YouTube (`http://www.YouTube.com`) is another community-driven site that hosts short movies and clips from amateur moviemakers. This content tends to be radically original and, in many cases, highly compelling (Figure 3-6).

YouTube provides both REST- and XML-RPC-based access to its APIs. The APIs fall into two main categories: user related and video related.

The user information available through YouTube services includes the following:

- ❑ User profile information
- ❑ Favorite videos for a given user
- ❑ Friends for a given user

The movie-related information available through YouTube includes the following:

- ❑ Searching videos by tag
- ❑ Listing videos for a given user
- ❑ Obtaining a list of currently featured videos

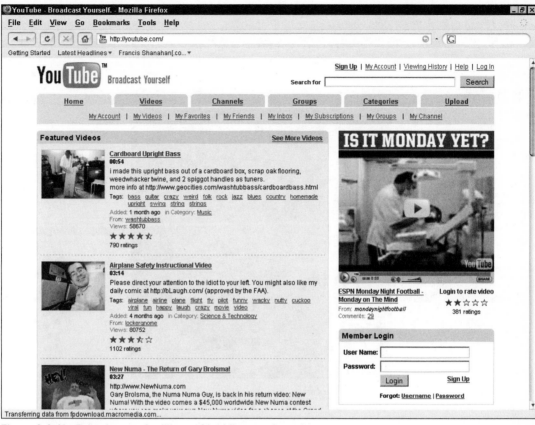

Figure 3-6: YouTube, home of millions of budding movie-makers

Chapter 9 shows you how to combine YouTube movies with Amazon data.

You can learn more about the YouTube developer program and obtain detailed documentation at the following URL:

```
http://www.YouTube.com/dev
```

TerraServer USA

Many years ago, Microsoft partnered with the United States Geological Survey (http://www.usgs.gov) to offer free satellite images of the United States via Web services. This was one of the earliest freely available Web services out there, and is still operating today (Figure 3-7).

Users can request photos in the form of tiles taken at a specific latitude and longitude for a given level of detail. For example, a tile might show a resolution of 1 mile for every pixel in the image. A more detailed tile might contain a resolution of 1 pixel per meter.

Figure 3-7: The Mapping tool built on TerraServer

Although limited to the United States, the content is both excellent and fascinating, and I encourage you to check it out.

Learn more about the TerraServer at the following location:

```
http://terraserver.microsoft.com/webservices.aspx
```

MSN Messenger Activities

MSN Messenger (`http://messenger.msn.com`) is Microsoft's instant messaging client and has an estimated user base of about 29 million active users. That's a lot of people.

MSN Messenger Activities are third-party applications accessible from within the MSN Messenger client. Activities are written as Web pages and can interact with the messenger client through the Messenger Activities API.

Once you've developed a messenger activity, you can register and deploy it for all messenger users to leverage. Alternatively, you can restrict the application's usage to only people you notify.

This approach of enhancing an existing application through a extensible architecture is quite prevalent in the mashup world. By not having to worry about messaging infrastructure, the developer is free to focus on the enhanced functionality brought about by an application.

Rather than being limited to the browser, a new delivery channel, that of the messaging client, is now available. You can learn more about the MSN Messenger Activity software development platform at the following URL:

```
http://msdn.microsoft.com/live/msnmessenger/default.aspx
```

Rhapsody

Rhapsody (`http://www.rhapsody.com`) is an online music provider. Rhapsody serves music to your desktop through its downloadable browser plug-in. Where Rhapsody differs from typical music providers is that Rhapsody does not charge for its service. The entire experience is free. There is no monthly fee and no credit card registration required.

The Rhapsody Web services platform allow developers access to Rhapsody's content. This includes artist and album information, as well as the ability to play music on your site.

Rhapsody's convenient linking scheme makes it easy to link to your favorite albums. An album link is constructed like this:

```
http://play.rhapsody.com/<artist name>/<album name>
```

So, a link to Radiohead's "Hail to the Thief" album would look like this:

```
http://play.rhapsody.com/radiohead/hailtothethief
```

You can also obtain data through RSS feeds using a similar URL structure. The following URL generates a feed of the tracks on Led Zeppelin's fourth album:

```
http://feeds.rhapsody.com/ledzeppelin/236870_ledzeppeliniv/tracks.rss
```

You can learn more about the available Rhapsody Web services at the following location:

```
http://webservices.rhapsody.com/
```

Second Life

Second Life (`http://www.SecondLife.com`) is a different kind of company with a different kind of offering. Second Life provides users with a full-blown three-dimensional world in which to live. Users can buy an area of virtual land within the Second Life meta-verse, and customize it as they see fit. Effectively build on it as you would in real life. You can build yourself a house, buy a car, drive around, talk to others, and carry out your day-to-day life all within the Second Life experience.

This type of virtual reality has been around for some time, but only now is achieving a critical mass of users to make participation worthwhile. You can change your appearance and dress how you'd like. You can set up a store, develop virtual products, and sell your wares. The world supports its own economy with currency and conversion rates between real life and Second Life dollars.

Events are also a major part of the world. Real-life concerts have been simultaneously broadcast into Second Life, allowing people to attend from all over the world. Real-world organizations such as the American Cancer Society have held fund-raising events. Book authors have held virtual signings, and real-world celebrities are beginning to make virtual appearances.

Amazon has also jumped on board by offering live presentations covering its Web service platform from within Second Life (Figure 3-8).

Figure 3-8: Jeff Barr from Amazon presenting within Second Life

Developers can now develop on top of the Second Life platform to integrate third-party site content into the world. Amazon's ECS has already been mashed into Second Life to create a virtual interface into the Amazon store.

With a user base as engaged and active as this, marketing companies are starting to take note. Events attract a highly diverse set of demographics, and a captive audience makes for a great marketing opportunity. As more and more marketers take note of this phenomenon, I expect the opportunities to monetize mashups within Second Life to grow.

Another example has combined `del.icio.us` with Second Life to allow you to bookmark a location with the virtual world, and store that bookmark on `del.icio.us`. Flickr has been mashed in to allow Flickr photos to appear in the virtual world.

Second Life is still in the early stages of development, but clearly the opportunity to create entirely new worlds through mashup techniques exists.

You can learn more about developing for Second Life at the following location:

```
http://www.secondlife.com/developers
```

Local Government

These are just a handful of the services available. Thousands of Web sites are now making content available, including local governments. Consider visiting your local government Web site to see what types of information are out there. You may find your local town is exposing traffic information, Megan's law registrants, or 911 calls via XML.

Summary

You've seen what Amazon has to offer, and this chapter has shown just a tiny fraction of the complementary APIs available. These services fall into all manner of categories, from Music to Search, Mapping to Messaging.

Almost all of these services are free to use, which is a theme I try to stick to in this book. Mashups are about experimentation, and no one wants to have to pay for the privilege.

There is a growing mashup community on the Web, and it generally is not a problem to find a provider of a given Web service. Just think about the *type* of data you need, then figure out who the leaders are in that space. Visit their Web sites; chances are they have a Web service offering.

If you find a company that doesn't yet expose its data to developers, I suggest emailing them and encouraging them to get on board. If you can obtain the content in a well-defined format that is easily parsed and manipulated (such as XML), then you can generally include the content into your application.

Whenever building mashups, take care to ensure that you are not breaching any copyright or usage restrictions with your mashups.

Now that you know what's available, the next few chapters cover the tools, technology, and techniques used to build the samples in this book.

The remaining chapters each focus on a given technique and walk you through building the sample applications that implement those techniques.

In Chapter 4, you'll set up the Visual Studio development environment and build your first application using ASP.NET. This is a great chapter if you're new to Microsoft and ASP.NET development.

Part II
Get Ready to Mash

In This Part:

Development Tools

Before you can create anything, you need a development environment. Although mashups can take many forms (including being either installable applications or Web sites), this book focuses on building mashups in the form of Web sites. For the examples in this book, you'll need specifically a compiler and a Web server.

In this chapter, you install the main development tools and build a sample Web site, complete with navigation and layout framework. In doing so, you'll become familiar with some of the advanced features of ASP.NET 2.0. The resulting Web site can be used as the basis for the other examples later on in the book.

Microsoft Express Editions

Microsoft has always led the way in terms of its Integrated Development Environment (IDE), and now its developer tools are even more accessible than ever before. For the first time ever, Microsoft now provides a free version of the Visual Studio IDE through what it calls the Express Editions. These are slimmed-down versions of the development environment available for download. I say "slimmed down" but you will find these tools to be quite feature-rich and more than adequate for students, hobbyists, and especially mashup developers.

Although this book focuses primarily on the Microsoft platform (including ASP.NET), the techniques described in this book can easily be adapted to a non-Microsoft world, such as LAMP (Linux, Apache, MySQL, and Perl) or Java 2, Enterprise Edition (J2EE).

The Express Visual Studio versions are available from the following location free of charge:

```
http://msdn.microsoft.com/vstudio/express/default.aspx
```

There are a number of tools in the Express suite. Each tool is a standalone product and can be downloaded on its own, if necessary.

Web Development

Mashup concepts are all about interoperability, and they are really technology-agnostic. You can develop Web services and XML in Java or Python just as well as .NET. You are free to use whichever tools you are comfortable with. For simplicity, I'll focus primarily on ASP.NET 2.0 development using Visual Web Developer 2005 Express Edition and, in some cases, SQL Server for database storage. As far as languages go, the examples in this text are provided in C#, although it is relatively easy to translate these into Visual Basic .NET.

Visual Web Developer 2005 Express Edition supports ASP.NET 2.0, C#, and Visual Basic .NET, including a full-featured Web development environment with a WYSIWYG (What You See Is What You Get) editor. This is the main development tool used throughout the book.

> **Visual Web Developer 2005 Express Edition is a real mouthful! For brevity, I will refer to this tool as simply Visual Studio or just Studio.**

If you have not done so already, download and install Visual Web Developer 2005 Express Edition.

Database Development

Inevitably, data storage is necessary to build a meaningful application. Data access is not a primary focus of this book, because you'll deal (for the most part) with *other* people's data. For those cases when data storage is needed, consider SQL Server 2005 Express Edition.

SQL Server 2005 Express Edition provides perfect lightweight data storage without needing to sacrifice features. All solutions developed in SQL Server Express are fully compatible with SQL Server Enterprise. This is great, because you can run the database right on a laptop without needing a huge "big iron" server.

Windows Development

The following tools are used exclusively for the Windows application development. Again, Windows forms can consume Web services just as well as Web forms.

❑ *Visual Basic 2005 Express Edition* — Visual Basic is probably one of the easiest languages to pick up, yet powerful enough to develop production-quality applications. If you are familiar with Visual Basic 6.0, this is the ideal tool for you. For Web applications, use Web Express with VB.NET as the default language.

❑ *Visual C# 2005 Express Edition* — Visual C# is the default language in the Visual Studio suite. You already saw C# mentioned in the "Web Development" section. Visual C# 2005 Express Edition is exclusively for Windows forms development. You cannot create an ASP.NET Web site with this edition of the toolset.

❑ *Visual C++ 2005 Express Edition* — C++ has long been the tool of choice when performance is required. C# has closed that gap significantly, but Visual C++ remains near and dear to many developers' hearts. Microsoft provides this lightweight version of its most popular compiler.

❑ *Visual J# 2005 Express Edition* — Visual J# is not necessarily going to have every J2EE feature the typical Websphere or Weblogic developer is used to but it might be a viable choice for those with prior Java language experience who are switching to Windows development.

A Simple Web Site

At this point you can build a simple ASP.NET page (Figure 4-1) to make sure Visual Studio is set up and working. The next sections build a generic Web site, which is an easy way to familiarize yourself with the Visual Studio IDE. If you are an experienced developer you'll find everything is in its right place. If you are new to Microsoft development, this will help you hit the ground running.

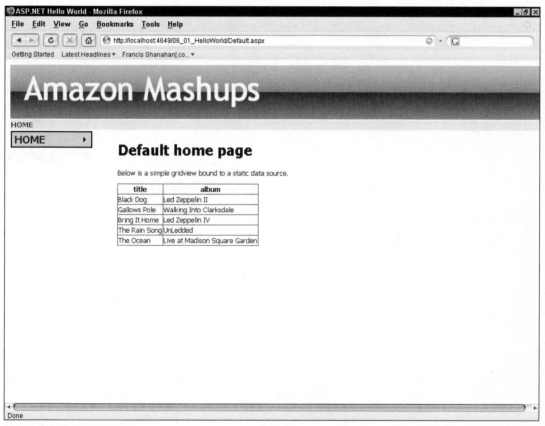

Figure 4-1: The end goal

You don't need Internet connectivity for the example in this chapter. The entire site runs locally on Visual Studio's Web server.

Try It Out   A Simple Web Site

Try creating a simple Web site with a single project and just one page. You'll build on this project throughout the remainder of this chapter.

1. Open Visual Web Developer Express Edition. Choose File→New Web Site (Figure 4-2)

   In the Create Web Site dialog, there are two drop-downs. The first drop-down controls where the project will be stored. There are three options: the file system, a Web server (HTTP), or an FTP server (FTP). You should store the project locally on the file system for now. Choose a location for the project along with a core source code language and click OK.

2. Click OK to create a simple project at that location. Of course, the project contains a single page named `Default.aspx` and little else.

3. Open the default page in the project `Default.aspx` and change to "Design" view (click the button at the bottom of the main window).

4. Type **Hello World** somewhere on the page and press F5 to build and run the solution. You will be prompted to add a `web.config` file to the project. The `web.config` file, as the name implies, stores configuration information for a given Web site, and you need one! Click OK to proceed.

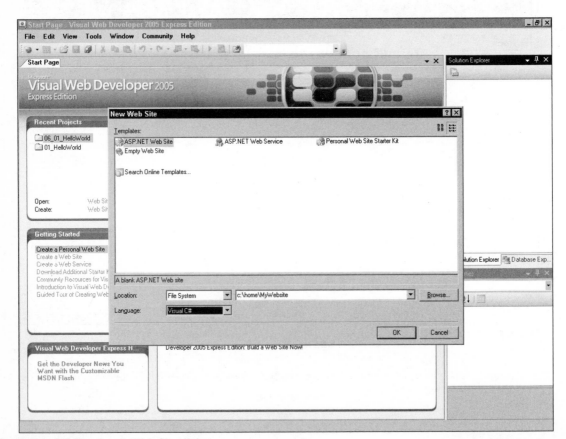

Figure 4-2: The Create Web Site dialog

Language Settings

Web developer source code language defaults to Visual C#. If you prefer coding in Visual Basic, just change the setting when creating the project. This will make every new page added to the project default to Visual Basic. Did you know that in ASP.NET 2.0 you can mix and match languages so that some pages might use Visual Basic and others C#?

The built-in Web server fires up and launches the solution in your default browser, displaying `Default.aspx`. Congratulations!!! You just built your first Web site!

ASP.NET 1.1 developers will notice a number of differences while using ASP.NET 2.0 (the native platform of VS Web Developer). For example, Internet Information Server is no longer needed. Studio installs its own lightweight Web server that is launched for a given project. You will also notice there is no longer a specific "project" file. Studio launches the Web site directly off of the file system. This makes development overhead much lower and makes the entire Web development environment more accessible.

Reviewing the Development Environment

This section reviews some of the features of the IDE. Figure 4-3 depicts the IDE as it appears out-of-the-box.

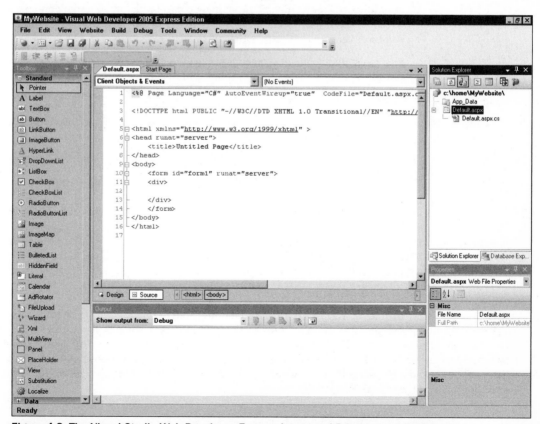

Figure 4-3: The Visual Studio Web Developer Express Integrated Development Environment

The center of the screen shows the particular file being edited. This might show an XML file, an ASP.NET page, the code for a given Web page (C# code), or even just a plain text file.

In the case of an ASP.NET page, the main area displays in either the *Source* or the *Design* view, allowing What You See Is What You Get (WYSIWYG) editing. Sometimes it's nice to be able to edit the page and see what it'll look like right away. In other situations, it's important to be able to edit the HTML or server tags directly. Studio supports both modes. Seasoned developers will be happy to learn that the IDE no longer attempts to format the HTML when switching from Source to Design mode.

On the left-hand side of the screen is the Toolbox window. The Toolbox contains all manner of controls for use on a given page. You can add these controls to your page simply by dragging and dropping from the Toolbox to a page's design surface.

Controls are grouped as shown in the following table.

Group Name	Description
Standard	Contains a default grouping of some of the more frequently used controls from all other sections.
Data	Includes both data access such as the SQLAdapter and data visualization controls such as the GridView.
Validation	Typically used for form validation, these controls allow you to limit entries in a form to specific values or patterns (for example, limiting text entered in a text box to ensure only valid email addresses are entered).
Navigation	Site Navigation features such as breadcrumbs and menus. ASP.NET 2.0 has powerful features here which I explore a little later.
Login	Dedicated set of controls focused around Authentication and Authorization.
WebParts	Portal functionality to let you build highly dynamic pages that the individual users can customize as they see fit.
HTML	Not controls per-se, but simple HTML tags. Sometimes the simplest things are the best.

The right side of the IDE contains the Solution Explorer window along with the Properties window.

In Visual Studio, a set of projects is grouped into a *solution*. A project might be a Web site, a Windows forms application, a Windows service, or simply a console application. Projects related to one another can be logically grouped into a solution. The Solution Explorer allows access to all of the elements of a given project, including all images, ASPX, ASMX, RESX, CS files, and so on.

ASP.NET makes it easy to quickly create a useful site containing a lot of functionality with very little code. Practically every Web site has certain features that are common across pages (for example, the layout, navigation menu, and so on). The next section shows how to build a common layout for your site, using a new feature in ASP.NET 2.0 known as Master Pages. The subsequent sections build on this by adding navigation and a breadcrumb. The resulting Web application can be used as a generic jumping off point for many of the examples in later chapters.

Master Pages

If you're building a Web site, it's a good idea to keep a common layout, look-and-feel, menu, and so on, across the pages of that site. A site where every page is completely different with no common elements makes users feel like they're on a different site with each page transition.

ASP.NET 2.0 solves this problem by allowing each page to be driven off of a Master Page. The common elements are defined in the Master Page, including the page layout. This also eases maintenance of the site. If you use Master Pages, each page driven off of the Master Page will automatically be updated once the Master Page changes.

Right-click in the Solution Explorer window and choose "Add New Item...". Choose Master Page from the resulting dialog and name it something like main.master. Make sure you check the "add code in a separate file" checkbox and then click OK. This will add a new Master Page to the project.

You'll notice that, by default, the Master Page contains a single contentPlaceHolder server tag. This area is important because it represents the non-generic content of the page. Whenever a page specifies this page as its Master, the contentPlaceHolder is populated with that page's actual content. This notion is called "visual inheritance," and it's a powerful concept, as you'll see in a moment.

Now you can add some code to the Master Page to help define the overall layout of the site. For example, you can add a Title for the page and perhaps a 3x3 table (3 rows, 3 columns).

Your page's source should look something like this:

```
<%@ Master Language="C#" AutoEventWireup="true" CodeFile="Main.master.cs"
Inherits="Main" %>

<!DOCTYPE html PUBLIC "-//W3C//DTD XHTML 1.0 Transitional//EN"
"http://www.w3.org/TR/xhtml1/DTD/xhtml1-transitional.dtd">

<html xmlns="http://www.w3.org/1999/xhtml" >
<head runat="server">
    <title>Amazon Mashups</title>
</head>
<body>
    <form id="form1" runat="server">
    <div>
        <table border="1">
            <tr>
                <td width="200"></td>
                <td><h1>Amazon Mashups</h1></td>
                <td width="200"></td>
            </tr>
            <tr>
                <td width="200">Left Side</td>
                <td><asp:contentplaceholder id="ContentPlaceHolder1"
runat="server"></asp:contentplaceholder>
                </td>
                <td>Right Side</td>
            </tr>
```

```
            <tr>
                    <td colspan="3">Bottom</td>
            </tr>
    </table>
    </div>
    </form>
</body>
</html>
```

Let's walk through what you've got here. The first line in the file is called a *page directive*. This one simply states that this is a Master Page by specifying the word `Master`. A page will use the word `Page` as the first word in the page directive.

```
<%@ Master Language="C#" AutoEventWireup="true" CodeFile="Main.master.cs"
Inherits="Main" %>
```

Next up is the `DocType` declaration. This tells the browser how strictly the subsequent tags in the page will adhere to the World Wide Web Consortium (W3C) XHTML specification:

```
<!DOCTYPE html PUBLIC "-//W3C//DTD XHTML 1.0 Transitional//EN"
"http://www.w3.org/TR/xhtml1/DTD/xhtml1-transitional.dtd">
```

The next section is mostly HTML defining the page head section, the body, and a three-column table. Notice I've placed the `ContentPlaceHolder` tag in the center-most cell of the table. This means any pages that use this page as their Master will render their content into the center of the page.

```
<td>
    <asp:contentplaceholder id="ContentPlaceHolder1"
runat="server"></asp:contentplaceholder>
</td>
```

Now that you have a Master Page, you need to hook up the `Default.aspx` page to use it. Open `Default.aspx` and delete all the content in there except the page directive (the first line in the file).

Add the following attribute to the `Page` directive:

```
MasterPageFile="~/Main.master".
```

This tells the compiler that this page is going to use `Main.master` as this page's Master Page. Your page directive should look like this:

```
<%@ Page Language="C#" AutoEventWireup="true" CodeFile="Default.aspx.cs"
Inherits="_Default" MasterPageFile="~/Main.master" %>
```

The tilde (~) in the path is a way to avoid hard-coding the path to the application within the files.

If you switch to Design view for `Default.aspx`, you'll notice the entire layout from the `Main.master` page is displayed and that it's grayed out. This is because you're editing `Default.aspx`, not the Master Page. ASP.NET lets you easily switch to the Master with the addition of a new menu item to the context menu (right-click and you'll see "Edit Master" in the context menu).

With the `default.aspx` page correctly wired up you can add some content to it. Right-click the `default.aspx` design surface and choose Create Custom Content. This adds a new tag, `asp:content`, to `default.aspx`. The content tag acts as a placeholder for the page-specific content. Try typing **Hello World** in this content area and press F5 to launch the application. A browser window launches with a page similar to Figure 4-4.

Figure 4-4: The Master Page in action

Before moving on, add a few more pages to the Web site. Make the Master Page for each one `main.master` while creating them by checking the Select Master Page checkbox from the Add New Item dialog box.

Though not mandatory, it is a best practice to name your Web pages all in lowercase. This adds an extra layer of interoperability and accessibility from case-sensitive sites and browsers.

Presenting XML Data

Admittedly, the Hello World example so far is the Web equivalent of polyester trousers. In this section, you add some XML data to the project and display that data using a `GridView` and ADO.NET.

The "ADO" in ADO.NET stands for "Active Data Objects." This is a huge area on which volumes have already been written and is the core framework that ASP.NET uses for data access.

Start by adding yet another item to the project, this time an XML file called `zeppelin.xml`. If you have not already noticed, I have a general affinity for Led Zeppelin and all things related. This XML file will contain some information about their songs:

```xml
<?xml version="1.0" encoding="utf-8" ?>
<songs>
  <song title="Black Dog" album="Led Zeppelin II"></song>
  <song title="Gallows Pole" album="Walking Into Clarksdale"></song>
  <song title="Bring It Home" album="Led Zeppelin IV"></song>
  <song title="The Rain Song" album="UnLedded" />
  <song title="The Ocean" album="Live at Madison Square Garden" />
</songs>
```

In this listing, the root node is `songs` and it contains five `song` nodes. Each song has a `title` attribute and an `album` attribute. Note the last two song nodes use a short-hand syntax of "`/>`" to close themselves.

Now you can use this data. Go back to the `default.aspx` and switch to Design view. Drag a `GridView` control to the page and rename it something like `myGrid`. Right-click on the `GridView` control and choose Show Smart Tag from the context menu.

The smart tag is a context-sensitive set of menu items that is different depending on the control you click or where you are in the editor. You can also bring up the smart tag menu by clicking the tiny "play" button, which appears above a control when you mouse over it.

Click the data source drop-down control in the `GridView`'s smart tag and choose <New Data Source>. The Data Source Configuration Wizard launches, as shown in Figure 4-5.

The following table describes the various data source possibilities in .NET.

Data Source	Description
Access Database	Microsoft Office's lightweight database.
Database	More robust storage, such as SQL Server or SQL Server Express.
Object	An instance of a class can be used as a data source. Members of the class are exposed as data items.
Sitemap	An ASP.NET XML document of a specific kind. You learn more about this in the upcoming sections.
XML File	A standard XML file. Note that you don't have to literally have a file. An in-memory XML document will work just fine.

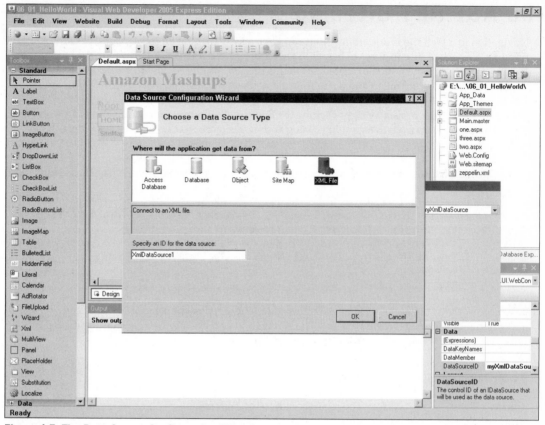

Figure 4-5: The Data Source Configuration Wizard

Because you are using an XML file as the data source, choose XML File from the wizard. A new dialog opens, allowing you to specify the location of the XML file and either an XSLT transformation file or an XPath expression. XSLT is covered in a later chapter, so for now, you should use a simple XPath expression. This expression is sort of a way to tell the `GridView` which pieces of the XML data to pull out. In this case you should enter `"songs/song"` to tell the `GridView` to present the song nodes in the XML file as its data rows.

When you finish the wizard and launch the solution, the `default.aspx` page presents the songs within the context of the Master Page.

The `GridView` (and, indeed, many of the controls) supports auto-formatting. Before moving on, it's worth right-clicking the `GridView` control in the document and playing with the Autoformat options in Visual Studio.

The ASP.NET Sitemap

Navigation in a Web site is important, but it can get tricky managing all those pages. Luckily, ASP.NET provides a bunch of nice features to help you keep track of the site. Among these are the menu, bread-crumb controls, and the notion of a sitemap. In this section, you learn how to create a sitemap and also how to use it to add cool menu and navigation elements to the site you just created.

Add a sitemap to the project by right-clicking the Solution Explorer window and choosing Add New Item. Choose Sitemap from the resulting dialog and name it Web.sitemap. This is the default name for a sitemap.

A new XML file is added to the project with a specific structure or schema. The sitemap should look like this:

```
<?xml version="1.0" encoding="utf-8" ?>
<siteMap xmlns="http://schemas.microsoft.com/AspNet/SiteMap-File-1.0" >
    <siteMapNode url="" title="" description="">
        <siteMapNode url="" title="" description="" />
        <siteMapNode url="" title="" description="" />
    </siteMapNode>
</siteMap>
```

Take note of the siteMapNode elements in this code. These represent pages in the site, and you should add a node for each page in the Web site. The Navigation and Breadcrumb controls are driven off of these. A siteMapNode has the attributes shown in the following table.

Attribute Name	Description
url	The relative path to the Web page.
title	The name that should show up for this page. Used by menu and breadcrumb controls.
description	Description of the page. Optional.

XML is case-sensitive. Ensure that you maintain the case of these elements. If there is an error in the case of the element names, the XML file will not validate against the expected structure.

Modify the Web.sitemap file to include nodes for your Web site. When you're finished, it should look something like this:

```
<?xml version="1.0" encoding="utf-8" ?>
<siteMap xmlns="http://schemas.microsoft.com/AspNet/SiteMap-File-1.0" >
    <siteMapNode url="Default.aspx" title="HOME" description="Main home page">
        <siteMapNode url="one.aspx" title="One" description="Page #1" />
        <siteMapNode url="two.aspx" title="Two" description="Page #2" >
            <siteMapNode url="three.aspx" title="Three" description="" />
</siteMapNode>
    </siteMapNode>
</siteMap>
```

The pages shown (one.aspx, two.aspx, and three.aspx) are just pages I added to the project. Yours might be named differently.

The sitemap is hierarchical in that a siteMapNode can contain other siteMapNodes nested within it. You can see in the preceding XML the root siteMap node contains a single siteMapNode for the default.aspx page. Underneath this there are two siteMapNodes for pages one and two. Page two contains page three underneath it. This is just an example, but you can see how it is possible to build a hierarchical navigation tree for a given site.

Navigation Controls

With the sitemap created, you can now add some navigation elements to the site. The natural place to do this is in the Master Page for the site.

Try It Out   **Adding a Menu**

1. Go back to the site Master Page, main.master. From the Toolbox, Navigation section, drag a Menu control to the table, replacing the "left side" text. I prefer the navigation on the left-hand side, but you are free to place it wherever you see fit. This adds the following tag to the source of the main.master page:

    ```
    <asp:Menu ID="myMenu" runat="server"></asp:Menu>
    ```

2. Before the menu will work, it must be bound to a datasource. Display the Smart Tag for the menu control and click the drop-down control next to Choose Data Source. Click New Data Source and the Data Source Configuration Wizard launches.

    This time, there are only two choices in this dialog, a sitemap or an XML file. Remember, any XML file can be used as a datasource in .NET, and coincidentally, the Web.siteMap file that you created in the last section is simply an XML file!

3. Click the Site Map icon and type **mySiteMapDS** as the identifier for this datasource. Click OK. The IDE adds a new datasource of type SiteMapDataSource to the main.master page. The menu control is now bound to this datasource.

4. Press F5 at this point to launch the application, and you will notice a fully functioning JavaScript menu, complete with mouse-over effects!

Of course, with no formatting, the menu is pretty boring to look at. You can quickly add some formatting from the Source view of the main.master page. Right-click the menu control and select Autoformat from the context menu. Choose a color scheme you like, and play around with the formatting until you're happy with it.

Most presentation-only changes in an ASPX page will not require stopping and restarting of the Web project. Try keeping the browser open while you modify the formatting of the menu. Save the results and press Refresh (F5) in the browser to see the results of your change. This little tip can save lots of time otherwise waisted on recompiling the app.

One other useful navigation control is the SiteMapPath control. The SiteMapPath control works in concert with the SiteMap itself to indicate where in a given site the user has navigated to. You've probably seen this feature on other Web sites, and it is traditionally known as a *breadcrumb*, presumably a reference to Hansel and Gretel.

Make a new row in the Master Page's table, just under the heading row. Drag a SiteMapPath control from the Navigation section of the Toolbox into this new row, and the following markup will be added to the source:

```
<asp:SiteMapPath ID="SiteMapPath1" runat="server"></asp:SiteMapPath>
```

The SiteMapPath control requires no other configuration, although there are many styles you can set to control the appearance of the breadcrumb.

At this point, it's worth launching the application to see the effects of your changes. A menu and breadcrumb control have been added, and they should be fully functional, allowing navigation from page to page.

Adding Some Style with CSS

Cascading Style Sheets (CSS) are a common mechanism for defining the style and appearance of your site. Using CSS files (versus defining styles within the page) is a best practice for the professional developer.

Try It Out   Adding a Style Sheet

1. Right-click the Solution window and choose Add New Item. Select Style Sheet from the resulting dialog and name it fun.css. A style sheet is added to the solution in the root of the Web project. This style sheet will store the style definitions for your Web site.

2. Open the style sheet. You will notice it contains a single style for the body tag and that style is empty. Add a new style for the siteHeading tag with the following code:

```
.siteheading
{
    background-image:url('images/banner_grey.png');
    background-repeat:no-repeat;
    height:100px;
}
```

HTML and CSS is not strictly case-sensitive, but it is a general best practice to stick to lowercase for your tags and CSS styles.

   This code simply states "format the content of the siteHeading tag so that it is 100 pixels high and uses the banner_grey.png background."

3. Open main.master and locate the following line:

```
<td colspan="2">
    <h1>Amazon Mashups</h1>
</td>
```

Rewrite the code so that it looks like this:

```
<td colspan="2" class="siteheading"> </td>
```

The addition of the class attribute to the <TD> tag means the heading will be driven off of the CSS file. You no longer need the <h1>Amazon Mashups</h1> tag because the background image specified in the CSS file contains this same text.

If you are new to CSS, there is good news in store. Visual Studio provides a wizard-like dialog window through which all properties of a given style rule can be edited. To launch this dialog, right-click any style and choose "build style...". Alternatively, if you prefer manually editing the CSS file, IntelliSense does a terrific job of presenting the available properties and their respective options.

4. Add a new folder named images to the project and place a new image in it named banner_grey.png. This is contained in the sample code accompanying this book.

5. The style sheet is now ready for use in the Web site. Open the main.master page, switch to Design view, and literally drag the fun.css file from the Solution Explorer window onto the design surface of the page. The editor is smart enough to know this is a CSS file, and regardless of where you drop the file, it will add a style sheet tag to the <head> section of the page. Check the source and you will find the following tag in the head of the page:

```
...
<head runat="server">
    <title>Amazon Mashups</title>
    <link href="fun.css" rel="stylesheet" type="text/css" />
</head>
...
```

When the page is retrieved by the browser, the link tag informs the browser to retrieve a CSS style sheet named fun.css and apply it to the page.

Of course, the best place to link the style sheet is in the Master Page so that all pages will use this style. In this manner, the link to the CSS is defined in a single place (the Master), but affects many pages.

Press F5 to run the project (or click the "play" button in the toolbar). The project will launch and the "Amazon Mashups" background image will be formatted according to the rule in the style sheet.

Themes and Skins

Unfortunately, there are a couple of issues with the pure CSS approach:

❑ The CSS style sheet is hard-coded into the Master. For example, if you wanted to provide two style sheets (one fun and one formal) for a Web site and let the user choose between them, you'd likely have to build in a little logic to modify which sheet was linked in.

❑ Customizing the style of server controls is a little messy. The only way to customize these is to assign styles to the controls, and then build CSS rules for these styles. This could get hairy.

ASP.NET themes and skins solve these problems by making the style information employed by a site configurable.

A *theme* is a collection of resource files (CSS, skin, and image files) that together define the appearance of a given site. In this section, you learn how to define a theme and associate it to the Web site.

Start by adding a new folder to the project. This is a special folder where the various themes will be stored and must be named `App_Themes`. Next, add a folder for each theme you are going to create. There will be two themes in this example, so create two folders under `App_Themes`, one named `fun` and the other `serious`.

Drag the `fun.css` file you created earlier into `fun` theme folder. Create a similar CSS file for the serious theme, named `serious.css`. Modify `serious.css` so that you'll be able to tell the fun and serious themes apart! You can have some fun here. For example, specify the Comic Sans MS font for the `fun` style sheet and the boring Times New Roman for the `serious`.

Figure 4-6 shows the IDE containing the `Themes` folder hierarchy for this example.

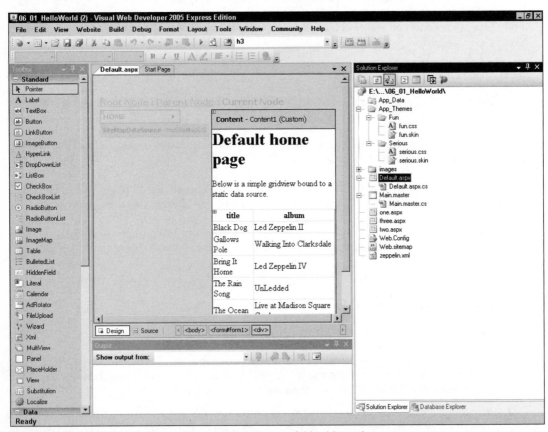

Figure 4-6: The Solution Explorer with expanded `Themes` folder hierarchy

One other thing to remember is to remove the style sheet definition from the `main.master` page. This is important, because it could override the theme and cause all sorts of confusion.

At this point, the themes simply contain CSS files. Now, you'll add a skin file to control the appearance of the menu server control created earlier in the chapter.

Add a new item to the "fun" theme, this time a skin file called `fun.skin`. The *skin files* control the appearance of server controls, overriding any formatting they might contain locally. For example, if you wanted all `asp:button` controls to have a similar appearance, you have two options: format each one individually or use a skin file.

Here's the skin file markup for `fun.skin`:

```
<asp:Menu runat="server" BackColor="#FFFBD6" DynamicHorizontalOffset="2"
BorderColor="black" BorderWidth="1" Font-Names="Tahoma" Font-Size="14pt"
ForeColor="#990000" StaticSubMenuIndent="10px" Font-Bold="True" Width="155px">
    <StaticMenuItemStyle HorizontalPadding="5px" VerticalPadding="2px" />
    <DynamicHoverStyle BackColor="#990000" ForeColor="White" BorderColor="black"
BorderWidth="1"/>
    <DynamicMenuStyle BackColor="#FFFBD6" BorderColor="black" BorderWidth="1"/>
    <StaticSelectedStyle BackColor="#FFCC66" BorderColor="black" BorderWidth="1"/>
    <DynamicSelectedStyle BackColor="#FFCC66" BorderColor="black" BorderWidth="1"/>
    <DynamicMenuItemStyle HorizontalPadding="5px" VerticalPadding="2px" />
    <StaticHoverStyle BackColor="#990000" ForeColor="White" />
</asp:Menu>
```

This markup will affect all menu controls in the site, wherever they might be. It simply specifies presentation styling information for those controls. The level of styling is different for each control (as you can see, for a menu there are many styling attributes).

At first blush, the markup for these files can look intimidating, but it's actually quite simple to create. The easiest way to do it is to edit the control on the page using the designer, then copy the source markup generated by the designer into the skin file. Remove the ID attribute and you're done.

Now, you have a theme containing a CSS and Skin file. Before you can set the theme to work, you must specify which theme the site should use. Open the `web.config` file and add the following line item:

```
<?xml version="1.0"?>
<configuration>
    <appSettings/>
    <connectionStrings/>
    <system.web>
        <compilation debug="true"/>
        <authentication mode="Windows"/>
        <pages theme="fun"/>
    </system.web>
</configuration>
```

This tag is pretty self-explanatory, and just sets the theme to be used by the site. Press F5 and you should find the theme correctly applied to the Web site. Without stopping the site, modify the `web.config` file to use the "serious" theme and refresh the browser. This time the site appears with a serious look and feel. Themes and skins are a powerful concept, and can really reduce development time for a complex site.

Summary

This chapter covered a lot of material, and, if you've followed along with the discussion, you now have a comprehensive framework into which you can plug your mashups.

The goals of the chapter were to get the development environment up and running and to familiarize you with some of the more powerful features in ASP.NET 2.0. In doing so, you created a working Web site complete with XML Data Access, Themes, a JavaScript Menu, breadcrumbs, and Master Pages.

Almost all sites you build need data access, navigation controls, and a structured approach to managing common elements. These are the core elements on which any site (including a mashup) is built, and the success of whatever new application you can dream up will be influenced by how well you have mastered these core competencies.

In upcoming chapters, you build various mashup Web sites that are far more interesting than the pages you created here. You may consider using the site you built in this chapter as the core platform on which the other mashups are built. For clarity, I will devote a single project to each mashup, but you will find they can easily be integrated into a single project should you so desire.

I have provided a simple framework here that I encourage you to experiment with, and experimentation is often where the best innovations are discovered.

Chapter 5 discusses the various technologies prevalent in the Web 2.0 world. That list includes RSS, OPML, XML, and XSL, among others.

Exercises

Here are some questions to test what you have learned. The answers to all exercises found at the end of chapters throughout the book are in Appendix B.

1. How do you add a style sheet to an ASP.NET page?

2. How does ASP.NET 2.0 support modifying the styles used in a given Web site?

3. What support for data sources does ASP.NET provide?

4. How do you access an XML data source using a `GridView`?

5. What options are there in ASP.NET for building navigation elements into a Web site?

6. What's the difference between a theme and a skin in ASP.NET?

7. What are Master Pages and how can they be used?

8. Do you need to use Microsoft tools to develop mashups?

The Technology

One thing is certain: The computing industry loves acronyms. In any given mashup, there are a myriad of technologies at work. To the uninitiated, this gobbledygook can be both intimidating and confusing. This chapter describes the main acronyms I use throughout the remainder of the book, along with some terms that you might encounter as you begin exploring mashups on a wider basis.

What Is a URI?

A *Uniform Resource Identifier (URI)* is slightly different from a URL, which you may be more familiar with. The URI refers to a page on the Web, including any code-fragment-specific identifiers.

A URL might look like this:

```
http://www.MySite.com/default.aspx
```

A *URI* might look like this:

```
http://www.MySite.com/default.aspx#mySection
```

`#MySection` is a named region of the Web page.

What Is HTTP?

HyperText Transfer Protocol (HTTP) is the main protocol used on the Internet. It rides on top of Transmission Control Protocol (TCP) and Internet Protocol (IP), which are low-level networking protocols.

HTTP is *connectionless*, meaning that if two parties are communicating, there is no dedicated connection between them. Think of your brother and sister tossing a ball in the backyard. The ball is the message. There is no dedicated connection between your brother and sister; they're just tossing and catching the ball.

HTTP uses two main methods of requesting data: GET and POST. In the GET method, request parameters are sent in the *querystring* of the URL. Here's an example:

```
http://www.mySite.com/myPage.aspx?CustomerId=1010
```

Here, the CustomerId is a parameter and its value is 1010.

In the HTTP POST method, parameters are written to the HTTP request itself, after the HTTP Header. The HTTP GET is limited in the amount of data it can pass, typically up to 4KB. On the other hand, the POST is practically unlimited, but requires some JavaScript to construct programmatically. Mashup developers typically use HTTP GET because it's slightly more accessible. You will see more on this in later chapters.

What Is XML?

When you first encounter the *eXtensible Markup Language* (XML), it takes a while to understand the benefits of it. XML is a way to express information in a structured manner. It's not really a language per se, but rather a meta-language, or a language to describe languages, and hence is very powerful.

A Sample XML Document

XML expresses information in a well-defined structured manner. This is extremely important if that data is to be processed by a computer. An XML document is made up of *elements*. Each element can have *attributes* and each element can contain elements. Consider the following example:

```
<?xml version="1.0" encoding="utf-8"?>
    <course subject="physics">
        <lesson>Introduction</lesson>
        <lesson>Mass & Weight</lesson>
        <lesson>Energy</lesson>
    </course>
```

XML documents typically begin with the following node to specify the encoding of the subsequent document:

```
<?xml version="1.0" encoding="utf-8"?>
```

The first element (or node) is course and it is said to be the *root node* of the document. course has child elements, in this case lesson nodes. The lesson nodes have values, Introduction, Mass & Weight, and so on.

The course sample document is *well-formed* because every element that is opened has a corresponding closing element, denoted by the backslash before the element name. Lastly, the course element also has an attribute called subject, and that attribute has a value, "physics".

All XML documents are well-structured. Library developers have created programming libraries to access the XML data using well-defined functions and syntax (XPath, for example). Once you understand how to use these, they can be used on any XML document, so there's some value in learning this stuff.

That's a very brief introduction into XML, but it's all you need to know for right now. I'll get into more complex examples in upcoming chapters.

What's the Point of It?

The point is to describe information in a consistent manner, so that no matter what type of information you're providing, it can be used and manipulated using a standard mechanism. For any XML document, I can define a *schema* (called a *Document Type Definition*, or *DTD*) or specification that defines the structure for that document. XML data can then be validated against the schema to ensure that the XML document is adhering to the specification that was intended.

What Is XHTML?

As we all know, *HyperText Markup Language* (HTML) has been used in various forms to build the Internet. The *eXtensible HyperText Markup Language* (XHTML) applies XML rigor to HTML.

Although HTML uses tags similar to XML, it is generally not well structured. For example, what is wrong with the following snippet?

```
<b>
   <p>
      After the sun
   </b>
   <p>
<br>
a little rain must fall<br>
```

This snippet might be acceptable in a typical browser such as Internet Explorer or Firefox. Browsers, in general, tend to be more forgiving than XML parsers. The previous snippet is invalid XHTML for a number of reasons, the first being that the <b> and <p> tags are nested invalidly. The second reason is that the <br> tag is not a valid XML tag.
 tags should really be written as <br/> in order to validate.

The XHTML DTD is included at the top of every HTML page. This provides a hint to the browser as to the markup contained therein.

XHTML comes in a couple of flavors, depending on how well-written your HTML is. You can validate your XHTML against an XHTML DTD. If you have a particularly well-structured site, you might consider using the xhtml1-strict DTD:

```
<!DOCTYPE html
PUBLIC "-//W3C//DTD XHTML 1.0 Strict//EN"
"http://www.w3.org/TR/xhtml1/DTD/xhtml1-strict.dtd">
```

Alternatively, you can use the transitional document type for pages that deviate from the XHTML specification:

```
<!DOCTYPE html
PUBLIC "-//W3C//DTD XHTML 1.0 Transitional//EN"
"http://www.w3.org/TR/xhtml1/DTD/xhtml1-transitional.dtd">
```

XHTML is important because it helps keep your document structure somewhat organized, and by adhering to the DTD, you can ensure that your page will render as expected in XHTML-compliant browsers.

Here's a more complex example based on Radiohead's music:

```
<?xml version="1.0" encoding="utf-8"?>
<artist name="Radiohead">
  <albums>
    <album name="Ok Computer">
      <songs>
        <song>Airbag</song>
        <song>Paranoid Android</song>
        <song>Subterranean Homesick Alien</song>
      </songs>
    </album>
    <album name="Hail To The Thief">
      <songs>
        <song>Sit down. Stand up.</song>
        <song>Scatterbrain</song>
        <song>Myxomatosis</song>
        <song>Wolf At The Door</song>
      </songs>
    </album>
  </albums>
</artist>
```

What Is XPath?

Along with XML to structure your data, you need some mechanism by which nodes in an XML document can be referenced. That's where XPath comes in. Look back to the previous sample XML document:

```
<course subject="physics">
    <lesson>Introduction</lesson>
    <lesson>Mass & Weight</lesson>
    <lesson>Energy</lesson>
</course>
```

To obtain a list of the lesson nodes, you might use an XPath expression such as //lesson. The double-slash // indicates that no matter where in the document the lesson node occurs, that node should be included in the result set.

Another example might be to precisely obtain the lesson node for Mass & Weight. This can be retrieved using the following syntax:

```
/course[lesson='Mass & Weight']
```

As you can see, XPath has a rich syntax that I won't regurgitate here. Rather, you will learn what you need as you progress through the samples in the book.

What Are XSL and XSLT?

The *eXtensible Stylesheet Language* (XSL) is a language that lets you *Transform* (XSLT) an XML document into something else. That something else might be more XML, or something completely different like XHTML or even straight text. XSL and XSLT as terms are generally used interchangeably.

By design, XSL is built using XML, and so you can validate an XSLT sheet just like you'd validate XML. Because companies such as Amazon expose their data through XML, and you want to transform that data into something else, XSL is an essential tool in your arsenal.

XSL uses a template- or rule-based approach. Every XSL sheet uses a set of templates that are applied or matched to XML nodes in the underlying XML document.

XSLT is used in almost every mashup in this book, and is something you'll become familiar with over the course of the text.

Try It Out **A Sample XSLT Document**

The following is an example XSL sheet that transforms the earlier Radiohead XML document:

```
<?xml version="1.0" encoding="utf-8"?>
<xsl:stylesheet version="1.0" xmlns:xsl="http://www.w3.org/1999/XSL/Transform">

  <xsl:template match="/">
    <html>
      <body>
        <xsl:apply-templates select="artist" />
      </body>
    </html>
  </xsl:template>

  <xsl:template match="artist">
    <h1>
      <xsl:value-of select="@name"></xsl:value-of>
    </h1>
    <table>
      <xsl:apply-templates select="albums" />
    </table>
  </xsl:template>

  <xsl:template match="albums">
    <xsl:apply-templates select="album" />
  </xsl:template>

  <xsl:template match="album">
    <tr>
      <td>
```

```
      <h2>
        <xsl:value-of select="@name"></xsl:value-of>
      </h2>
    </td>
  </tr>
  <xsl:apply-templates select="songs" />
</xsl:template>

<xsl:template match="songs">
  <xsl:apply-templates select="song" />
</xsl:template>

<xsl:template match="song">
  <tr>
    <td>
      <xsl:value-of select="."></xsl:value-of>
    </td>
  </tr>
</xsl:template>

</xsl:stylesheet>
```

How It Works

This transformation formats the results into HTML. The XSL outputs each song in each album into a row in an HTML table.

If you're writing XML in Visual Studio Web Developer, you can easily format the document you're working on by pressing Ctrl+K followed by Ctrl+D.

Notice the presence of `<xsl:template>` tags. Each template represents a rule or pattern that is applied whenever a node in the underlying document is found. Documents are processed from the top down, so each pattern is only applied to the XML node that's being processed at the time.

By referencing this sheet in the Radiohead XML document, the document is transformed when viewed in a browser (Figure 5-1):

```
<?xml version="1.0" encoding="utf-8"?>
<?xml-stylesheet type="text/xsl" href="radiohead.xslt"?>
<artist name="Radiohead">
  <albums>
    ...
```

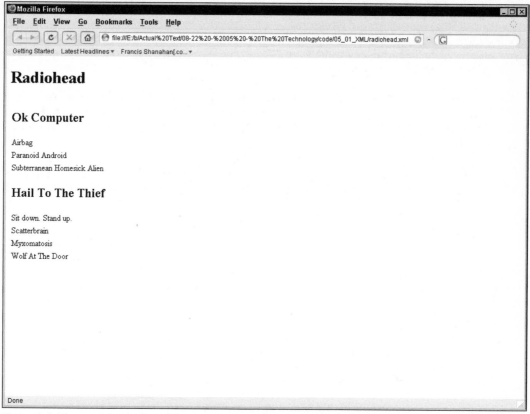

Figure 5-1: The resulting HTML generated from the Radiohead XML data

What Are Web Services?

Defining *Web services* used to be really easy, but as time marches on, the definition has become more difficult to pin down. A *service* is basically any method exposed by an application, which allows other applications to consume that system's functionality. So, if you shine shoes for a living, you're exposing a shoe-shine service. A Web service is that same service exposed digitally on the Internet.

What Is WSDL?

Web services also employ a mechanism called *Web Service Description Language* (WSDL) that tells other systems how to interact with the methods provided by the Web service. That's confusing, so imagine the shoe-shine scenario as an example.

If you're a shoe-shine guy, you need a way to accept shoes. It'd be nice if accepting shoes was standardized so that you're not looking all over the store for shoes to shine. You tell your customers, "Drop your dirty shoes off at the countertop in my store." That's your interface, and it becomes a part of your service description.

The same thing applies to Web services. Web services use WSDL to say things such as, "I can calculate interest on a loan," and, "Pass me the terms of the loan in this XML structure and in these parameters."

The Amazon ECS WSDL is located here:

```
http://webservices.amazon.com/AWSECommerceService/AWSECommerceService.wsdl
```

The following is a snippet taken from the Amazon WSDL:

```
<xs:element name="ItemLookup">
    <xs:complexType>
        <xs:sequence>
            <xs:element name="MarketplaceDomain" type="xs:string" minOccurs="0"/>
            <xs:element name="AWSAccessKeyId" type="xs:string" minOccurs="0"/>
            <xs:element name="SubscriptionId" type="xs:string" minOccurs="0"/>
            <xs:element name="AssociateTag" type="xs:string" minOccurs="0"/>
            <xs:element name="Validate" type="xs:string" minOccurs="0"/>
            <xs:element name="XMLEscaping" type="xs:string" minOccurs="0"/>
            <xs:element name="Shared" type="tns:ItemLookupRequest" minOccurs="0"/>
            <xs:element name="Request" type="tns:ItemLookupRequest" minOccurs="0"
maxOccurs="unbounded"/>
        </xs:sequence>
    </xs:complexType>
</xs:element>
```

This snippet describes the ItemLookup method. As you can see, this doesn't look like much. It's barely readable to the human eye. Almost all development platforms such as Eclipse or Visual Studio can understand WSDL and use it to generate a proxy class tailored to a particular Web service.

The proxy class has the information from the WSDL embedded in it, so function calls on the proxy class transparently invoke the Web service over the network. Thus, calling Web services is as easy as instantiating a class and calling functions on this class.

You'll use WSDL later in the book with Amazon and Google.

What Is SOAP?

The *Simple Object Access Protocol* (SOAP) is a specification that helps Web services structure the data as it's exchanged between them. SOAP is a lengthy and complex specification that is still under development. Luckily, it's not necessary to memorize all the gory details of SOAP and WSDL to leverage Web services.

The SOAP specification details how to convert objects into XML (serialization) and how to invoke methods on those objects using a well-defined schema, or XSD.

Development tools are at a level of sophistication now that consuming SOAP is a routine operation, and one that can greatly enhance the functionality in your application without requiring the voodoo of yesteryear.

Typically, Web services operate across HTTP, although SOAP can travel on TCP as well. Most of the applications in this book are Internet facing, and, hence, will leverage HTTP.

What Is REST?

REST stands for "Representational State Transfer," and is more of an architectural style than a specification. REST, in the context of mashups, is loosely defined as any communication that takes place without the trappings of a sophisticated protocol such as SOAP.

REST asks that when you invoke a method, you send that method all the necessary information for processing to take place. The method you've invoked will not retain any of the information beyond the scope of its processing. It's a *stateless method* in the sense there is no state or session information maintained from one call to the next. The job of maintaining session state is up to the caller.

Where SOAP converts objects and method calls to a well-defined XML document, REST is a quick-and-dirty (sometimes more efficient) translation of information to an accessible form. The form could be comma-separated values, or any other format that meets your needs.

Try It Out   A Sample REST Call

Here's a sample REST API call going against Amazon's ECS API:

```
http://webservices.amazon.com/onca/xml?Service=AWSECommerceService&Operation=Custom
erContentSearch&Name=Fred&AWSAccessKeyId=[YOUR KEY HERE]
```

Figure 5-2 shows the response from that invocation. You can generate this response yourself with just a Web browser.

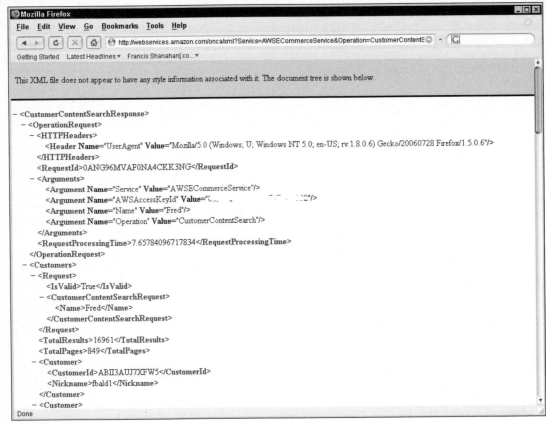

Figure 5-2: REST XML response from Amazon

What Is a Remix?

The terms *remix* and *mashup*, I suppose, came from the music world. A *remix* is the same song, sung to an updated beat; the same applies to Web services. For example, Amazon exposes its product data, and, typically, you'd expect that data to be used to build shopping Web sites.

You could use that data to draw a picture of Jeff Bezos (head of Amazon) using pictures of products related to Jeff's personal interests (space, physics, science, and so on). That's not what Amazon intended, but it is fairly artistic nonetheless. That's a remix.

What Is a Mashup?

A *mashup* is similar to a remix. You might have heard examples again from the music world where elements of Led Zeppelin are combined with Jayzee, for example, to form a weird rap/rock song. That's a mashup.

The same can be done with data from the Internet. In this book, I cover all sorts of ways in which you can combine data from disparate sites to form new and innovative applications.

What Is RSS?

Really Simple Syndication (RSS) is an XML specification that describes a mechanism whereby data such as news headlines can be syndicated across sites. RSS has enjoyed huge success in the world of blogging, and is being more and more tightly integrated into the fabric of the Web.

Much of RSS's success is owed to its simplistic structure. The availability of XML libraries has made loading and processing XML and, therefore, RSS documents very easy. Application developers do not have to waste time developing file formats, transfer protocols, and software to implement syndicating content — they can focus on developing content-consuming applications with functionality.

Remixes and mashups are now seeing success because the technology is at a point where the developer can focus on adding greater value to the content, or using this content in interesting ways, and doesn't have to spend time implementing the plumbing to move the content around.

You can provide an RSS *aggregator* (or *reader*) a list of *feed URLs*, each of which exposes RSS. The reader will then aggregate these together and periodically poll for updates, allowing you to monitor content from multiple sites all at the same time.

RSS structure is relatively simple, although there are few different versions of the specification at this point. This book uses the RSS 2.0 specification exclusively. At the very basic level, an RSS feed consists of a `<channel>` node containing a series of `<item>` nodes, as shown here:

```
<?xml version="1.0" encoding="iso-8859-1"?>
<rss version="2.0">
  <channel>
    <title>News by Shanahan</title>
    <link>http://www.FrancisShanahan.com</link>
    <description>Shanahan delivers up-to-the-minute news and info from the far
reaches of the web.</description>
    <language>en-us</language>
    <copyright>(c) 2006 Francis Shanahan</copyright>
    <pubDate>Wed, 10 Jan 2007 21:17:42 EST</pubDate>

    <item>
      <title>Man Bites Dog</title>
      <link>http://www.FrancisShanahan.com/details.aspx?cid=100</link>
      <description>A man bit a pooch today in Johnstown Mall...</description>
      <pubDate>Wed, 9 Jan 2007 21:17:42 EST</pubDate>
    </item>

    <item>
      <title>Potatoes to rule Earth</title>
      <link>http://www.FrancisShanahan.com/details.aspx?cid=101</link>
      <description>Scientists have discovered tiny aliens living in
potatoes...</description>
```

```
        <pubDate>Wed, 8 Jan 2007 20:12:02 EST</pubDate>
      </item>
    </channel>
  </rss>
```

Later in this book you learn more about RSS and build your own remix that transforms Amazon product information into a live feed.

What Is OPML?

Outline Processor Markup Language (OPML) and is just one more format that's powering the adoption of XML across the Internet. OPML was originally developed to capture document outlines, similar to a table of contents. Since its initial development, it is has been widely adopted for use with RSS readers.

As mentioned, you can set up an RSS reader with a set of URLs, each of which is then monitored by the reader and polled for updates. This collection of RSS URLs is typically stored in OPML format.

OPML consists of just four required nodes shown in the following table; the rest are optional.

Node Name	Description
opml	The root node.
head	Stores metadata pertaining to the body of the document.
body	Contains a series of one or more outline nodes.
outline	The actual content of the document.

Here's a sample OPML document that depicts a number of RSS feed files:

```
<?xml version="1.0" encoding="utf-8" ?>
<opml>
  <head>
    <title>Start.com Subscriptions</title>
  </head>
  <body>

    <outline title="Francis Shanahan[.com]"
htmlUrl="http://www.FrancisShanahan.com/"
xmlUrl="http://francisshanahan.com/rss.aspx" type="rss"/>

    <outline title="Living in a World of Connected Systems"
htmlUrl="http://www.marcmercuri.com/"
xmlUrl="http://www.marcmercuri.com/syndicationservice.asmx/getrss" type="rss"/>

    <outline title="Amazon Customer Reviews"
htmlUrl="http://BaeBo.FrancisShanahan.com" xmlUrl="
http://baebo.francisshanahan.com/g.aspx?x=acustrss&w=arss&operation=ItemLookup&resp
onsegroup=Large&itemid=b000ff9poc" type="rss"/>
  </body>
</opml>
```

As mentioned, OPML is not an RSS-specific specification, although it has enjoyed widespread adoption through the proliferation of news in the form of XML and news aggregators.

What Is Atom?

Atom is another format for syndicating content, similar to RSS. Although this book does not implement an Atom interface, it's mentioned in this context as another technology you will encounter in the news syndication space.

What Is GeoRSS?

GeoRSS is an extension of RSS, this time to provide additional geographic information along with the RSS item. Mapping APIs (such as Yahoo or Google Maps) use GeoRSS because it facilitates positioning markers on a map. You use GeoRSS in Chapter 11 to display restaurant locations on a Yahoo Map.

What Is Ajax?

Asynchronous JavaScript and XML (Ajax) is probably the most over-hyped term in the mashups world. Ajax lets you communicate from a Web page back to a Web server without requiring a page refresh. This fundamental capability is quite powerful, and has been used to great effect in all manner of applications. Microsoft was the first major company on the scene by Ajax-enabling the Web interface of Microsoft Outlook. A number of years later, Google broke new ground by leveraging Ajax to create Google Maps.

The notion of being able to provide smooth access to an enormous set of data such as a map captured the imagination of developers worldwide. It didn't take long for the Google Maps interface to be dissected, and mashups started cropping up all across the Net.

Chapter 10 explains Ajax in great detail, and uses it to build an Ajax-powered Wish List.

What Is JSON?

JavaScript Object Notation (JSON) is essentially a format for specifying JavaScript objects so that they can easily be transported. You could think of it as a way of serializing JavaScript objects. Note that I said JavaScript objects, not Java objects — there's big difference there.

So, what does it look like? JSON writes objects down as a hierarchical series of name-value pairs. Here's an example.

```
{
   "Album": {
     "Title": "Are You Experienced?",
     "Artist" : "The Jimi Hendrix Experience"
   }
}
```

This particular example could be represented as XML like this:

```
<Album>
    <Title>Are You Experienced?</Title>
    <Artist>The Jimi Hendrix Experience"</Artist>
</Album>
```

JSON is slowly gaining ground on XML, although is not intended to replace it. As a notation, it is clearly less verbose than XML, requiring less markup to convey the same data structure. Less data being transmitted on the wire leads to better performance of the application.

You can learn more about JSON in Chapter 12, which explains how to build a JSON-powered Customer Browser.

What Is Serialized PHP?

Serialized PHP is similar in notion to JSON. It allows a piece of PHP script to be converted (serialized) into a string, and then passed around as a variable. The resulting string can then be de-serialized back into PHP code by the receiver.

What Is POX?

Pox is a serious disease that can be fatal if left untreated. As it pertains to mashups though, Plain Old XML (POX) is one of those "fun" acronyms necessitated by the multitude of acronyms that all mean more complicated things. Plain Old Java Objects (POJO) is another example.

What Is RDF?

The *Resource Description Format* (RDF) is a cornerstone of the notion of the *semantic Web*. RDF provides an XML-based syntax by which data or resources can be described. RDF data can be read by machines and used to infer a meaning or semantic description of the resource in question.

If you consider the Internet in its current form, every Web site is an island. Humans can interact with these sites, but it's very difficult for a computer to process or understand the content and context of a given site.

Companies such as Google have made billions of dollars by just building a means by which pages can be ranked against a set of criteria. RDF would enable a far richer classification of information than simple page ranking.

By using a scheme such as RDF, when widely adopted, it would allow creation of inferences based on the data. Here's a scenario:

❑ Site A describes a resource such as Jimmy Page born in West London.

❑ Site B describes Jimmy Page as the guitarist from Led Zeppelin.

❑ By combining these two resources and recognizing they are related you can infer that Led Zeppelin's guitarist was English.

In this manner, the whole of the information gathered using RDF would exceed the sum of its parts.

What Is FOAF?

Friend of a Friend (FOAF) is an emerging specification focused on publishing machine-readable information on the Web.

Here's an example document describing myself:

```
<foaf:Person>
  <foaf:name>Francis Shanahan</foaf:name>
  <foaf:mbox_sha1sum>1332113b0e6289f92815fc210f9e9137262c252e</foaf:mbox_sha1sum>
  <foaf:homepage rdf:resource="http://www.FrancisShanahan.com" />
</foaf:Person>
```

This FOAF snippet just describes my name and home page.

The vision is that some day the Internet will be populated with such information. Applications can then be written that parse this information and make inferences based on it. You'll be able to ask, "Who is Billy and who does he know?"

What Is WML?

Desktops and laptops are no longer the only means of accessing the Internet. Hand-held devices and cell phones are getting in on the act as well. A standard browser uses HTML or XHTML, JavaScript, Cascading Style Sheets (CSS), and so on, to render the content.

Because of space and interface restrictions, mobile devices need a smaller, more compact markup language. Enter *Wireless Markup Language* (WML), which is based on XML. WML uses a different model than HTML for page structure. *Pages* are known as *decks*, and a *deck* can contain multiple *cards*.

Here's a sample WML page described in markup:

```
<?xml version="1.0" ?>
<!DOCTYPE wml PUBLIC "-//PHONE.COM//DTD WML 1.1//EN"
"http://www.phone.com/dtd/wml11.dtd">
 <wml>
   <card id="main" title="BaeBo Amazon Search">
     <p mode="wrap"><b>Enter Keywords to Search Amazon</b></p>
     <p>
        <input name="Keywords" value="iPod"/><br/>
        <do type="accept" label="Search Amazon">
             <go href="http://BaeBo.francisshanahan.com/g.aspx?Keywords=($Keywords)"
method="get">
                  <postfield name="x" value="amazonsearchwml.xml"/>
                  <postfield name="w" value="awml"/>
                  <postfield name="Operation" value="ItemSearch"/>
                  <postfield name="ResponseGroup" value="Medium"/>
                  <postfield name="SearchIndex" value="Blended"/>
             </go>
        </do>
        Search: <a
href="g.aspx?x=amazonsearchwml.xml&amp;w=awml&amp;j=&amp;Operation=ItemSearch&amp;R
esponseGroup=Medium&amp;SearchIndex=Books&amp;ItemPage=1&amp;Keywords=$(Keywords)">
[Books]</a>
        <a
href="g.aspx?x=amazonsearchwml.xml&amp;w=awml&amp;j=&amp;Operation=ItemSearch&amp;R
esponseGroup=Medium&amp;SearchIndex=DVD&amp;ItemPage=1&amp;Keywords=$(Keywords)">[D
VDs]</a>
        <a
href="g.aspx?x=amazonsearchwml.xml&amp;w=awml&amp;j=&amp;Operation=ItemSearch&amp;R
esponseGroup=Medium&amp;SearchIndex=Music&amp;ItemPage=1&amp;Keywords=$(Keywords)">
[Music]</a>
        <a
href="g.aspx?x=amazonsearchwml.xml&amp;w=awml&amp;j=&amp;Operation=ItemSearch&amp;R
esponseGroup=Medium&amp;SearchIndex=Electronics&amp;ItemPage=1&amp;Keywords=$(Keywo
rds)">[Electronics]</a>
        <br/>
        http://www.FrancisShanahan.com<br/>
     </p>
   </card>
 </wml>
```

Figure 5-3 shows the same page when displayed in a BlackBerry simulator.

WML is a lot like HTML, but with a reduced feature set and a stricter syntax. You learn more about WML in Chapter 14, which provides a mobile interface into Amazon.

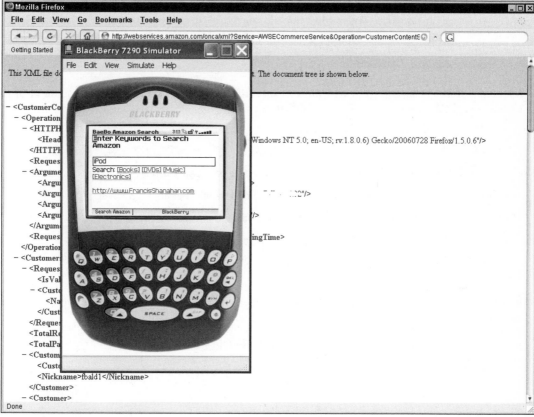

Figure 5-3: A Sample WML page

What Are Microformats?

Microformats are relatively new and build on existing standards such as RSS and XHTML to create simple new conventions for representing data of various types. An example might be the *hCards*, which are simple conventions for displaying personal contact information.

Here's an example hCard for me:

```
<div class="vcard">
 <a class="url fn" href="http://www.FrancisShanahan.com">Francis Shanahan</a>
 <div class="adr">
  <div class="street-address">Main Street</div>
  <span class="locality">Anytown</span>
  <span class="country-name">USA</span>
 </div>
</div>
```

As you can see, this isn't a strict specification like a DTD or XML-Schema representation. It's simply a set of HTML tags with associated styles. Most microformats take this simple approach.

Microformats are extremely targeted solutions, meaning they are not designed or intended to be infinitely extensible and extendible.

Many microformats have been created, all with specific problems and specific solutions in mind. The following table lists some currently existing microformats.

Microformat Name	Purpose
hCard	Describing people or organizations
hCalendar	Describing calendars and events
hReview	Describing opinions, ratings, and reviews
rel-tag	Describing tags, keywords, or categories
XOXO	Describing lists and outlines

This is not intended to be a full list. Microformats are relatively new and you should start seeing them crop up in various places over time. Consider using them in your own mashups.

You can learn more about microformats at the following URL:

```
http://www.MicroFormats.org
```

What Is XML-RPC?

XML-RPC is a simple mechanism to issue a method call on a remote system. It works by transmitting both the function name and parameters as an XML structure. The "RPC" in XML-RPC stands for *Remote Procedure Call* and harkens back to a time before SOAP. XML-RPC is a far simpler protocol than SOAP, and still in use in many companies.

Summary

The terms in this chapter are just a handful of the more common acronyms you'll find thrown around as you explore the world of service-oriented architectures and mashups. There is always something else to learn, but these terms will at least serve as a foothold to facilitate your reading and understanding of the remaining chapters.

In this chapter, I have made reference to many of the mashup applications contained in future chapters. You can jump to those chapters now, or consider reviewing the following questions to ensure your understanding of this chapter's content.

Next up, in Chapter 6, you uncover the architectural "plumbing" behind mashups. You learn the main techniques for mashing data together, as well as the pros and cons of each approach.

Consider reviewing the following questions before moving on.

Exercises

1. What is the difference between XHTML and HTML?
2. What do RSS and Atom have in common?
3. What is a REST-style API?
4. What do XML-RPC and SOAP both have in common?
5. What is hCard?
6. Does REST have to use the `Querystring`?
7. Is REST a protocol?
8. What are microformats?
9. Which is better — SOAP or a REST-style interface?

Mashup Techniques

This book is all about mashups — in other words, combining data and services from various sources to create new applications. Of course, there are many ways to approach this problem, each with its own pros and cons. In this chapter, you learn about some of the more typical approaches to mashing services together, and I'm sure by the time you're finished reading, you will have dreamt up a few more techniques of your own.

Keep in mind that while mashups are typically associated with fun applications, the technology that powers them is actually quite sophisticated. These are powerful techniques that combine sophisticated technologies and, hence, have broad applicability in the context of a corporate enterprise. The major vendors (IBM and Microsoft) are already realizing this and making inroads in this area.

This chapter covers the use-cases for these techniques and suggests the appropriate (and inappropriate) usage for each case.

Mashing on the Web Server

Every site sits on a Web server. It's the thing that serves up the page, typically Internet Information Server (IIS) in the Microsoft world. In the pure vanilla use case, the faithful Web server does all the work of mashing while the browser just sits and waits for a response. Don't dismiss this fundamental approach though, because it has its place, particularly when dealing with alternatives to the traditional desktop browser (for example, mobile devices).

---

iFrames — Sorry, Doesn't Count

In the days before Web services and XML, people were combining Web sites together using frames and iFrames. The following HTML snippet takes the contents of the `src` tag (in this case, a Google URL) and presents it in a 400 pixel by 400 pixel box in the browser:

```
<iframe width="400px" height="400px"
src="http://www.google.com/search?hl=en&q=mashups&btnG=Google+Sea
rch">
</iframe>
```

In all seriousness, this technique really doesn't count as a mashup, although you can still find it in use if you look hard enough. There's no re-purposing of the content, no re-branding, no alterations of the content, and no aggregation with other data. The `iframe` has met its match I'm afraid.

Understanding the Architecture

Figure 6-1 shows a typical HTTP page request. From an architectural perspective, this is the simplest form of mashup.

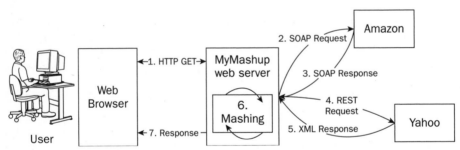

Figure 6-1: Browser, server, and partner site interactions with a typical mashup

How It Works

This use case is definitely the most straightforward:

1. The Web browser communicates with the server, requesting a page using straight HTTP or HTTPS.

2. That page is constructed by the Web server, which reaches out to what I'll call the *source* or *partner sites* (for example, Amazon, Yahoo, or Google, and so on). The first request in this example is to Amazon using the Simple Object Access Protocol (SOAP) over HTTP.

3. Amazon returns back a SOAP response.

4. The second request in this example is to Yahoo using a Representational State Transfer (REST) style approach.

5.   Yahoo responds with Plain Old XML over HTTP.

6.   Lastly, the Web server aggregates the responses, combining and rationalizing the data in whatever manner makes sense.

7.   The resulting data is bound to the HTML and inserted into the response, which is sent back to the browser.

Pros and Cons

The benefits of this approach are that the browser is decoupled entirely from the partner sites supplying the data. The Web server acts as a proxy and aggregator for the responses. As a developer, you don't have to worry about whether or not the browser supports a certain aspect of eXtensible Stylesheet Language Transformation (XSLT) in JavaScript, for example.

Furthermore, you don't have to support multiple versions of Dynamic HTML (DHTML) to make up for differences in the browser's implementation.

> In Chapter 10, when you start dealing with Ajax, you'll find that, in certain cases, to implement a specific feature in JavaScript, the browser support for that feature is inconsistent. For example, Firefox implements XML parsing its own way, and Internet Explorer uses a completely different set of objects. In cases like these, you must actually code the same feature two different ways, and execute the right one depending on the browser the user is using.

Disadvantages of this approach are that the browser requests an entire page, which typically is acceptable, but as you'll see in the next section, it's not as clean or as sophisticated as it could be.

Second, the Web server is doing all the work in terms of data manipulation. Though this is good in terms of maintenance, it's not so good in terms of scalability. When your mashup gains popularity and starts being viewed by thousands of users, the amount of work the server's doing increases, while the browser residing at the client is relatively idle.

When to Use

This is a good approach to use when you can't predict the type of client requesting the mashed data. For example, most people will think of mashups as being accessed entirely from a browser. Now, imagine a ubiquitous computing world when the user might be using a device such as a BlackBerry, Pocket PC, or even cell phone interface to consume your mashup. The real power is in the ability to mash data on the server, and spit it out in a way the client will understand, whether it's a browser or not.

> You implement this technique in Chapter 14 to produce a Wireless Markup Language (WML) interface from Amazon data so that you can browse Amazon from a cell phone!

Rich User Interface using Ajax

This approach has been hyped beyond belief in recent times, but has actually been around many years. The first widely distributed use of Asynchronous JavaScript XML (Ajax) was in the Microsoft Outlook Web Interface, but for whatever reason, it was not noticed until many years later.

Understanding the Architecture

This is certainly the snazziest of mechanisms. This approach allows a far richer of experience for the user if implemented well. Be careful, however, because usability is king in the mashup world, and there are many pitfalls to avoid when you start dealing with asynchronous requests. Figure 6-2 shows the flow of data in an Ajax implementation.

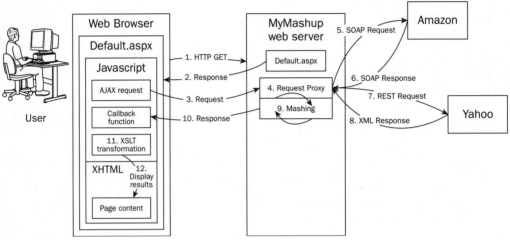

Figure 6-2: Browser, server, and partner site interactions using Ajax

How It Works

The browser is really the workhorse in this use case:

1. As before, the sequence begins with the browser requesting a page from the Web server. That page is served in the standard manner.

2. At the point when the browser first loads the page, there is no mashup content present. Some JavaScript is downloaded to the browser, along with the HTML for the page.

3. The next step is for the browser to issue a request back to the server for additional content. This might be a SOAP request or REST- or XML-RPC-style request, but it's all the same basic principal. The real nuance here (and it's a big nuance) is that this request is done through JavaScript and happens asynchronously, behind the scenes, so to speak. Because it's asynchronous, the page is not refreshed in the browser, nor is the browser blocking until the call is processed. In fact, the whole thing can happen without the user ever even noticing! This particular topic is covered in detail in Chapter 10.

4. The server in this case is acting as a proxy. The browser has asked for some content, perhaps a stock quote from Yahoo. The server typically does nothing more than forward that request on to the intended recipient.

5. A SOAP request is made to Amazon.

6. Amazon responds with a SOAP response.

7. A REST request is made to Yahoo.

8. Yahoo processes the request and returns the data back to the server, as in the first scenario.

9. Some mashing may occur on the server. This is really an optional step because the data might just be sent directly back to the browser.

10. Once the data is ready, it's sent back to the browser. Meanwhile, back at the browser, life has moved on. A JavaScript callback function that was named in the original request handles the response when it finally arrives from the server.

   A callback function is simply a function that is assigned to execute when a particular event fires. In this case, the callback executes when the response is received by the browser.

11. Typically, at this point, a transformation is applied to the XML data to convert it into XHTML, which includes data and presentation markup. (Remember, XHTML is simply well-formed HTML).

12. That snippet is then inserted into the page's structure and appears before the user!

You might ask, "Well, why doesn't the browser talk directly to the partner site?" This is by design. The reason is because of Web browser security. Because of the built-in security restrictions in all browsers, an `XmlHttpRequest` object can only retrieve data from the site that served that page. You cannot go out to other sites using `XmlHttpRequest` and, hence, the need for a response handler or proxy on the Web server in the Ajax scenario. JSON solves this issue, as you will see later in this chapter.

Pros and Cons

As you can infer from the explanation, this is a complicated mousetrap with many moving parts. Developers will face JavaScript challenges, server communication issues, and asynchronous methods that are difficult to predict, and so on. Maintenance of the solution can be challenging, along with debugging during development.

You should ensure that this technique is applied where it makes sense, and only where it makes sense. For example, it makes sense to use Ajax to refresh a portion of a page; it doesn't make sense to refresh an entire page using this technique.

Lastly, on the "con" side of things, when you use JavaScript to modify a page's state in this manner, the browser's built-in navigation mechanisms (such as the Back button and History) are bypassed. If users bookmark an Ajax page, they are only bookmarking the URI, not the actual content of the page. This can cause confusion on the part of the user.

On the positive side of things, this technique, when combined with a little imagination, can enable a terrific experience within the browser. In many cases, you can replicate a full-featured rich client experience. You gain the maintenance benefits of an application that doesn't need to be installed (zero-footprint), but the sophistication of a rich client application.

Another benefit with this approach is that the presentation of the results, meaning the way the results appear on the screen and the associated HTML markup is all driven by the XSLT style sheet that is applied to the XML data. This means there is no presentation logic embedded in the actual C# code that powers the application. The C# server code is kept nice and clean and, if you do need to modify how the results look, it's a simple case of editing the XSLT file. There is no recompilation necessary.

Furthermore, the browser is doing the majority of the work. This means less work for the server to do, and, consequently, more time for it to serve more pages. The less work your Web server is required to do, the more scalable the resulting application is. The more scalable the application, the more users you can handle before you need to go buy additional hardware.

Lastly, because all data (regardless of which partner site it is coming from) is routed through a common point on the server, the aggregation and combination of results is possible. As you will see later in this chapter, with JSON, this kind of data processing is only possible within the browser itself.

When to Use Ajax

Ajax is a powerful technique that opens up a lot of possibilities. For example, you can apply Ajax to help you solve the following problems:

❑ Traverse impossibly large datasets (for example, Google Maps, where it's clearly impossible to download every satellite image to the browser).

❑ Provide real-time updates to dynamic data (stock quotes are a perfect example, where the user shouldn't need to fully refresh the page to get accurate information).

❑ Report user interactions back to the server (for example, click tracking for gathering marketing information).

❑ Enrich search interfaces by providing results as the user types (commonly known as a Live Search).

When Not to Use Ajax

Of course, you are free to use Ajax whenever you'd like, but take care, lest it ends up becoming the new "blink" tag.

❑ Consider the user experience. Will adding Ajax confuse the user? Will it be clear to the user that the data is being refreshed?

❑ Don't use Ajax to refresh an entire page, because what's the point? You can just use the Refresh button in the browser!

❑ Remember that Ajax modifies the state of the page. If you bookmark an Ajax-enabled page and then go to that bookmark, the page might not contain the same content that was originally bookmarked. There are a few hacks around this that involve modifying the querystring of the page to contain state information, but I do not recommend this approach for all but the simplest of scenarios.

This completes the overview of Ajax as a mashup technique. In Chapter 10, you build a mashup using Ajax and become intimately familiar with its inner workings. Before leaving this chapter there is one more topic to discuss: JSON.

Mashing with JSON

JavaScript Object Notation (JSON, pronounced "Jay-son") is a notation that is gaining popularity in the mashup community mainly because of its readability and simplicity. This section familiarizes you with the communication mechanism of a mashup using JSON.

Understanding the Architecture

JSON itself is just a notation, a way of writing down objects in a manner that is easily readable by humans and easily processed by machines. The built-in JavaScript capabilities of most browsers are actually what enable JSON as a viable mashup technology. Figure 6-3 shows the architecture and interactions in a JSON implementation.

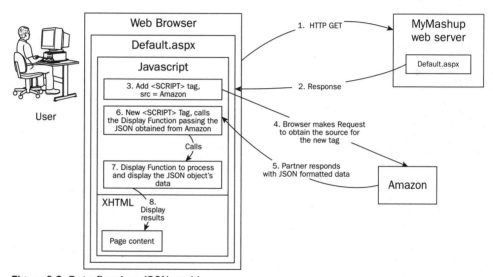

Figure 6-3: Data flow in a JSON world

How It Works

Most JSON mashups make use of an approach known as the *Dynamic Script method*. It follows a flow similar to the following:

1. As always, the flow starts with a browser request for a page using HTTP GET.

2. A page is served by the Web server that contains a couple of key JavaScript functions:

   a. A parsing function expects a JavaScript object as a parameter. This function examines the object passed into it and inserts the data contained in the object into the HTML of the page.

   b. An "initiation" script is the genius of the Dynamic Script method. It adds a *new* script tag to the page, and specifies the source for that script tag as being a URL at some partner site (for example, Amazon.com). That URL will render not HTML nor XML, but JSON.

3. The browser attempts to load the source code for the new script tag.

4. By loading the script, an HTTP GET request is made out to Amazon (or whatever the source was).

5. The partner site (in this case, Amazon) responds with a JavaScript object serialized into JSON notation.

6. This JSON script becomes wrapped in a function call to the render function, and the entire JavaScript blob becomes the content for the script tag added in Step 2b.

7. The browser now attempts to execute this new piece of JavaScript. This results in a call to the render method from Step 2a.

8. The render method is invoked and the JSON script is evaluated and turned into a JavaScript object. The render method uses this new JavaScript object in its execution, and pumps the data it contains into the page.

The Dynamic Script method is actually pretty simple but, unfortunately, doesn't lend itself well to an easy explanation. You will see this method in action in Chapter 12.

Pros and Cons

The main benefit with the JSON approach is communication path. The browser communicates directly with the partner site with no need to go through the server. As a result, load on the server is reduced because the browser is in charge of the communication.

Developers often find using the pre-made objects supplied in JSON to be easier than processing XML using XSL or XPath in JavaScript. In many cases there are fewer cross-browser compatibility issues as well.

It's rather a subjective observation, but there are those who feel JSON is easier to read. I don't find this myself, but I will leave it to your judgment.

On the down side, because the browser talks directly to the partner site, there is no opportunity for consolidation of the data on the server. With Ajax, you have an opportunity to consolidate data, depending on how you implement your proxy. This possibility doesn't exist with JSON.

Finally, JSON is not supported by many APIs, Yahoo being the biggest supporter of this notation. Amazon, for example, will not serve JSON natively. In Chapter 10, I walk through an option for converting Amazon data into JSON using XSL, and then consuming this data using the Dynamic Script method.

When to Use JSON

JSON is a useful tool to use if you need to get something working fast. Clearly, there are fewer moving parts with the Dynamic Scripting method than in, for example, Ajax. There's no proxy, and the browser elegantly executes the partner query without all of the additional JavaScript required in an Ajax implementation.

When Not to Use JSON

Don't use JSON when you need to process the partner data and, perhaps, aggregate or combine it with other partner sites before displaying it. If you need to perform an XML/XSL transformation on it, the Ajax or server-side transformation options will be a better fit.

A Word of Warning

A word of caution is necessary when using these techniques. When the partner is someone like Amazon or Yahoo, you can be assured they will not pass you back malicious script. If you are unsure of the partner, take extra care that you validate the returned data for any values that might inadvertently harm the page (or the user's browser). Remember, the content that gets displayed is not determined until runtime. It's your responsibility to ensure that you don't inadvertently open up a security hole with your page. If the partner sends malicious script (for example, JavaScript that implements a worm-type virus) and you display that in your code, then you've accidentally propagated a virus, and that's *bad*! In fact, the first Ajax-based self-propagating worm has already hit the Internet. Security should always be top-of-mind when creating new and engaging Web sites.

Summary

In this chapter, you learned about some of the main techniques for mashing Web service data from an architectural perspective, including the following:

- ❑ Mashing on the server
- ❑ Mashing in the browser using Asynchronous JavaScript and XML
- ❑ Mashing in the browser using JSON

When ramping up on new techniques such as mashups, it's useful to get the 50,000-foot overview before diving into the code.

I am not the inventor of these techniques, and my ways are not the only ways. Be conscious of the fact that there are always going to be new ways of doing things. These techniques are not the final word on how to do things by any means. Variations are constantly springing up, and creative individuals like you are continuing to push the possibilities of what can be done with data. This chapter and the diagrams herein should prove to be a valuable resource as you go beyond this book to create your own dynamic Web sites.

In the next few chapters you go beyond the theory and learn how to apply these techniques in the real world.

Chapter 7 walks you though building your first remix, an automated mechanism to convert Amazon search results into RSS feed data using SOAP.

Before continuing, review the following exercises, which test your familiarity with the content of this chapter.

Exercises

1. What are three possible approaches to creating mashups?
2. What is Ajax?
3. What are the pros and cons of Ajax?
4. List the pros and cons of a JSON/Dynamic Scripting approach to mashing data.

Creating Your First Remix

It has been said that I am a bit of a scrooge. I prefer the term "frugal." When I make a purchase, I like to know I'm getting the best price for an item. I also do a lot of research using customer reviews from Amazon before deciding what to buy. Amazon prices and customer reviews generally fluctuate over time. RSS is a great way of monitoring data, so it made sense to me to combine the two.

In this chapter, you build your first remix; an automated Really Simple Syndication (RSS) feed of Amazon product information using Simple Object Access Protocol (SOAP). This remix will produce a feed of XML in the form of RSS. That RSS feed can then be monitored just like a blog so that when the price drops, you'll know it. You're going to create an "Amazon blog" of sorts.

The feed can be subscribed to by any RSS 2.0–compliant News Reader. It's a really fun little remix and might even save you some money.

The Battle Plan

This chapter shows two separate examples that are each applications in their own right. Each example builds on the previous one.

The first example is a single page, entirely self-contained. The plan here is to create a simple search form. The form submits and displays the results in HTML. This is no big deal, but this example illustrates the SOAP calls to Amazon.

The next example builds on the first and modifies the search form to provide an option to produce an RSS feed instead of the search results in HTML. This allows the user to subscribe to the results using an RSS reader. In this example, you build a generic RSS generator.

Understanding the Architecture

Before diving in, it's important to have a mental image of the end result. Figure 7-1 shows the architecture of the solution.

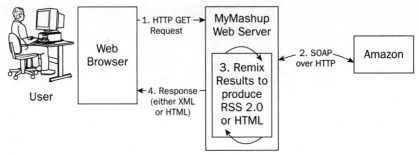

Figure 7-1: The Amazon RSS remix architecture

How It Works

Because this is a remix, there are not as many moving parts as a typical mashup:

1. The user fills out a simple search screen and selects the Submit button. The request (a typical HTTP GET or POST) is sent back to the server hosting the remix.

2. The server processes the request and issues an ItemSearch query to Amazon's Web Service (AWS) platform. The AWS replies back with the results.

3. Depending on what was requested (HTML or RSS), the response is then parsed on the server and converted into XML that complies with the RSS 2.0 specification.

4. The remixed response is then sent down to the browser.

There are a few schemas or specifications for syndicating content. One of the more popular is RSS version 2.0 but you could easily modify this example to produce Atom, RSS 1.0, or whatever format you'd like.

The format of RSS is really simple, hence the name (Really Simple Syndication), but thoroughly effective, as you will see.

The User Interface

The interface is pretty simple in this case, just a simple form. Create a new project using Visual Studio Web Developer (or reuse the project from Chapter 4) and add a new Web page named default.aspx to the project.

If you'd like to hook this into the Web site you created in Chapter 4, simply add the code developed in this chapter to that project, and add the new page to the sitemap file. The page will automatically show up in the navigation menu. You can go a step further and apply the main.master Master Page to the page as well.

The user interface is shown in Figure 7-2. It has a table to control the layout. The table contains a text box for the Keywords search terms and a drop-down control to allow the user to specify the search index to be queried.

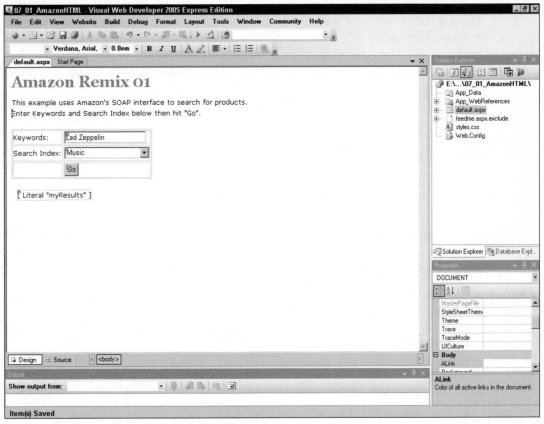

Figure 7-2: The Amazon RSS interface at design time

Try It Out — Build the Form

The HTML and layout of the form is entirely at your discretion. I'll present some guidelines here to get you started. Once the application is working I encourage you to deviate from this script to incorporate as much sophistication as you wish into the project.

1. To add the form-fields, switch to the page's Design view and drag a `TextBox` onto the page. Name this control by setting its ID in the Properties window to `Keywords`.

2. Drag a `DropDownList` onto the page and name this `SearchIndex`.

3. To add the drop-down option items you can switch to Source view and enter them manually, or right-click the drop-down control and use the properties dialog, as shown here:

```
...
<option value="DVD">DVD</option>
<option value="Books">Books</option>
...
```

As stated in Chapter 4, there's a rather large set of search indices within the Amazon catalog. I have specified them all, but you might consider limiting the choices to the most popular (for example, Books, Music, DVDs).

4. The last thing to add is the Submit button. Drag and drop an HTML Input (Submit) control onto the form and change its ID to cmdSubmit. In the next section, you build the code behind this button.

5. Add a Literal control named myResults that will be used to print out the results.

I have purposefully kept this page simple for clarity, but you can get as creative as you want and add further fields (such as Locale and Sorting) so that the result set would be further refined.

One important note here is that, although you could use traditional HTML controls like <input> to build this form, or ASP.NET controls like <asp:TextBox>, this example uses server-side HTML controls.

To create a server-side HTML control, start by building the form out of standard HTML controls. This will create markup like this:

```
<input id="Text1" type="text" />
```

Then, right-click this control and select the "Run As Server Control" option in the context menu. This will modify the previous markup as follows:

```
<input id="Text1" type="text" runat="server" />
```

Make sure you're using server-side HTML controls and not their HTML equivalents, or the example won't make sense. When complete, the ASPX page source code should look similar to Listing 7-1.

Listing 7-1: The Search Entry Screen Source

```
<%@ Page Language="C#" AutoEventWireup="true" CodeFile="default.aspx.cs"
Inherits="_default" %>

<!DOCTYPE html PUBLIC "-//W3C//DTD XHTML 1.0 Transitional//EN"
"http://www.w3.org/TR/xhtml1/DTD/xhtml1-transitional.dtd">

<html xmlns="http://www.w3.org/1999/xhtml" >
<head runat="server">
    <title>Amazon Search using SOAP</title>
    <link href="styles.css" rel="stylesheet" type="text/css" />
</head>
<body>

    <form id="form1" method="post" runat="server" >
        <h1>
            Amazon Remix 01</h1>
        This example uses Amazon's SOAP interface to search for products.
        Enter Keywords
        and Search Index below then hit "Go".<br />
        <br />
    <table>
    <tr><td>Keywords: </td><td><input type=text value="Led Zeppelin"
name="Keywords" id="Keywords" runat="server" /></td></tr>
```

```
    <tr><td style="height: 27px">Search Index: </td><td style="height:
27px"><select name="SearchIndex" id="SearchIndex" runat="server" >
    <option value="Blended">All</option>
    <option value="Electronics">Electronics</option>
    <option value="Music" selected>Music</option>
    <option value="DVD">DVD</option>
    <option value="Books">Books</option>
    <option value="Apparel">Apparel</option>
    <option value="Baby">Baby</option>
    <option value="Beauty">Beauty</option>
    <option value="Classical">Classical</option>
    <option value="DigitalMusic">Digital Music</option>
    <option value="ForeignBooks">Foreign Books</option>
    <option value="GourmetFood">Gourmet Food</option>
    <option value="HealthPersonalCare">Health & Personal Care</option>
    <option value="HomeGarden">Home & Garden</option>
    <option value="Jewelry">Jewelry</option>
    <option value="Kitchen">Kitchen</option>
    <option value="Magazines">Magazines</option>
    <option value="Merchants">Merchants</option>
    <option value="Miscellaneous">Miscellaneous</option>
    <option value="MusicalInstruments">Musical Instruments</option>
    <option value="MusicTracks">Music Tracks</option>
    <option value="OfficeProducts">Office Products</option>
    <option value="OutdoorLiving">Outdoor Living</option>
    <option value="PCHardware">PC Hardware</option>
    <option value="PetSupplies">Pet Supplies</option>
    <option value="Photo">Photo</option>
    <option value="Restaurants">Restaurants</option>
    <option value="Software">Software</option>
    <option value="SportingGoods">Sporting Goods</option>
    <option value="Tools">Tools</option>
    <option value="Toys">Toys</option>
    <option value="VHS">VHS</option>
    <option value="Video">Video</option>
    <option value="VideoGames">Video Games</option>
    <option value="Wireless">Wireless</option>
    <option value="WirelessAccessories">Wireless Accessories</option>
    </select></td></tr>
        <tr>
            <td>
            </td>
            <td>
    <input type="submit" runat="server" Value="Go" id="cmdSubmit"
onserverclick="cmdSubmit_ServerClick" causesvalidation="false" /></td>
        </tr>
    </table>
    <br />
     
        <asp:Literal ID="myResults" runat="server"></asp:Literal>
    </form>
</body>
</html>
```

As you can gather from the listing, there are a large number of SearchIndexes in the Amazon catalog. Feel free to customize these as you see fit. (Not everyone wants to search on "Pet Supplies," for example.)

The Server-Side Code

With the user interface defined, you can turn your attention to the logic behind it. Double-click the button you just added to the form. Studio automatically adds an event handler for the click event of this button and changes focus to the code-behind of the page.

<hr>

Try It Out   **ASP.NET's Event Model**

ASP.NET uses an event-driven model, just like you'd see in the Windows rich client programming environment. Events (such as the button click) fire on the client (the browser) but are executed on the server. This is an interesting programming model that you should fully understand before moving on. You can try a simple experiment to play with this feature. Enter the following code in the event handler you just created:

```
protected void cmdSubmit_ServerClick(object sender, EventArgs e)
{
        this.Keywords.Value = "Hello Event Driven World";
}
```

This code simply sets the text of the TextBox control. Run the project at this point and click the button. The text is set by the server and the new page is sent back to the browser.

Storing Configuration Data

In this example, there are a couple of data fields (namely, your Amazon Associate ID and your Developer Network Subscriber ID) that will be used in every call you make to the Amazon E-Commerce Service (ECS) platform. Rather than including these keys in each call, it would make more sense for these to be placed in a configuration file and reference them as configuration settings. In the old days, this would have meant placing the keys in the registry and writing some access class to obtain them at run-time.

ASP.NET uses the web.config file located in the root of every ASP.NET project as the primary storage for configuration data of this sort. This sort of data is known as an *application setting*. There is a set of classes within the .NET Framework that, when provided with a key name, will automatically retrieve an application setting value from the web.config file.

To store this (or any setting) in the web.config, add the following lines to the appSettings section of the web.config file:

```
<add key="AWSAccessKeyId" value="your_aws_key" />
<add key="AssociateTag" value="your_associate_tag" />
```

You can also use the ASP.NET Configuration Wizard to add these settings. Click the ASP.NET Configuration icon in the top of the Solution Explorer window to launch the wizard. Click the Application tab and choose Create Application Settings. Enter the appropriate fields (name and value) and the wizard will add the appropriate fields in the web.config for you. Personally, I find it quicker to edit the web.config than to use the wizard.

With the configuration settings stored in the `web.config` file, you can now reference these settings with the `ConfigurationManager` object. Replace all references to the configuration data in your code with the following function:

```
ConfigurationManager.AppSettings["AWSAccessKeyId"];
```

For example, this line of code would retrieve the value of the `AWSAccessKeyId` key from the `web.config` file.

You should consider using this approach whenever you have data that is application-specific and might change.

Retrieving Amazon Data using SOAP

It's time now to write the code to query the Amazon platform. In the next "Try It Out" section, you add the Web reference to the AWS. The code communicates to Amazon through an automatically generated Web service proxy class.

Try It Out   Generating the SOAP Proxy

There are two options to generating the proxy class. The following steps show the first option:

1. Using the IDE, right-click the Solution Explorer and select Add Web Reference. The Add Web reference dialog appears.

2. Type in the following URI into the Web service dialog and click OK:

```
http://webservices.amazon.com/AWSECommerceService/2005-03-23/US/AWSECommerceService.wsdl
```

The URI is recognized by Visual Studio as a Web Services Description Language (WSDL) endpoint, and so the Add Reference button becomes enabled (Figure 7-3).

3. Click Add Reference and the proxy code is generated.

The second option is to generate this proxy class manually using a command-line utility called `wsdl.exe`. This utility is part of the .NET Software Development Kit (note this is different from the .NET Framework). The default installation path for `wsdl.exe` is `C:\Program Files\Microsoft Visual Studio 8\SDK\v2.0\Bin`.

Use the following command to query the Amazon WSDL endpoint and create a client proxy class in the default language, C#:

```
wsdl
http://webservices.amazon.com/AWSECommerceService/2005-03-23/US/AWSECommerceService
.wsdl
```

Visual Basic users can use the following:

```
wsdl /language:VB /out:AWSECommerceService.vb
http://webservices.amazon.com/AWSECommerceService/2005-03-23/US/AWSECommerceService
.wsdl
```

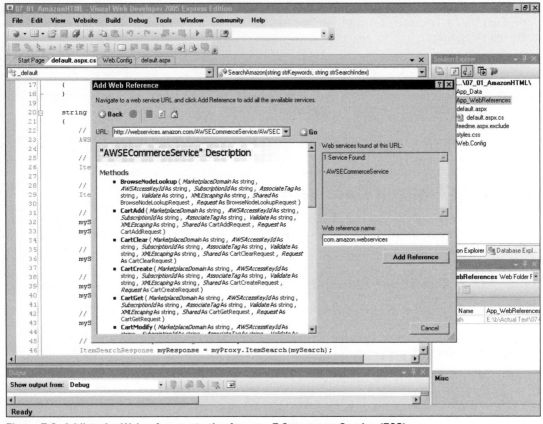

Figure 7-3: Adding the Web reference to the Amazon E-Commerce Service (ECS)

Of course, you don't have to create the proxy in this manner, but I find it is always useful to see the inner workings of what the IDE is doing for you.

You will use this reference, or proxy class, to invoke the methods available on the Web service. The class models the service with a function for each action that can be invoked on the service.

A Note on UDDI

When you have a wide array of Web services, managing those services and actually finding out what they are and where they are located becomes a challenge. Universal Description, Discovery and Integration (UDDI) is an initiative to facilitate management of a directory of Web services. You might think of it as the Yellow Pages for Web services. In this case, UDDI is not needed because you already have the URI of Amazon's Web service description as per the Amazon documentation.

Searching in a Different Locale

Amazon data is organized by region and locale. In this book, I have implemented the US locale primarily, but I recognize the need to be able to implement mashups using Amazon data pertaining to various regions around the globe. In general, the Amazon ECS platform implementation follows a similar approach, regardless of the locale being used.

If you would like to search against data from other regions, simply substitute the correct WSDL endpoint in place of the US locale. The following table documents the current locales available from Amazon.

Locale	WSDL Endpoint URI
US	http://webservices.amazon.com/AWSECommerceService/AWSECommerceService.wsdl
UK	http://webservices.amazon.com/AWSECommerceService/UK/AWSECommerceService.wsdl
DE	http://webservices.amazon.com/AWSECommerceService/DE/AWSECommerceService.wsdl
JP	http://webservices.amazon.com/AWSECommerceService/JP/AWSECommerceService.wsdl
FR	http://webservices.amazon.com/AWSECommerceService/FR/AWSECommerceService.wsdl
CA	http://webservices.amazon.com/AWSECommerceService/CA/AWSECommerceService.wsdl

These URLs are case-sensitive. Typing uk instead of UK will result in a server 404 error (missing page), and the endpoint you seek will not show up.

Using the Proxy

Now, you can use this proxy to invoke the AWS. The first step is to add a `using` statement to the code-beside class for the `default.aspx` page:

```
using com.amazon.webservices;
```

The `using` statement allows you to reference classes of that namespace without fully qualifying the namespace in every instance.

AWS provides a request-and-response class, depending on the operation you are executing. In this case, you will issue an `ItemSearch` request, so instantiate the `ItemSearchRequest` object. Add a new function to your code-beside class. The code for this function is shown in Listing 7-2.

Listing 7-2: The `SearchAmazon` **Function**

```
string SearchAmazon(string strKeywords, string strSearchIndex)
    {
        // Create a new instance of the proxy class
        AWSECommerceService myProxy = new AWSECommerceService();

        // Create a new instance of the ItemSearch class
        ItemSearch mySearch = new ItemSearch();

        // ItemSearchRequest stores the actual request parameters
```

(continued)

Listing 7-2: *(continued)*

```
        ItemSearchRequest mySearchRequest = new ItemSearchRequest();

        // Set some parameters, Keyword and Search Index
        mySearchRequest.Keywords = strKeywords;
        mySearchRequest.SearchIndex = strSearchIndex;

        // Just need Small results, not the full enchilada
        mySearchRequest.ResponseGroup = new string[] { "Medium", "Request"};

        // Set the subscription and associate tags here
        mySearch.AWSAccessKeyId=
 ConfigurationManager.AppSettings["AWSAccessKeyId"];
        mySearch.AssociateTag = ConfigurationManager.AppSettings["AssociateTag"];

        // Setup request
        mySearch.Request = new ItemSearchRequest[] { mySearchRequest };

        // Execute the request and get the response
        ItemSearchResponse myResponse = myProxy.ItemSearch(mySearch);

        // Parse the response and return the results in HTML
        string strHTML = "";
        foreach (Items myItems in myResponse.Items)
        {
            foreach (Item myItem in myItems.Item)
            {
                // Get the results in HTML
                strHTML += FormatAsHTML(myItem);
            }
        }
        return strHTML;
    }
```

How It Works

The SearchAmazon function begins by creating an instance of the Amazon Service Proxy.

Next, it begins to construct the request with the ItemSearch and ItemSearchRequest objects. The ItemSearchRequest is used to specify the Keywords and SearchIndex for the query. You could further narrow the search at this point with additional parameters such as Actor, Brand, Composer, and so on, depending on what you are searching for.

The next step is to specify the ResponseGroup. In this example you are just interested in the Medium response group, but if you wanted the response to include the original request, you would specify it as an additional ResponseGroup like so:

```
    mySearchRequest.ResponseGroup = new string[] { "Medium", "Request"};
```

The AWSAccessKeyId and AssociateTag (optional) are specified as shown. The AWSAccessKeyId is required in all requests.

The request is then prepared and executed through the service proxy.

Finally, the results are iterated through and written out to the page using the Literal control defined earlier. Each result item that is found is converted into HTML using the FormatAsHTML function (Listing 7-3).

I have omitted error checking from this code for clarity. You should add in checks for null object references, and a check to ensure there are results present before attempting parsing to ensure a robust code base.

Listing 7-3: The FormatAsHTML Function

```
string FormatAsHTML(Item myItem)
    {
        // Will contain the results
        string strHTML ="";

        // Check for null
        if (myItem != null)
        {
            // Begin the item HTML
            strHTML += "<div class=\"item\">";
            // Add the title
            strHTML += "<h2>" + myItem.ItemAttributes.Title + "</h2>";

            // Add the item image if present
            if (myItem.SmallImage != null)
            {
                strHTML += "<img src=" + myItem.SmallImage.URL;
                strHTML += " width=" + myItem.SmallImage.Width.Value;
                strHTML += " height=" + myItem.SmallImage.Height.Value;
                strHTML += " align=\"left\" >";
            }

            // Add the ASIN
            strHTML += "<b>ASIN:</b> " + myItem.ASIN + "<br/>";

            // Add the price if present
            if (myItem.OfferSummary != null)
            {
                if (myItem.OfferSummary.LowestNewPrice != null)
                {
                    strHTML += "<b>Lowest Price:</b> " +
                        myItem.OfferSummary.LowestNewPrice.FormattedPrice
                        + "<br/>";
                }
            }
            // Add a link to the details
            strHTML += "<a href=\"" + myItem.DetailPageURL + "\">View
Details</a><br/>";

            // Close the output
            strHTML += "</div>";
        }
        return strHTML;
    }
```

The FormatAsHTML function takes an Item as a parameter and returns a string as a result. It simply interrogates a single Amazon Item for each of the relevant properties. Each one in turn is added to the output as a new HTML tag.

Feel free to experiment here with the various properties such as SalesRank, EditorialReviews, and so on. Be aware that different properties will be populated depending on the search criteria and the response group combination. For example, a Garden Tool would not have an Author, but it would certainly have a Manufacturer.

At this point, you are ready to execute the application. Press F5 and perform a search. The results will be added to the page wherever you placed the Literal control. If all is well, your screen will look similar to Figure 7-4.

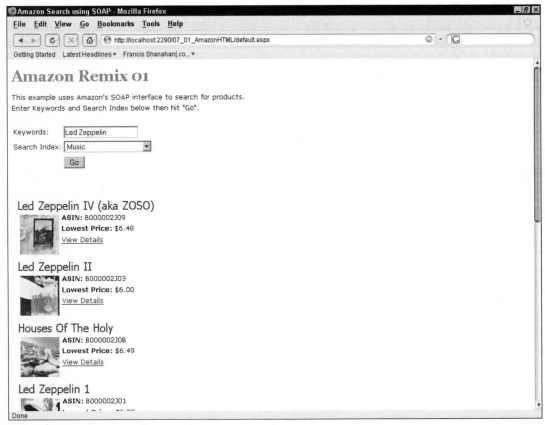

Figure 7-4: The search application in action

If this was all you wanted to achieve, you could stop right here and have a functional Amazon Search application. The next section shows how to take this application and convert it to generate RSS.

Building the RSS Generator

With the success of the Amazon Search under your belt, it's time to move on to the RSS portion of this remix. You can reuse the code you have so far.

Try It Out   Adding the AmazonUtility Class

Right now, the page submits to itself using an HTTP POST and prints out HTML. RSS readers typically use HTTP GET to obtain updated feed data which is, of course, in XML, so there are some changes necessary.

> *HTTP* GET *differs from HTTP* POST *in that all parameter and form information is sent in the querystring of the URI. The querystring is everything to the right of the first question mark in a given URI.*

A parameter will be added to the querystring to control whether the application will respond with HTML or RSS. If the parameter is present, RSS will be generated. Otherwise, the application just generates HTML as usual. This "Try It Out" example walks you through adding this new page, and the modifications to the default.aspx page:

1. Add a new class to the project and name it AmazonUtility.cs. You will use this class to store generic functionality that is not necessarily related to an individual page.

2. Cut (Ctrl+X) the SearchAmazon function from default.aspx.cs and paste it into the AmazonUtility class you just created.

3. Move (cut and paste) the FormatAsHTML function into the AmazonUtility class.

4. The last few lines in SearchAmazon pertain to parsing and formatting the results in HTML. Because these are not really related to the core capabilities of this function, move them into their own function called GetResultsFromResponse (Listing 7-4).

Listing 7-4: The GetResultsFromResponse **Function**

```
public static string GetResultsFromResponse(ItemSearchResponse myResponse)
{
    // Parse the response and return the results in HTML
    string strResults = "";
    foreach (Items myItems in myResponse.Items)
    {
        if (myItems.Item != null)
        {
            foreach (Item myItem in myItems.Item)
            {
                // Get the results in HTML
                strResults += FormatAsHTML(myItem);
            }
        }
    }
    return strResults;
}
```

GetResultsFromResponse simply iterates through the result set and invokes FormatAsHTML for each item it locates in the ItemSearchResponse.

5. Change `SearchAmazon`'s signature so that it returns the `ItemSearchResponse` object, `myResponse`. To do this, locate the following definition:

```
public string SearchAmazon(string strKeywords, string strSearchIndex)
```

Now, change that definition to the following definition:

```
public static ItemSearchResponse SearchAmazon(string strKeywords,
string strSearchIndex)
```

The idea here is that you will have a function for obtaining the results, and a separate function for parsing them.

6. Modify the `return` statement in `SearchAmazon()` to return the `ItemSearchResponse` object:

```
...
// Execute the request and get the response
        ItemSearchResponse myResponse = myProxy.ItemSearch(mySearch);

            return myResponse;
    }
```

7. Make all the methods in `AmazonUtility` static. To do this, simply place the `static` keyword after the `public` access modifier for each method.

8. Change the `AmazonUtility` class itself to be static by changing its definition to include the `static` keyword like so:

```
public static class AmazonUtility
```

9. You can now modify the `default.aspx.cs` page to use this new class by changing the code in the Submit button's event handler. Here is the initial code:

```
protected void cmdSubmit_ServerClick(object sender, EventArgs e)
    {
        string strKeywords = Request.Params["keywords"];
        string strSearchIndex = Request.Params["searchIndex"];
        myResults.Text = SearchAmazon(strKeywords, strSearchIndex);
    }
```

Following is the revised code using the new class:

```
protected void cmdSubmit_ServerClick(object sender, EventArgs e)
    {
        string strKeywords = Request.Params["keywords"];
        string strSearchIndex = Request.Params["searchIndex"];

    ItemSearchResponse myResponse = AmazonUtility.SearchAmazon(strKeywords,
    strSearchIndex);

    myResults.Text = AmazonUtility.GetResultsFromResponse(myResponse);
    }
```

It's a good idea to compile, run, and test your code regularly. This helps ensure that you take smaller steps while coding and don't get too lost in things. Try running the application again at this point. It should work just as it did in the previous section, without any new functionality.

How It Works

With these changes, you have a new static class with three static public methods, `SearchAmazon`, `GetResultsFromResponse`, and `FormatAsHTML`. If you wanted to search Amazon from an additional page, you could simply reuse the `AmazonUtility` class.

You also have a function that purely searches Amazon and returns the results. These results can be processed to create HTML using `GetResultsFromResponse`. This function iterates through the `ItemSearchResponse` and uses `FormatAsHTML` to obtain snippets of HTML, which together form the response. You should see now the benefits of structuring things this way.

> *The Solution Explorer shows the project's files and resources. Each page in ASP.NET represents a class. To view a class's methods and properties, you can utilize a different window named the Class Viewer. This window depicts the project as a set of classes, not files. Each class shows a set of methods and a set of properties just as you'd expect in an object model. Click View→Class View to open this useful Tool window.*

In the next few sections, you'll add a new function named `FormatAsRSS` to obtain RSS-formatted XML. Before creating this function, you must modify the `default.aspx` page slightly.

Try It Out   **Modifying the Form**

1. Open the code-beside for the form you created in the first part of this chapter (`default.cs`).

2. Create a new function `GetResults()`:

```
void GetResults()
    {
        string strKeywords = Request.Params["keywords"];
        string strSearchIndex = Request.Params["searchIndex"];

        // Check for null and set the default (music)
        if (strSearchIndex == null) strSearchIndex = "Music";
        ItemSearchResponse myResponse = AmazonUtility.SearchAmazon(strKeywords,
strSearchIndex);

        if (Request.Params["type"] == "rss")
        {
            Response.Clear();
            Response.Write("RSS Goes Here");
            Response.End();
        }
        else
        {
            myResults.Text = AmazonUtility.GetHTMLFromResponse(myResponse);
        }
    }
```

The reason for this function is to provide a layer of abstraction between the functionality to query Amazon and the event handler. By putting this code in a function, you can now call it from other events.

This function has a few additional features on top of the previous code. Notice the use of the `Request.Params` collection to obtain the `keywords` and `searchIndex` parameters. The `Request.Params` collection is a combination of the form post parameters and the querystring. By using this collection, regardless of whether the page was submitted from the form or whether it was retrieved by an RSS reader, the correct parameters will be obtained.

This function also will default to a `SearchIndex` of `Music` if none is provided.

3. Change the event handler for the Submit button to use the new function:

```
protected void cmdSubmit_ServerClick(object sender, EventArgs e)
    {
        GetResults();
    }
```

4. Add code to the `Page_Load` event to call `GetResults` if the page is passed any `keywords`:

```
protected void Page_Load(object sender, EventArgs e)
    {
        // If this page was passed any keywords, then GetResults
        if (Request.Params["keywords"] != null)
        {
            GetResults();
        }
    }
```

This code checks for the `keywords` parameter in the request. If `keywords` are present, the page attempts to find some results.

How It Works

In the first example, it was only possible to view `default.aspx` in the browser, select Submit, and get back search results. There was no way of going directly into this page and obtaining the results without selecting the Submit button. The goal of the last few changes in this example has been to provide an alternative means into this page.

At this point, the code can accept keyword and search index parameters in either the querystring or through the form-post. The code is set up structurally to produce RSS XML, although right now this is just a placeholder.

Now, if you type the URL, you will get back an empty page with just a placeholder message stating "RSS goes here."

```
http://yourPathHere/default.aspx?keywords=Radiohead&SearchIndex=Music&Type=rss
```

If you change the `Results` parameter to `normal`, you get back a page resembling Figure 7-5:

```
http://yourPathHere/default.aspx?keywords=Radiohead&SearchIndex=Music&Type=normal
```

The function `GetResults` takes the keywords and the search index from the querystring and automatically performs a search against Amazon using the `AmazonUtility` class.

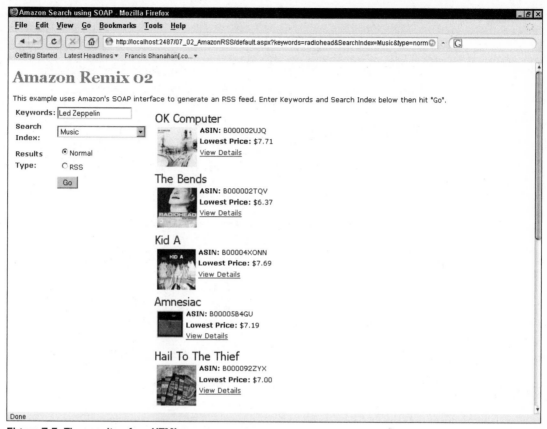

Figure 7-5: The results of an HTML query

The Structure of RSS 2.0

A given RSS 2.0 document or feed is made of up two main components: a channel and one or more items. The *channel* defines the feed content, title, publication date, and so on. It's analogous to a channel on your television. The *items* represent the actual content. Each item might contain the details of a particular news item or, in this case, some product information.

> *An RSS document is typically referred to as an "RSS feed."*

Listing 7-5 illustrates a sample RSS document.

Listing 7-5: Sample RSS Document

```
<?xml version="1.0" encoding="utf-8"?>
<rss version="2.0">
  <channel>
```

(continued)

Listing 7-5: *(continued)*

```
<title>Francis Shanahan[.com]</title>
<link>http://www.FrancisShanahan.com/</link>
<description>Blog feed of Francis Shanahan[.com]</description>
<copyright>Copyright 1999-2007 Francis A. Shanahan</copyright>

<item>
  <title>Man Bites Dog!</title>
  <link>http://www.FrancisShanahan.com/detail.aspx?cid=1003</link>
  <description>
    In today's news a hungry man grabbed a passing dachshund. Horror ensued.
  </description>
  <pubDate>Wed, 3 Jun 2006 12:00:00 GMT</pubDate>
</item>

<item>
  <title>Weird Dream</title>
  <link>http://www.FrancisShanahan.com/detail.aspx?cid=1002</link>
  <description>
    Last night I had a weird dream about a man biting a dog.
  </description>
  <pubDate>Tue, 2 Jun 2006 11:00:00 GMT</pubDate>
</item>

<item>
  <title>Really Hungry</title>
  <link>http://www.FrancisShanahan.com/detail.aspx?cid=1001</link>
  <description>
    God I'm so hungry. I could really go for some food.
  </description>
  <pubDate>Mon, 1 Jun 2006 10:00:00 GMT</pubDate>
</item>
</channel>
</rss>
```

Listing 7-5 shows a typical RSS feed consisting of a channel element and multiple item elements. The channel has a title, link, description, and a copyright notice. There are three item elements in this document; each one contains a `pubDate` or publication date, a description, a link to the individual story, and a title.

Remember, RSS stands for "Really Simple Syndication." It grew out of a need for content (typically a news headline or story) to be syndicated. Hence, the elements in a valid RSS are centered around storytelling and news headlines.

The following table describes the required XML elements for an RSS channel.

Element Name	Description
title	The name of the RSS feed.
link	The link to the Web site serving the feed.
description	A description of the feed's content.

These are the mandatory fields. Without them, your RSS feed is not valid. Of course there are other elements that you might consider adding to ensure the feed can be easily understood by users; for example, the native language of the feed, the publication date, or a contact email address.

The item element also has a number of mandatory and optional fields. The following table describes the required and optional elements of an item element.

Element Name	Description
title	The name of the item.
link	The link to the Web site serving the item.
description	A summary of the item's content.
author	(Optional) Typically, the name or email address of the author.
category	(Optional) Each item can be assigned to one or many categories.
comments	(Optional) A link to a page containing comments on this item.
enclosure	(Optional) A link to a rich-media file such as an MP3 file related to this item.
guid	(Optional) A unique identifier for this item.
pubdate	(Optional) The item publication date.
source	(Optional) The RSS channel that this item came from.

As it turns out, the elements required to describe a channel are exactly the same as those required to describe an item. In other words, title, link, and description are all that are required. The only difference is the content of the elements, which, in this case, is item-specific. Of course, additional fields such as author and publication date help readers make sense of the data.

For a complete overview of RSS 2.0, you can refer to the following URL:

```
http://blogs.law.harvard.edu/tech/rss
```

Try It Out   Creating an XML Document from Scratch

The .NET Framework provides a number of classes and facilities within the System.Xml namespace for creation and manipulation of XML. The sample code includes an additional page entitled sample_xml.aspx, which creates a simple XML structure.

The following steps walk you through the code behind the sample_xml.aspx Web page:

1.   Create a new page, named sample_xml.aspx.

2.   In the Page_Load event, add the following code, which clears the response stream and tells the browser to expect a content type of XML:

```
Response.Clear();
Response.ContentType = "text/xml";
```

3. Create a new XML document as follows:

```
XmlDocument myXml = new XmlDocument();
```

4. Create the album node using the newly created XML document:

```
XmlNode myAlbum = myXml.CreateNode(XmlNodeType.Element, "album", "");
```

5. Create a new attribute for this node, again using the XML document:

```
XmlAttribute albumName = myXml.CreateAttribute("title");
albumName.Value = "BBC Sessions";
```

6. Assign this attribute to the album node:

```
myAlbum.Attributes.Append(albumName);
```

7. Assign the album node to the document:

```
myXml.AppendChild(myAlbum);
```

8. Create some song nodes using the same approach as before:

```
XmlNode mySongA = myXml.CreateNode(XmlNodeType.Element, "song", "");
XmlNode mySongB = myXml.CreateNode(XmlNodeType.Element, "song", "");
XmlNode mySongC = myXml.CreateNode(XmlNodeType.Element, "song", "");
mySongA.InnerText = "Out on the Tiles";
mySongC.InnerText = "Achilles Last Stand";
```

9. Add these song nodes as children of the album node:

```
myAlbum.AppendChild(mySongA);
myAlbum.AppendChild(mySongB);
myAlbum.AppendChild(mySongC);
```

10. Add a new function to the AmazonUtility class to format an XML document as a string:

```
public static string GetStringFromXml(XmlDocument myDoc)
{
    StringWriter myStringWriter = new StringWriter();
    XmlTextWriter myXmlTextWriter = new XmlTextWriter(myStringWriter);

    // Write the Xml document out to a string
    myDoc.WriteTo(myXmlTextWriter);

    string strResults = myStringWriter.ToString();
    return strResults;
}
```

This function uses an XmlTextWriter tied to a StringWriter to convert the XML document into a string and return the result.

11. Lastly, write out the XML document:

```
Response.Write(AmazonUtility.GetStringFromXml(myXml));
Response.End();
```

How It Works

When you run the `sample_xml` page, the following XML structure is produced:

```
<album title="BBC Sessions">
    <song>Out on the Tiles</song>
    <song />
    <song>Achilles Last Stand</song>
</album>
```

This is a four-node document, the first (or root) node being an album element with a single attribute (a title whose value is "BBC Sessions"). The album node itself contains three other song nodes. The first and third song's inner text have been assigned a value.

The second song node, however, has not been assigned a value and, hence, is a self-closing element. This optimization was done by the framework, and is one of the advantages of using the `System.Xml` classes over creating this XML using string concatenation.

Notice also that it does not matter the order in which the nodes were added. The song nodes were added to the album node *after* the album node was added to the XML document. Yet, all nodes made it into the output.

Try It Out **Outputting RSS**

In this "Try It Out" example, you build the RSS output. You will create an XML document containing the RSS data, convert it into a string, and then stream it to the browser using the `Response` object.

1. Start by adding a new function named `FormatAsRSS` to the `AmazonUtility` class. This function will be called from within `GetResultsFromResponse` to format an Amazon response as RSS. This function begins by creating the channel information, then iterates through the result set to create new RSS items nodes.

Listing 7-6 shows the code for `FormatAsRSS`.

Listing 7-6: The `FormatAsRSS` **Function**

```
...
using System.Xml;
    ...
    public static class AmazonUtility
{

    /// <summary>
    /// Returns RSS XML for a specific Amazon Item
    /// </summary>
    /// <param name="myItems">The Items instance</param>
    /// <returns>a string of XML</returns>
    public static string FormatAsRSS(Items myItems)
    {
        XmlDocument myDoc = new XmlDocument();

        // Create the root RSS node
```

(continued)

Listing 7-6: *(continued)*

```
        XmlNode myRSS = myDoc.CreateNode(XmlNodeType.Element, "rss", "");

        // Add the version attribute
        XmlAttribute rssVersion = myDoc.CreateAttribute("version");
        rssVersion.Value = "2.0";
        myRSS.Attributes.Append(rssVersion);

        // Create a new element node named "channel"
        XmlNode channel = myDoc.CreateNode(XmlNodeType.Element, "channel", "");

        // Create a new element node named "title"
        XmlNode title = myDoc.CreateNode(XmlNodeType.Element, "title", "");
        title.InnerText = "First Amazon Remix";

        // Create a new element node named "link"
        XmlNode link = myDoc.CreateNode(XmlNodeType.Element, "link", "");
        link.InnerText = "http://www.FrancisShanahan.com/";

        // Create a new element node named "description"
        XmlNode description = myDoc.CreateNode(XmlNodeType.Element, "description",
"");

        description.InnerText = "Amazon results through RSS 2.0";

        // Append the channel specific elements
        channel.AppendChild(title);
        channel.AppendChild(link);
        channel.AppendChild(description);

        // Iterate through the products
        foreach (Item myItem in myItems.Item)
        {
            // Create a new item node for each one
            XmlNode myNode = CreateRSSItem(myDoc, myItem);
            // Append the resulting item to the channel
            channel.AppendChild(myNode);
        }

        // Finally append the channel and the RSS node
        myRSS.AppendChild(channel);
        myDoc.AppendChild(myRSS);

        return GetStringFromXml(myDoc);
    }
}
```

2.   Next, add another new function, `CreateRSSItem`, to parse each item in turn. This function
     takes an Amazon `Item` and creates a new RSS item node to be added to document. The new
     node contains all relevant Amazon product information such as description, price, and so on.
     `CreateRSSItem` is shown abbreviated as follows:

```
private static XmlNode CreateRSSItem(XmlDocument myDoc, Item myItem)
{
    // Create a new element node named "item"
```

```
    XmlNode rssItem = myDoc.CreateNode(XmlNodeType.Element, "item", "");

    // Create a new element node named "title"
    XmlNode title = myDoc.CreateNode(XmlNodeType.Element, "title", "");
    title.InnerText = myItem.ItemAttributes.Title;

    // Create a new element node named "link"
    XmlNode link = myDoc.CreateNode(XmlNodeType.Element, "link", "");
    link.InnerText = myItem.DetailPageURL;

    // Create a new element node named "description"
    XmlNode description = myDoc.CreateNode(XmlNodeType.Element, "description", "");

...additional details omitted for brevity...

    // Append the new elements to this rss Item.
    rssItem.AppendChild(title);
    rssItem.AppendChild(link);
    rssItem.AppendChild(description);

    return rssItem;
}
```

3. Add a new `using` statement to the `AmazonUtility` class to leverage the `System.Xml` namespace. This namespace houses the `XmlDocument` and related objects:

```
using System.Xml;
```

4. You will need to modify the `GetResultsFromResponse` function to allow the caller to specify whether or not results should be provided as RSS. This is easily accomplished with an additional parameter and an `if` statement:

```
public static string GetResultsFromResponse(
   ItemSearchResponse myResponse,
   bool doRss)
   {
       // Parse the response and return the results
           if (doRss)
           {  // Get the results in RSS
               strResults += FormatAsRSS(myItems);
           }
           else
```

When you run the application, you can now specify (through the default form) whether you would like the results in RSS or Normal format. The RSS output will be as shown in Listing 7-7.

Listing 7-7: Sample RSS Output for a Given Search

```
<rss version="2.0">
  <channel>
    <title>First Amazon Remix</title>
    <link>http://www.FrancisShanahan.com/</link>
    <description>Amazon results through RSS 2.0</description>
    <item>
```

(continued)

Listing 7-7: *(continued)*

```
        <title>Led Zeppelin IV (aka ZOSO)</title>
        <link>http://www.amazon.com/exec/obidos/redirect?...</link>
        <description>Lowest Price:$6.55
...Also known as the "rune" album or Zoso because of the medieval symbols adorning
the inner sleeve,...</description>
        <pubDate>6/24/2006</pubDate>
    </item>
    <item>
        <title>Led Zeppelin II</title>
<link>http://www.amazon.com/exec/obidos/redirect?...</link>
        <descriptionLowest Price:$6.79...Riff rock had been what Jimmy Page's former
band, the ...</description>
        <pubDate>6/24/2006</pubDate>
    </item>
    <item>
        <title>Houses Of The Holy</title>
<link>http://www.amazon.com/exec/obidos/redirec... </link>
        <description>Lowest Price:$5.65...Buoyed by the runaway commercial success of
...</description>
        <pubDate>6/24/2006</pubDate>
    </item>
  </channel>
</rss>
```

Consuming the RSS Data

With the application complete, it's time now to test. Start by testing the output from the browser. Run the application and enter the following URL:

```
http://YourPathHere/default.aspx?Keywords=radiohead&SearchIndex=Music&type=rss
```

The browser will display the RSS data, as shown in Figure 7-6.

There are a number of ways of consuming RSS data, the most typical, of course, being through an RSS reader such as SharpReader. You can obtain SharpReader through the following URL:

```
http://www.SharpReader.net
```

With the application running on your local machine, fire up SharpReader and type the same URI as before. SharpReader will go out, retrieve your XML data, and display it as a list of headlines similar to Figure 7-7.

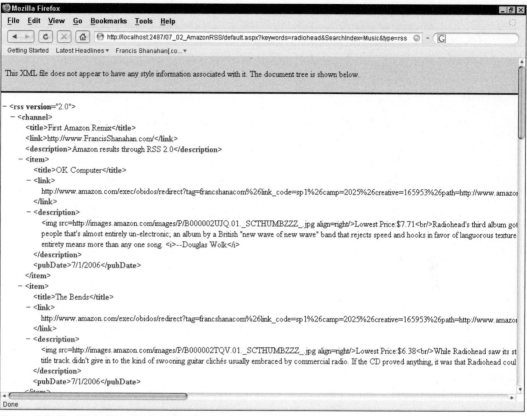

Figure 7-6: The RSS data displayed in the browser

Other Things to Try

If you have deployed your application to a public Web site (for example, http://www.Francis Shanahan.com) and it is no longer running on your localhost Web server, you can consume this feed using any RSS reader that understands RSS 2.0. This includes sites like Google Reader, Start.com, or Live.com.

To add a feed to Start.com, open up the Start.com Web site in a browser and make sure the Left-menu is displayed. Click "Add Feeds and Gadgets" and enter the URL to your application in the text area. When you submit the form, the Start.com Web site adds this as a new feed in your profile. Results will be automatically refreshed periodically.

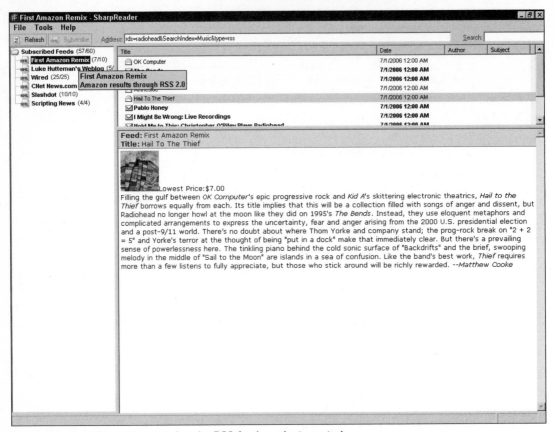

Figure 7-7: SharpReader consuming the RSS feed you just created

Validating the RSS

As mentioned earlier, RSS is a specification and, as such, a well-formed RSS document will adhere to a specific XML Schema. To ensure your application is producing XML that follows the rules of the RSS schema, you can validate your feed using a number of freely available RSS validators. Try navigating to http://www.feedvalidator.org, entering your feed, and clicking OK. This Web site checks the format of your RSS document to ensure that you have accurately implemented the specification. Any errors or deviations from the official RSS schema will be highlighted by the Web site, along with suggestions on how to correct these errors.

Searching in a Different Locale

As mentioned earlier (while building the Amazon SOAP proxy), various WSDL endpoints are available, depending on the locale you wish to search by. One additional piece of information here is that it is possible to reuse the code you have created, with no modifications, to search by a different locale. In other words, you have coded this example against the US locale, but it is possible with a simple configuration change to point the application code at the United Kingdom (UK), French (FR), or Japanese (JP) (Figure 7-8) databases, for example.

Figure 7-8: The Amazon Remix displaying Japanese data

When you added the Web reference to the project, Visual Studio generated the Web proxy class. In addition to this, a new application setting was added to the `web.config` file. This setting looks like this:

```
<appSettings>
    <add key="com.amazon.webservices.AWSECommerceService"
value="http://soap.amazon.com/onca/soap?Service=AWSECommerceService"/>
    </appSettings>
```

By modifying the value of the Web service key, you can point the entire proxy class at a new locale. Change the value to the following:

```
<appSettings>
    <add key="com.amazon.webservices.AWSECommerceService"
value="http://soap.amazon.co.uk/onca/soap?Service=AWSECommerceService"/>
    </appSettings>
```

This change points the proxy at the UK locale. When you run the application, products and prices are displayed from the UK database and using British pounds sterling.

Because this is a configuration setting, you can change this setting without stopping the application and without recompiling the application. Try running the application, then changing the value while keeping the browser open. Selecting Refresh in the browser will bring back a new set of results formatted accordingly.

The following table details the valid endpoints by locale. Note these are different from the previous table, which detailed WSDL endpoints.

Locale	WSDL Endpoint URI
US	`http://soap.amazon.com/onca/soap?Service=AWSECommerceService`
UK	`http://soap.amazon.co.uk/onca/soap?Service=AWSECommerceService`
DE	`http://soap.amazon.de/onca/soap?Service=AWSECommerceService`
JP	`http://soap.amazon.co.jp/onca/soap?Service=AWSECommerceService`
FR	`http://soap.amazon.fr/onca/soap?Service=AWSECommerceService`
CA	`http://soap.amazon.ca/onca/soap?Service=AWSECommerceService`

The Japanese locale (Figure 7-8) uses a special character set to display the Yen currency symbol. This will not display with the existing code, and you may need to set the character set of your page to be different from the default.

Other Ideas to Try

As mentioned earlier, RSS is everywhere. You might consider taking this example even further by providing a means to sort the data, or to further refine the search criteria beyond simply specifying a `keyword` and `searchindex`.

I also recommend exploring the RSS features available in both Internet Explorer version 7 and the upcoming release of Windows Vista. Vista includes a wide range of support for RSS and feed management, including a new `sidebar gadget`, which can consume and display RSS data right on the desktop.

Summary

In this chapter, you built your first Amazon remix. You built two complete working applications that each leverage Amazon's data using SOAP. In the process, you learned a great many aspects of Web service technology, including the following:

- ❏ How to create a SOAP proxy for a given WSDL endpoint
- ❏ How to store configuration data in the `web.config` file
- ❏ How to iterate through an Amazon search result set

❑   How RSS is structured

❑   How to build an XML document from scratch

In Chapter 8, you will use what you have learned here to build your first real mashup. Chapter 8 integrates Yahoo search results into the Amazon example and illustrates how to make REST API calls using the .NET Framework.

Before proceeding, try the exercises that follow to test your understanding of the material covered in this chapter. You can find the solutions to these exercises in Appendix B.

Exercises

The following questions will test your knowledge of the content contained in this chapter.

1.   How can you easily change the locale used by the Amazon SOAP proxy (for example, to search UK product listings instead of the US listings)?

2.   How can an XmlDocument be created using C#?

3.   How can you construct a search query against Amazon using the Amazon SOAP interface?

4.   Where can you store configuration information in an ASP.NET Web site?

Part III
The Mashups

In This Part:

Building Your First Mashup

Now that you have conquered your first remix, the tools are in place for you to tackle your first real mashup. In this chapter, you use the both Amazon's and Yahoo's REST APIs for the first time. You learn two separate techniques for binding the resulting data to the presentation layer. The first uses an ASP.NET Repeater; the second uses standard HTML. You learn how to use both and create a killer mashup in the process.

The techniques in this chapter teach you how to do the following:

❑ Call REST-style APIs using C#

❑ Convert ASP.NET server controls to traditional HTML

❑ Bind data to a `Repeater` control

❑ Build a mini-browser within a browser using HTTP GET

❑ Merge Amazon and Yahoo XML data together into a single document

The Battle Plan: Yahoo Plus Amazon

In this mashup, you build a search interface that searches both Yahoo and Amazon from the same screen. The source data will be consolidated into a single XML document and transformed into XHTML. The results will be presented to the user in a standard search-results type table.

Understanding the Architecture

In Chapter 7, you used SOAP to request and retrieve data from Amazon. In this chapter, you use a REST-style interface. Figure 8-1 shows the various elements involved and the flow of data between each party.

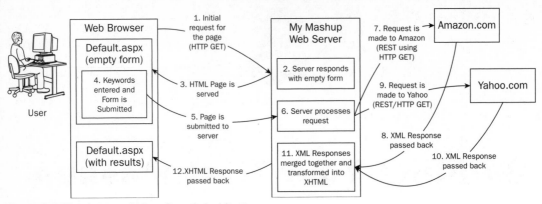

Figure 8-1: The Amazon/Yahoo Search Architecture

How It Works

As you can see from Figure 8-1, there are quite a few steps involved in this mashup. Thankfully, each one is relatively simple and should not pose any problems:

1. The browser requests the page in the usual manner, HTTP GET.

2. The server processes this request and builds the default.aspx page as requested.

3. The built page, entirely HTML (no JavaScript in this example), is streamed to the browser.

4. The user types in a few keywords to search on and presses Submit.

5. The page form is submitted to the server.

6. The Web server processes this new request and realizes there is more work to be done.

7. The keywords entered in Step 4 are used as part of a REST-style request to Amazon's API.

8. Amazon responds with the results formatted in XML.

9. The server now makes a REST-style call to Yahoo.

10. Yahoo also responds with its own XML.

11. The Web server now mashes these two results into a single XML document, and transforms that document using an eXtensible Stylesheet Language Transformation (XSLT) into a snippet of XHTML. This XHTML is inserted into the page.

12. The page is served once more, this time with result content. The page is displayed complete with the results from the searches.

In Chapter 7, you retrieved some data from Amazon using SOAP. In this chapter, you will start with the Yahoo interface, which uses REST-style APIs.

The Approach

Because there are two sources of data in this mashup (Amazon and Yahoo), it's simplest to build an interface to each datasource independent of the other. This step-by-step approach makes development much easier. Once you get each one working in isolation, you can mash them both together.

In the first exercise in this chapter, you build the Yahoo interface. It's important to understand the multitude of ways mashup data can be retrieved from the Internet and presented. This chapter examines two approaches.

The first technique will retrieve Yahoo data using REST and then bind that data to an ASP.NET `Repeater` control similar to the `GridView` example in Chapter 4. This time, the data is coming from a remote source and not a local XML file.

The second technique will retrieve Amazon data using a non-ASP.NET-specific mechanism that employs standard HTML controls and a generic REST interface.

Finally, the two examples will be mashed together to produce a consolidated set of results and complete your first mashup.

The User Interface for Yahoo Search

The client interface is as complicated as you want to make it. For clarity, I'll keep things simple with the form in Figure 8-2.

The interface is simply a `TextBox` to enter search keywords and a `Button` control to execute the search. You should build this interface with ASP.NET server controls, as opposed to HTML controls.

The Amazon interface that you build later in this chapter will use pure HTML controls and, hence, could be seen as being a little more "technology agnostic." There really is nothing that necessitates the use of ASP.NET for a mashup, and my job is simply to illustrate the possibilities. It's up to you as the developer to use the right approach for a given situation.

The Repeater Control

In this first example, you'll display the results from Yahoo in an ASP.NET `Repeater` control. The `Repeater` is a much lighter-weight control than the `GridView` that you used in Chapter 4. Ensure that the page is opened in Design view, and then drag and drop a `Repeater` onto the page:

```
<asp:Repeater ID="Repeater1" runat="server" DataSourceID="">
</asp:Repeater>
```

This markup is added to the page and simply instantiates a basic `Repeater`. Normally, you would bind this control to a datasource contained on the page, as you did in Chapter 4. However, in this case, the datasource will be an XML response from Yahoo that will not exist until run-time. The `DataSourceID` is set to nothing in the previous markup. As a result, there is nothing to bind to at design time and, hence, no design-time binding support.

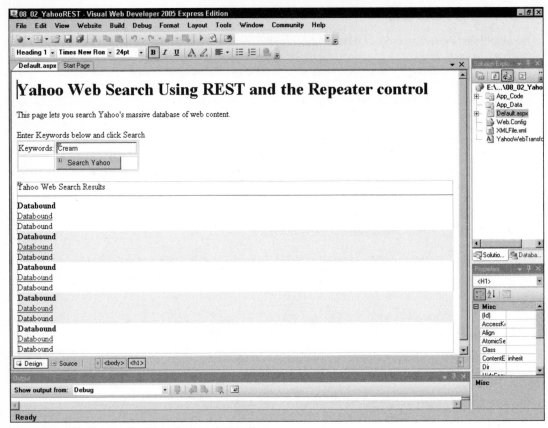

Figure 8-2: The Yahoo client interface at design time

The Repeater control works by allowing you to define various templates as per the following table.

Template Name	Description
HeaderTemplate	The first row in the rendered Repeater. Use this to define headings or open an HTML table tag.
ItemTemplate	The main template, used to bind the data to the control.
AlternatingItemTemplate	Similar to the ItemTemplate, this provides a mechanism to format alternating rows for clarity.
FooterTemplate	The opposite of header.
SeparatorTemplate	Occurs in between items, again for ease of formatting.

Each template can be bound to a data element in the underlying datasource. The template structure provides great flexibility in terms of the way you bind to the data, and the resulting markup is much lighter-weight than the equivalent content rendered using a `GridView`.

You could try creating this same screen using a `GridView` *for comparison.*

Define a `HeaderTemplate` as follows:

```
<HeaderTemplate>Yahoo Web Search Results</HeaderTemplate>
```

Next up is the main `ItemTemplate`, which looks like the following:

```
<ItemTemplate>
    <b><%# DataBinder.Eval ( Container.DataItem, "Title" ) %></b><br />
    <a href="<%# DataBinder.Eval ( Container.DataItem, "ClickUrl" ) %>"><%#
DataBinder.Eval ( Container.DataItem, "Url" ) %></a><br />
    <%# DataBinder.Eval ( Container.DataItem, "Summary" ) %>
</ItemTemplate>
```

Looking at this code, you see the `ItemTemplate` declaration. Inside the `ItemTemplate` are several `DataBinder` statements. Each `DataBinder` expression takes the following form:

```
<%# DataBinder.Eval( Container.DataItem, "COLUMN_NAME" ) %>
```

`COLUMN_NAME` is the name of the data item to display. When you execute this and successfully bind to a datasource, the `DataBinder` expression is replaced with the relevant data from that datasource. The column names `"Title"`, `"ClickUrl"`, `"Url"`, and `"Summary"` are specified in the Yahoo API's XML response, as per the Yahoo API documentation.

You can also define an `AlternatingItemTemplate`, which should use the same markup as the `ItemTemplate`. You should modify this markup with perhaps a different background color so that every other row in the `Repeater` will appear highlighted. This provides a useful visual cue to the user that greatly aids readability.

The `SeparatorTemplate` is omitted here, but it's typically just a simple HTML horizontal row that looks like this.

```
<SeparatorTemplate><hr /></SeparatorTemplate>
```

The `separator` is inserted in between each item and `alternatingItemTemplate`.

That completes the markup for the client page. Next up is the logic behind the page.

Querying Yahoo Through REST

In this next section, you'll turn your attention to the code-behind file for this Web page. You'll implement the REST interface into Yahoo and learn how to convert the resulting XML into a dataset that can be bound to the repeater.

A Sample Yahoo REST URI

Here's a simple experiment. Insert your Yahoo developer Application ID into the following URL and try pasting the result that follows into the browser:

```
http://api.search.yahoo.com/WebSearchService/V1/webSearch?appid=<INSERT YOUR APP ID
HERE>&query=cream&results=10&start=1
```

> **This is important. You will need to insert your own Application ID for this URI to work. I cannot distribute my personal Application ID because it is against the terms of the Yahoo Developer Network policy. This applies to all APIs used in this book.**

When you paste this or *any URL* into a Web browser, the browser issues what's called an HTTP GET request to that URI. The result is an XML file served directly from Yahoo's network. You can play with the query keywords themselves, but the response will look similar to Listing 8-1.

Listing 8-1: Sample Yahoo Results

```
<ResultSet xsi:schemaLocation="urn:yahoo:srch
http://api.search.yahoo.com/WebSearchService/V1/WebSearchResponse.xsd"
totalResultsAvailable="93100000" totalResultsReturned="2" firstResultPosition="1">
<Result>
   <Title>...</Title>
      <Summary>...</Summary>
      <Url>...</Url>
      <ClickUrl>...</ClickUrl>
      <ModificationDate>...</ModificationDate>
      <MimeType>...</MimeType>
      <Cache>
         <Url>...</Url>
         <Size>...</Size>
      </Cache>
   </Result>
</ResultSet>
```

The document nodes themselves will, of course, contain actual data, but I have omitted this data for clarity.

Notice the presence of the "Title", "ClickUrl", "Url", and "Summary" nodes. These will become columns and have already been specified in the Repeater control for data-binding purposes.

> *This is a sample of the data you can expect from the Web Search API. From it, you can clearly read the structure of the xml schema. This method of issuing URI calls in a browser to get some test data is a useful technique when debugging your mashups, and will work with all REST-style interfaces that support HTTP GET.*

Yahoo has specific URIs for each of its APIs. This example uses the Web interface, but you can search for Images, Audio, Movies, and so on. Refer to Chapter 5 for more details on the data available from Yahoo.

Before moving on, you should review the structure of the request:

❑ First is the path to the Yahoo server:

```
http://api.search.yahoo.com/
```

❑ Then the API you're looking for (in this case, webSearch):

```
WebSearchService/V1/webSearch
```

❑ Finally, the Querystring that appears after the question mark in a given URI:

```
?appid=<INSERT YOUR APP ID HERE>&query=cream&results=10&start=1
```

This breaks down as shown in the following table.

Querystring Keyname	Description
Appid	The application ID, required for all Yahoo API calls.
query	The keywords of the search.
results	The number of results to retrieve.
Start	The position to start delivering results from. This is useful if you're implementing pagination of the result set.

Try It Out Build a Mini-Browser in C#

If the browser can do it, so can you. To build even the most basic of mashups, you must be able to issue GET requests from within your C# code. Luckily, the .NET Framework provides a comprehensive set of classes to accomplish this task. In this example, you build a simple page that retrieves any URI you specify and displays the results. This simple code will be reused to retrieve XML from Yahoo later in the chapter.

1. Create a new Web site with a single page named default.aspx.

2. Open default.aspx and drag a textbox onto the page. Rename it txtUri.

3. Drag a button onto the page and rename this cmdGo.

4. Drag a Literal control onto the page and name this myLiteral.

5. Double-click the button to open the code-behind for the control.

6. Add the following two using statements at the top of the C# file:

```
using System.Net;
using System.IO;
```

These statements are necessary because the HttpWebRequest and HttpWebResponse classes are both contained in the System.Net namespace. The Stream classes are located in the System.IO namespace.

7. Enter the following code into the `cmdGo_Click` event handler:

```
protected void cmdGo_Click(object sender, EventArgs e)
{
    HttpWebRequest myRequest = (HttpWebRequest)WebRequest.Create(this.txtUri.Text);
    HttpWebResponse myResponse = (HttpWebResponse)myRequest.GetResponse();
    Stream myResponseStream = myResponse.GetResponseStream();
    StreamReader myReader = new StreamReader(myResponseStream);

    this.myLiteral.Text = ((StreamReader)myReader).ReadToEnd();
}
```

8. Press F5 or click Play to run the project. If prompted to add a `web.config` to the project, choose "Yes" to add one in.

9. When the application launches, type a URI (for example, `www.amazon.com`) into the textbox and click Go. The page refreshes after loading the page you requested into the `Literal` control, and should look like Figure 8-3.

Figure 8-3: The mini-browser in action

How It Works

The code for this example is very simple. When the user clicks Go, the page returns to the server and the `Click` event for the `cmdGo` button fires. A new `HttpWebRequest` object is created using the URI that the user entered in the form:

```
HttpWebRequest myRequest = (HttpWebRequest)WebRequest.Create(this.txtUri.Text);
```

Next, the request is actually executed, meaning the application goes out and retrieves the URI specified in the request:

```
HttpWebResponse myResponse = (HttpWebResponse)myRequest.GetResponse();
```

At this point, you have a valid `HttpWebResponse`. The response itself does not yet contain the content for the request, and this is retrieved using the `GetResponseStream()` method. `GetResponseStream` returns a `Stream` that can then be used to read the body of the response from the server:

```
Stream myResponseStream = myResponse.GetResponseStream();
```

You read the response stream with a `StreamReader`:

```
StreamReader myReader = new StreamReader(myResponseStream);
```

The last thing to do is simply read the HTML from the response stream:

```
this.myLiteral.Text = ((StreamReader)myReader).ReadToEnd();
```

The Yahoo Code Beside

Now that you have successfully retrieved HTML, you can use this same code to retrieve XML from Yahoo! If you built the mini-browser sample, it's time to switch back to the Yahoo code base.

> *In ASP.NET 1.1 the code behind a page was entirely its own class, hence the name "code-behind." The ASPX portion of the page sub-classed the C# code-behind class at run-time to create a new class. In ASP.NET 2.0, the code file associated with a page is actually a partial class that is shared across the ASPX file and the C# file. For this reason, ASP.NET 2.0 code files are known as "code besides," but I am still stuck with the original terminology.*

Adding the Generic Helper Class

Earlier, you wrote a small piece of code to obtain any Web URI and convert it into a string. This is incredibly useful, so you should reuse it by placing it into its own class.

Right-click the project and add a new item, a class named `WebUtility.cs`. Visual Studio will prompt to store this class in a special subfolder named `App_Code`. This makes sense because the class itself is not associated with any specific page. This approach helps maintain order in the project and keeps code organized (Listing 8-2).

Listing 8-2: The New WebUtility **Class**

```
using System;
using System.Xml;
using System.Net;
using System.IO;
using System.Text;
using System.Configuration;
using System.Xml.Xsl;
using System.Collections.Specialized;

    /// <summary>
    /// Simply Helper class with many useful Mashup functions
    /// </summary>
    public static class webUtility
    {
        static webUtility()
        {
        }

    /// <summary>
    /// Retrieves a Uri using HTTP GET and returns the results as XML
    /// </summary>
    /// <param name="strURL">Uri to retrive</param>
    /// <returns>Xml document results</returns>
      public static XmlDocument GetUri(string strURI){

        // Create a request object
            HttpWebRequest myRequest =
(HttpWebRequest)WebRequest.Create(strURI);

        // Obtain the response from the server
        HttpWebResponse myResponse = (HttpWebResponse)myRequest.GetResponse();
        Stream myResponseStream = myResponse.GetResponseStream();

        // Load the result into an XML document
        XmlDocument myDoc = new XmlDocument();
        myDoc.Load(myResponseStream);

        // return the XML document
            return myDoc;
    }
    }
```

Because this is a helper class and will not store data of its own, it's a good idea to make it static. A static class does not need to be instantiated. This is a nice coding convenience, and works well given the nature of the functionality that the class provides.

When you have a static class, there is only ever one instance of that class available at run-time. This pattern is known as the Singleton Design Pattern. Be careful with static classes in a high-performance environment because if many threads are attempting to access the same instance, they may act in contention with one another.

You can make a class static with the addition of the `static` keyword to the class definition:

```
public static class webUtility
```

Notice the following two additional lines of code at the bottom of the `GetUri` function:

```
// Load the result into an XML document
XmlDocument myDoc = new XmlDocument();
myDoc.Load(myResponseStream);
```

These convert the response stream to an `XmlDocument` before returning it. This is a little more useful (as you'll see) for transforming the data. Of course, as you experiment, you might consider making a copy of this function that simply returns a string. Strings are easier to deal with, but more difficult to transform. XML is perfect for transformations.

Now you have a very useful little helper function. This `WebUtility` class will be reused in many of the subsequent chapters.

Converting an XML Document to a DataSet

`DataSets` are the primary class involved in data access in ADO.NET. Unlike ADO `Recordsets`, ADO.NET `DataSets` are disconnected, meaning they do not maintain a live connection to their data-sources. The `DataSet` serializes its data as XML, which makes it very easy and useful to serialize and deserialize the data.

> *"Serializing" means taking an object and converting all its data into a string. Why would you want to do this? An object exists in memory. To store that object, you need some way of examining its state (meaning all its data elements) and saving them. This is serialization. "De-serialization" is the exact opposite, taking a string and instantiating an object from it. The string in this case is usually XML data, although you will find in later chapters that it might take other forms (for example, JSON).*

If you have an XML document, you can easily populate a `DataSet` from XML as follows:

```
XmlNodeReader myReader = new XmlNodeReader(myDoc);
DataSet ds = new DataSet();
ds.ReadXml(myReader);
```

This code creates an `XmlNodeReader` based on the `XmlDocument`, `myDoc`. It then instantiates a new `DataSet` that starts out life empty but in the final line of code is populated using the original XML document.

Behind the Submit button, you need to do the following:

1. Obtain the Yahoo REST API response.
2. Convert it into an XML document.
3. Fill a `DataSet` using the XML document as the datasource.
4. Bind the `DataSet` to the `Repeater` control to display the results.

Listing 8-3 shows the code behind the Submit button, which implements these steps.

Listing 8-3: The Event Handler for the Submit Button

```
protected void Submit1_ServerClick1(object sender, EventArgs e)
    {
        string strKeywords = this.Text1.Value;

        if (strKeywords != "")
        {
            XmlDocument myDoc =
webUtility.GetUri("http://api.search.yahoo.com/WebSearchService/V1/webSearch?appid=
<INSERT YOUR APP ID HERE>&query=" + strKeywords + "&results=10&start=1");

            XmlNodeReader reader = new XmlNodeReader(myDoc);
            DataSet ds = new DataSet();
            ds.ReadXml(reader);
            this.Repeater1.DataSource = ds.Tables[1].DefaultView;
            Repeater1.DataBind();
        }
    }
```

Run the application, enter a keyword or a search term in the text box, and click the button. If all is well the page will refresh itself and display a set of the results in the Repeater control, as shown in Figure 8-4.

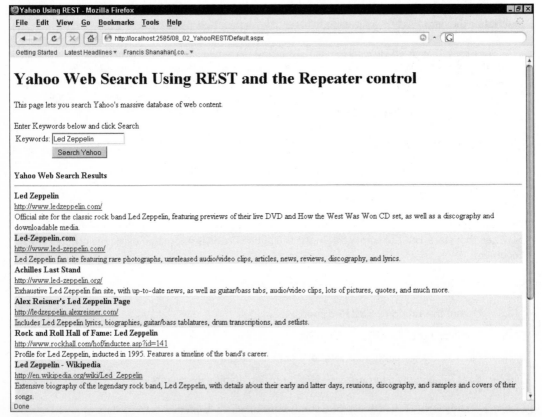

Figure 8-4: The Yahoo Repeater example in action

Play around with this until you are comfortable with what is going on here. Essentially, you have achieved the same result as you did in Chapter 7, only this time using a different approach.

The nice thing about this REST/XML/DataSet approach is that the presentation of the results is entirely based on the Repeater control. You don't need to recompile the application to modify how the results are presented or styled.

Congratulations! You are 50 percent of the way through your first mashup! With the Yahoo portion of the mashup complete, it's time to turn your attention to Amazon. Remember, you simply want to be able to search both sites at the same time, and return a consolidated list of results. In the next section, you reuse the WebUtility helper class to obtain an XmlDocument of Amazon Search results.

The Amazon Client User Interface

In the previous section, you built a perfectly good search interface with ASP.NET server controls. In this section, you build the same interface, but with pure HTML controls. If you'd like to reuse the Yahoo interface, you are free to do so, but I want to point out that ASP.NET server controls are in no way required when building mashups.

The easiest way to convert the Yahoo sample is to take the HTML source for the page and remove the runat=server attributes from the form element:

```html
<body>
    <form id="form1" runat="server"></form>
    <h1>
        Amazon + Yahoo</h1>
    This page lets you search Amazon and Yahoo at the same time!!!<br />
    <br />
    Enter Keywords, Search Index and click Go.
    <form action="default.aspx" method="get" target="_blank">
    <table>
    <tr>
        <td>Keywords: </td>
        <td><input type=text value="Zeppelin" name="Keywords" /></td>
    </tr>
    <tr>
        <td>Search Index: </td>
        <td>
            <select name=SearchIndex>
<option value="Blended">All</option>
<option value="Electronics">Electronics</option>
<option value="Music" selected>Music</option>
<option value="DVD">DVD</option>
<option value="Books">Books</option>
    ...
    </select>
        </td>
    </tr>
    <tr>
        <td>
        </td>
        <td>
```

```
        <input type=submit name="Go" value="Go" id="Submit1"/>
    </td>
</tr>
</table>
<br />
    <asp:Literal ID="myLiteral" runat="server"></asp:Literal>
</form>
</body>
```

In the HTML code for this form, there are a couple of things to note. The first is that the ASP.NET server `form` is empty. Every ASP.NET page needs a server `form`, so you cannot remove this tag, but there is nothing stopping you from leaving it empty.

The next thing to note is the addition of the HTML `form` that drives the example. This `form` is set to submit using the GET method, and the action is set to the name of the page. Lastly, the ASP.NET `Literal` control at the bottom of the listing will store the results of the search.

XSL Transformations

Transforming data with eXtensible Stylesheet Language (XSL) style sheets is a powerful data-manipulation technique that you'll use over and over again in your mashups. This is the first time you are encountering it, so you'll spend a little extra time on this first transformation.

Conceptual Overview of XSL

XSL transforms an XML document from one form to another by examining the source document, looking for patterns, and then providing output according to a set of rules contained in the XSL style sheet.

The heart of XSLT is the template. A *template* is a way of specifying a pattern and telling the XSL processor, "any time you see this pattern, do the following."

If you examine a simple XSL template, it looks like the following:

```
<xsl:template match="/">
    <!-- Do something -->
</xsl:template>
```

This template is looking for the root node of the underlying document. The match value (in this case, a slash "/") is an XPath expression that matches a portion of the XML document:

```
<xsl:template match="Title">
 <!-- Do something -->
</xsl:template>
```

This template matches the "Title" node.

The `xsl:` portion of these elements simply denotes that this `template` tag is part of the XSL namespace. `xsl:` is actually a namespace prefix, as specified in the `xsl:stylesheet` tag:

```
<xsl:stylesheet version="1.0" xmlns:xsl="http://www.w3.org/1999/XSL/Transform">
```

Restating this in non-XML/XSL jargon this means "any time you see an `xsl:` in an element, the following element is part of the `http://www.w3.org/1999/XSL/Transform` schema."

Specifying the XSL Output Type

When you do a transformation, you end up with another document, typically an XML document, but it could be HTML or text or almost anything. You can specify the output as HTML quite easily using the `<xsl:output>` node as follows:

```
<xsl:output method="html"/>
```

Accurate XPath with Namespaces

To obtain the value of a specific XML node, you use the `<xsl:value-of>` element. This element contains an attribute that specifies the XML node to output. The following statement would output the value of the `"Title"` node:

```
<xsl:value-of select="Title" />
```

This differs from the following:

```
<xsl:value-of select="n:Title" />
```

In the second example, the element name `"Title"` is prefixed by a namespace prefix `n:`. You must look back up the document tree to obtain the find the `xmlns` namespace declaration that specifies which namespace the `n:` prefix represents.

In this case, you might find the following:

```
xmlns:n="urn:yahoo:srch"
```

This is how XML scopes elements. Without scoping, if two XML documents used the same node name (for example, `"Title"`), and those documents were combined into a single document, there would be no way of specifying which particular node you want.

With namespaces you can accurately specify exactly which node you're looking for. Remember, even if you don't see a namespace prefix, that node still belongs to a namespace. This special namespace is known as the *default namespace*.

Triggering a Template

In order for a template to execute on a given node, that template must be invoked. XSL does this through the `apply-templates` node:

```
<xsl:apply-templates select="Title"/>
```

This tells the parser to go out, find any templates that match this node (the `"Title"`), and execute them. When it's finished, the result of these templates will be placed at the `apply-templates` location in the resulting document.

An XSL Performance Tip

It's a best practice to keep your XPath expressions as small as possible. For example, consider the following:

```
<xsl:template match="nodeA/nodeB/nodeC">
    <!-- do something -->
</xsl:template>
```

It's more efficient for the parser to process the following:

```
<xsl:template match="nodeA">
    <xsl:apply-templates select ="nodeB"/>
</xsl:template>

<xsl:template match="nodeB">
    <xsl:apply-templates select ="nodeC"/>
</xsl:template>

<xsl:template match="nodeC">
    <!-- do something -->
</xsl:template>
```

This might be counterintuitive at first because the second method looks like a lot more code. The most expensive operation the XML parser does is to evaluate the XPath expressions contained in every node.

"nodeA/nodeB/nodeC" is a more complicated expression than simply evaluating "nodeA" then "nodeB" then "nodeC" in turn. With this in mind, the second syntax becomes a better approach.

The Amazon XSL Style Sheet

With your new-found understanding of XSL, let's walk through the sample style sheet as shown in Listing 8-4.

Listing 8-4: The Amazon Listing Results Style Sheet

```
<?xml version="1.0" encoding="UTF-8"?>
<xsl:stylesheet version="1.0" xmlns="http://www.w3.org/1999/xhtml"
xmlns:tns="http://www.w3.org/1999/xhtml"
xmlns:xsl="http://www.w3.org/1999/XSL/Transform"
xmlns:a="http://webservices.amazon.com/AWSECommerceService/2005-10-05">
  <xsl:output method="html"/>
  <xsl:template match="/">
    <table>
      <tr>
        <td>
          <h2>Results from Amazon</h2>
        </td>
      </tr>
      <tr>
        <td valign="top">
          <xsl:apply-templates select="a:ItemSearchResponse/a:Items"/>
        </td>
      </tr>
```

```
      </table>
    </xsl:template>

    <xsl:template match="a:Items">
      <table>
        <xsl:apply-templates select="a:Item"/>
      </table>
    </xsl:template>

    <xsl:template match="a:Item">
      <tr>
        <td>
          <img>
            <xsl:attribute name="src">
              <xsl:value-of select="a:SmallImage/a:URL" />
            </xsl:attribute>
            <xsl:attribute name="alt">
              <xsl:value-of select="a:ItemAttributes/a:Title" />
            </xsl:attribute>
            <xsl:attribute name="align">left</xsl:attribute>
          </img>
          <a>
            <xsl:attribute name="href">
              <xsl:value-of select="a:DetailPageURL" />
            </xsl:attribute>
            <xsl:value-of select="a:ItemAttributes/a:Title" />
          </a>
          <br/>
          <xsl:apply-templates select="a:OfferSummary"/>
          <br/>
        </td>
      </tr>
    </xsl:template>

    <xsl:template match="a:OfferSummary">
      <b>Lowest Price:</b><xsl:value-of select="a:LowestNewPrice/a:FormattedPrice"
/><br/>
      <b>Total New:</b><xsl:value-of select="a:TotalNew" /> |
      <b>Total Used:</b><xsl:value-of select="a:TotalUsed" />
    </xsl:template>
```

This style sheet has been kept purposefully simple with little actual HTML or formatting.

The first line in the file simply denotes that this is an XML file:

```
<?xml version="1.0" encoding="UTF-8"?>
```

The next line is the XSL style sheet declaration that sets up any namespaces specific to the document, along with the XSL namespace itself:

```
<xsl:stylesheet version="1.0" xmlns="http://www.w3.org/1999/xhtml"
xmlns:tns="http://www.w3.org/1999/xhtml"
xmlns:xsl="http://www.w3.org/1999/XSL/Transform"
xmlns:a="http://webservices.amazon.com/AWSECommerceService/2005-10-05">
```

This line also dictates the target namespace or `xmlns:tns`, which is XHTML, because this style sheet will output HTML. Next, I specify the output of the XSL transformation, which in this case, is HTML:

```
<xsl:output method="html"/>
```

Next is the root template, which, as always, matches to the root node of the XML document:

```
<xsl:template match="/">
  <table>
    <tr>
      <td>
        <h2>Results from Amazon</h2>
      </td>
    </tr>
    <tr>
      <td valign="top">
        <xsl:apply-templates select="a:ItemSearchResponse/a:Items"/>
      </td>
    </tr>
  </table>
</xsl:template>
```

The root template writes out some HTML markup and then applies another XSL template to match against the Items node:

```
<xsl:template match="a:Items">
  <table>
    <xsl:apply-templates select="a:Item"/>
  </table>
</xsl:template>
```

The Items template applies yet another template that matches against each Amazon Item. Each Item node in the document is processed in the order encountered:

```
<xsl:template match="a:Item">
  <tr>
    <td>
      <img>
        <xsl:attribute name="src">
          <xsl:value-of select="a:SmallImage/a:URL" />
        </xsl:attribute>
        <xsl:attribute name="alt">
          <xsl:value-of select="a:ItemAttributes/a:Title" />
        </xsl:attribute>
        <xsl:attribute name="align">left</xsl:attribute>
      </img>
      <a>
        <xsl:attribute name="href">
          <xsl:value-of select="a:DetailPageURL" />
        </xsl:attribute>
        <xsl:value-of select="a:ItemAttributes/a:Title" />
      </a>
```

```
            <br/>
            <xsl:apply-templates select="a:OfferSummary"/>
            <br/>
        </td>
    </tr>
</xsl:template>
```

You will notice the odd `<img>` and `<a>` tags. These are straight out of HTML but converted here into valid XML. To display an HTML link tag using XSL, you use the following syntax:

```
<a>
    <xsl:attribute name="href">http://www.Amazon.com</xsl:attribute>
    Click Here
</a>
```

This XSL results in the following HTML:

```
<a href="http://www.Amazon.com">Click Here</a>
```

Note the `<a>` tag is simply another XML node — more output that should be displayed. The `href` is an attribute of that a node. In this example, the actual URL is hard-coded to be `Amazon.com`. If you were to obtain the actual URL from the underlying XML document, the syntax would be as follows:

```
<a>
<xsl:attribute name="href">
    <xsl:value-of select="myUrl"/>
</xsl:attribute>
Click Here
</a>
```

Notice the use of `xsl:value-of` to retrieve the value from the underlying XML. This same approach is applied to the `<img>` tags in the Amazon style sheet.

Now the stage is set, the back-end code to obtain the data is in place, and the XSL style sheet to transform that data is in place. In the next section, you transform that data in C# and output the results.

Applying an XSL Style Sheet in C#

The .NET Framework provides a comprehensive set of classes for processing XML and XSL. With the data present in an `XmlDocument` as returned by the `GetUri` method of the `WebUtility` class, the next step is to transform this data using the XSL file you just created. Listing 8-5 shows a new function, `DoXSLTransformation`, that you should add to the `WebUtility` class. This function takes an XML document as input, along with the name of the XSL file to apply to the document. The results are returned as a string for use in the calling page.

Listing 8-5: Processing an XML File with XSL in C#

```csharp
public static string DoXSLTransformation(XmlDocument myDoc, string strXsl)
{
    // Create an XSL transformation
```

(continued)

Listing 8-5: *(continued)*

```
        XslCompiledTransform myProcessor = new XslCompiledTransform();

        // Load the XSL document
        myProcessor.Load(System.Web.HttpContext.Current.Server.MapPath(strXsl));

        // Create a text writer for use in the transformation
        StringWriter myWriter = new StringWriter();

        // Transform the source XML document
        myProcessor.Transform(myDoc, (XsltArgumentList)null, myWriter);

        // Return the result as a string
        return myWriter.ToString();
    }
```

How It Works

1. The `XmlDocument myDoc` holds the source XML file as returned by the Amazon REST API.

2. To create the XLST an `XslCompiledTranform` object is required. This actually processes the XSL.

3. The processor loads the XSL style sheet from a file. `StrXsl` stores the name of the XSL style sheet file. The code `Server.MapPath(strXsl)` maps the path of the file to the actual file on the Web server.

4. The next line creates a `StringWriter` object for use in the transformation.

5. The processor applies the XSL style sheet to the XML document. XSL can accept arguments for use in the sheet itself, but, in this case, there are none.

6. Finally, the results of the transformation are converted into a string and returned from the function.

The function is called from the code-besides and the return value (which, at this point, is a string of HTML) is added to the page through the `Literal` control you added earlier:

```
string strResults = webUtility.DoXSLTransformation(myResults, "AmazonYahoo.xsl");
this.myLiteral.Text = strResults;
```

Figure 8-5 shows the Amazon results produced from the transformation. Notice that this looks very similar to the Yahoo example. However, the inner workings are quite different.

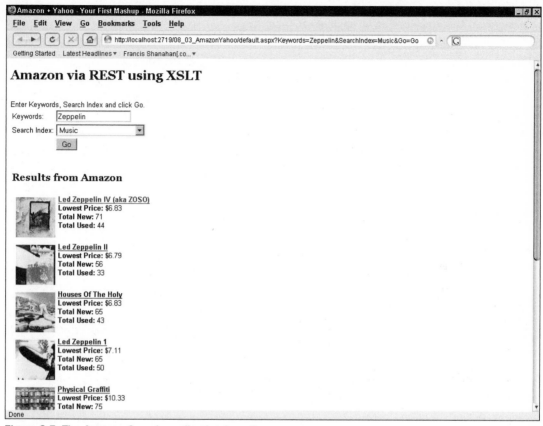

Figure 8-5: The Amazon Search application in action

Mashing the Results

It's been a long time coming, but with both the Yahoo and Amazon searches working independently, you finally come to the magic moment when the data is mashed together. Rather than rewrite everything again, you should just reuse the Amazon code you already have.

If you've been following along, you'll realize that you already have the necessary tools in place to simply plug Yahoo (or any valid XML provider with a REST interface) into the mashup.

Building on the Amazon code base, the first step is to obtain additional data after the Amazon call has been made. This is achieved with another call to GetUri:

```
XmlDocument myYahooDoc =
webUtility.GetUri("http://api.shopping.yahoo.com/ShoppingService/V1/productSearch?a
ppid=<INSERT APPLICATION ID HERE>&query=" + strKeywords + "&results=10&start=1" );
```

This code retrieves another document (this time named myYahooDoc) and simply reuses the URI from the earlier Yahoo example.

At this point, you'll have two valid XML documents, and they need to be combined into a third, consolidated XML document. Create this third document as follows:

```
XmlDocument myResults = new XmlDocument();
```

The document is completely empty upon creation. Add a root node as follows:

```
XmlNode myRoot = myResults.CreateElement("MashupRoot");
myResults.AppendChild(myRoot);
```

These lines first create a root node named "MashupRoot" and subsequently add it to the myResults document.

With the root node in place, you can "hang" the other two documents off of it:

```
// Add the amazon results to the main doc
XmlNode amazonTmp = myResults.ImportNode(myAmazonDoc.DocumentElement, true);
myResults.DocumentElement.AppendChild(amazonTmp);

// Add the yahoo results to the main doc
XmlNode yahooTmp = myResults.ImportNode(myYahooDoc.DocumentElement, true);
myResults.DocumentElement.AppendChild(yahooTmp);
```

In each case, the entire document is converted into an XmlNode using ImportNode. This node is added to the document as a child off the main root of the document. What you end up with is an XML document that looks like this:

```
<MashupRoot>
    <... Amazon document ...>
    <... Yahoo document ...>
</MashupRoot>
```

Of course, before you can transform this document, you must modify the XSL style sheet as follows:

1. Add a new namespace prefix to the xsl:stylesheet node of the document:

```
<xsl:stylesheet version="1.0" xmlns="http://www.w3.org/1999/xhtml"
    xmlns:tns="http://www.w3.org/1999/xhtml"
    xmlns:xsl="http://www.w3.org/1999/XSL/Transform"
    xmlns:a="http://webservices.amazon.com/AWSECommerceService/2005-10-05"
    xmlns:y="urn:yahoo:prods">
```

This denotes that all nodes prefixed with an `a:` are from the Amazon schema and those with a `y:` are from the Yahoo schema. This avoids conflicts in the style sheet rules.

2. Add new templates for processing Yahoo results:

```xsl
<xsl:template match="y:Result">
    <table>
      <xsl:apply-templates select="y:Catalog"/>
    </table>
</xsl:template>

<xsl:template match="y:Catalog">
    <tr>
      <td>
        <img>
          <xsl:attribute name="src">
            <xsl:value-of select="y:Thumbnail/y:Url" />
          </xsl:attribute>
          <xsl:attribute name="alt">
            <xsl:value-of select="y:ProductName" />
          </xsl:attribute>
          <xsl:attribute name="align">left</xsl:attribute>
          <xsl:attribute name="width">
            <xsl:value-of select="y:Thumbnail/y:Width" />
          </xsl:attribute>
          <xsl:attribute name="height">
            <xsl:value-of select="y:Thumbnail/y:Height" />
          </xsl:attribute>
        </img>
        <a>
          <xsl:attribute name="href">
            <xsl:value-of select="y:Url" />
          </xsl:attribute>
          <xsl:value-of select="y:ProductName" />
        </a><br/>
        Prices from $<xsl:value-of select="y:PriceFrom"/> to
$<xsl:value-of select="y:PriceTo"/><br/>

      </td>
    </tr>
  </xsl:template>
```

The first template effectively "calls" the other. I have done nothing new here, but added more instructions for processing the additional Yahoo nodes from the underlying XML.

3. Lastly, apply the new templates from the root node of the document:

```xsl
<xsl:apply-templates select="MashupRoot/y:ResultSet/y:Result"/>
```

You will notice here I have added `"MashupRoot"` as the root node of the document. You must add this to the earlier Amazon template instruction as well:

```xsl
<xsl:apply-templates select="MashupRoot/a:ItemSearchResponse/a:Items"/>
```

This completes the code changes for the mashup. You can press F5 and run the application. When you search on a keyword, the results will be mashed together into a single HTML table, which should look just like Figure 8-6.

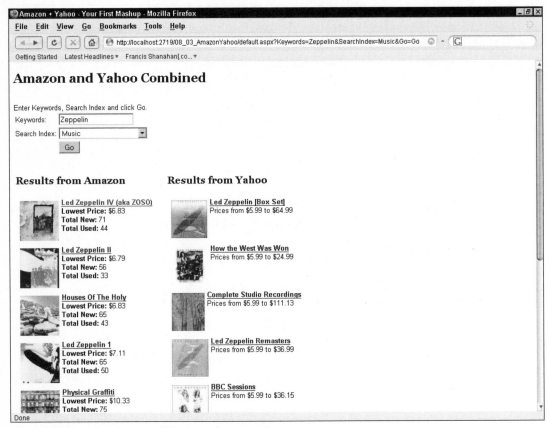

Figure 8-6: Your first Amazon/Yahoo mashup in action

Summary

In this chapter you have gone from a standing start to breaking the mashup quarter mile. You learned how to do the following:

❑   Retrieve data from Amazon using REST

❑   Transform XML data using XSLT. (You will learn more on this topic in future chapters.)

❑   Merge XML datasources

❑   Bind XML to a `Repeater` control using ASP.NET

You have obtained data from two disparate sources and combined them together into a useful application. In doing so, you learned useful techniques for processing XML and making HTTP GET calls, and you have begun building a useful helper class that can be leveraged in later chapters.

From this chapter, I am sure you are thinking about how building upon the Internet as a platform has changed. In the old world, you had centralized databases and built monolithic client-server or n-tier applications on top of them.

Now, you are building complex distributed systems using lightweight techniques to incorporate data from many different sources.

This is a relatively simple and classic example that combines search results. The real power of such techniques becomes apparent when you apply the technique to a problem that has never been thought of in this manner. With these new-found skills, I find some data and combine it with something else to create a new and interesting use for the Internet.

This chapter showed how to mash data on the Web server. In Chapter 9, you begin using JavaScript and the browser to push processing off of the Web server and onto the user's desktop.

Before continuing, consider the following exercises to test your knowledge of the information covered in this chapter. You will find the answers to these and other exercises in Appendix B.

Exercises

1. How can an XML document be loaded into a `DataSet`?

2. How can an XSLT be executed in .NET?

3. How can an HTTP GET request be issued in C#?

Putting the Browser to Work

Mashups are really changing the way the Web works. At their core, mashups enable a far richer experience in the browser than ever before. So what does that "richer" really mean? Well, if you think back to the early days of the Web, you had a content page, with a link on it. If you wanted to reach out to another site, you added a link. The user clicked the link and moved to the new page. That's a fairly plain-vanilla user experience, plodding along from site to site. The downside is the moment your users click that link, they are gone, no longer on your site, and no longer a customer!

Asynchronous JavaScript enables you to build clickable links or buttons on your site that pull in information and add it to the page. The user views this info on your site. They never leave! A user that doesn't leave is a user that might click an advertisement, read more content, or fulfill a purchase.

In this chapter, you learn how to pull data into your site dynamically and provide users a really interesting experience.

Specifically, you learn how to do the following:

❑   Use the YouTube API to obtain movies and short films

❑   Pull data from Amazon's Movie database

❑   Display information in a Web page without ever refreshing the page

The Battle Plan

The idea in this chapter is to create a simple mechanism to enhance a content-driven page. The example code associated with this chapter will implement a mockup of a movie review site. The site content will contain various underlined links to denote that these areas are clickable.

Instead of navigating the user to a separate page, clicking a link will trigger a series of steps behind the scenes to retrieve additional content from YouTube and Amazon leaving the user on the same page. In this manner, the user will be able to augment the content of the page by clicking links within it. The user never leaves the page, however, because all content is pulled in using asynchronous JavaScript. Figure 9-1 shows the finished site displaying content from Amazon.

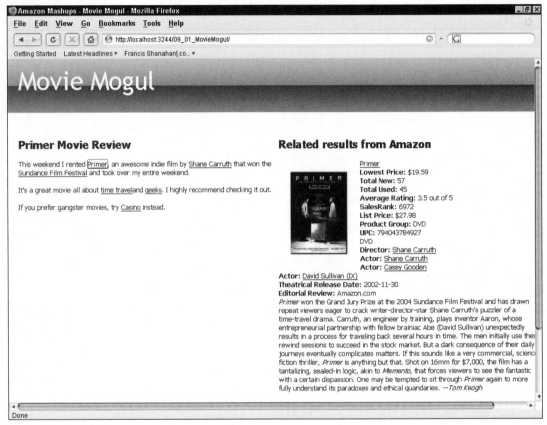

Figure 9-1: The Movie Mogul site in action

I will use Amazon and YouTube in the examples in this chapter, but you should be comfortable enough to change these based on the nature of the content in your specific scenario. For example, a news site might pull content from the "blog-o-sphere" using Technorati.

Understanding the Architecture

Figure 9-2 shows the overall data flow within the Movie Mogul example.

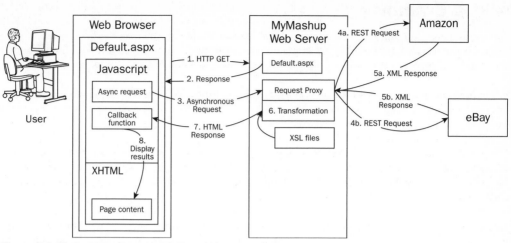

Figure 9-2: The architecture of the Movie Mogul example

How It Works

Here's how it works:

1. The first thing that happens is that users visit the Web site using a browser.

2. The page is served up by the Web server and includes a small JavaScript library.

3. As users click through the site, they might hit a button or a link on the page that triggers a JavaScript event. Rather than submitting a form and refreshing the entire page, this JavaScript issues an asynchronous call to the server without blocking the users.

4. This request is received by a proxy (a pass-through) on the server, which then reaches out to either Amazon (Step 4a) or YouTube (Step 4b) for data. These are REST-style HTTP GET requests.

5. The partner sites respond with XML (either Step 5a or Step 5b) and send it back to the server.

6. Each site responds with XML data back to the mashup domain's Web server. This data is then transformed on the Web server into HTML using XSL style sheets that reside locally on the Web server.

7. The resulting HTML is sent back to the browser.

8. The browser handles this response with a `javascript` function and simply inserts it into the page, perhaps as the `innerText` of a `Div` tag.

Those reading ahead would ask why this chapter isn't called "Ajax." Well, this paradigm isn't quite Ajax because the transformation is happening on the Web server. In this chapter, the server is serving ready-made XHTML snippets. As you'll see in Chapter 10, in Ajax, the server sends vanilla XML and the transformation is done in the browser.

Working Examples

Although there is no official naming commission, this technique has become known as Just Asynchronous HTML (JAH). This technique uses asynchronous communication with the Web server through JavaScript, made possible through a specific JavaScript object, `XmlHttpRequest`.

If you haven't already done so, it's a good idea at this point to take a look at some working examples out on the Web. Google Suggest (`http://www.google.com/webhp?complete=1&hl=en`) and Google Maps (`http://maps.Google.com`) are two excellent examples.

Google Maps allows a user to navigate a map interactively using the browser. The user enters a location or address and is shown a map of that location in the browser. The user can then drag and move the visible area of the map in any direction. This is something you normally would not associate with a browser experience.

Google Suggest uses the same technique of asynchronous communication, but in a completely different manner. A search form is displayed into which a user can type a query. With every keystroke the user enters, a list of possible matches appears (Figure 9-3). These are "suggestions" and afford the user the convenience of less typing. If the intended search term appears in the list of suggestions, the user can simply click that and go directly to the search results.

Figure 9-3: Google Suggest uses asynchronous communication to present search options

Setting Up the Project

Now that you have a few projects under your belt, I'm going to assume you are quite comfortable with routine tasks such as project setup and so on. If you need guidance in this area, see Chapter 4 for development environment setup.

To set up the project for this chapter, follow these steps:

1. Create a new Web site using Visual Studio, or reuse the site you created in Chapter 4.

2. This site will rely on JavaScript, and it's a good idea to store all of this in a single location. Add a new folder named `js` to store the JavaScript files used by the application.

3. Add a new file to the `js` folder named `request.js`. This file will store the JavaScript for this example.

4. Reuse the `webUtility.cs` file you created in Chapter 8 by adding it into the project.

5. Create a simple Web page containing some blurb of content. This page will serve as the container for additional data pulled in from YouTube and Amazon. This is named `default.aspx` in this example.

6. Link the `request.js` JavaScript file to the `default.aspx` page by adding the following in the `<head>` section:

```
<script type="text/javascript" src="js/request.js"></script>
```

7. Add a `<div>` tag to the `default.aspx`:

```
<div id="results">Results go here</div>
```

   The `div` tag will house the result data when it comes back from the server.

8. Reuse the `amazonUtility.cs` class you created in Chapter 7 by adding it to the project.

Figure 9-4 shows the `default.aspx` page in design mode.

> *The printing industry has used a piece of generic content that looks like Latin literature as filler text before the final copy is available. This text begins with the words "Lorem ipsum dolor sit amet..." and goes on to fill a number of pages with content. There is some confusion as to whether or not this is actual Latin and, if so, whether or not it translates to anything meaningful. Consider Googling for "Lorem Ipsum" if you need some generic content to fill a void.*

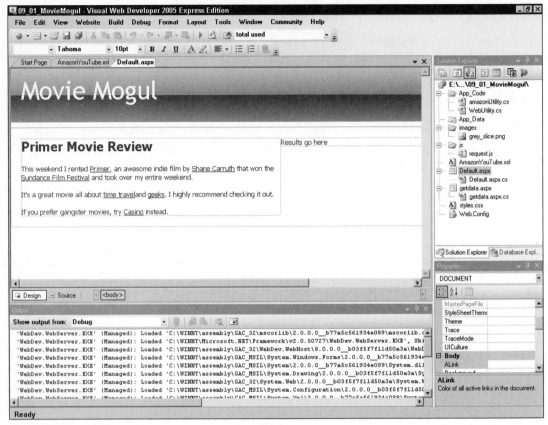

Figure 9-4: The project strawman, `default.aspx` **is shown**

The Data Provider

To retrieve the data from either Amazon or YouTube, this example uses a dedicated page named `getdata.aspx` as the data provider/proxy. In this section, you build the `getdata` page and implement the interfaces into Amazon and YouTube.

You should examine the YouTube API before moving on. The following table describes the available methods through the YouTube REST interface.

API Name	Description
`youtube.users.get_profile`	Displays data on a specific YouTube user.
`youtube.users.list_favorite_videos`	Provides a user's favorite videos.
`youtube.users.list_friends`	Lists a user's friends on YouTube.
`youtube.videos.get_details`	Obtains the details for a specific video.

API Name	Description
`youtube.videos.list_by_tag`	Returns a list of videos for a specific tag or keyword.
`youtube.videos.list_by_user`	Returns a list of videos for a specific user.
`youtube.videos.list_featured`	Returns a list of videos most recently added to the YouTube site.

I'll use the `list_by_tag` method, which obtains movie details based on how they have been tagged by YouTube users. This is as close to a *search by keyword* type method as the API supports.

To use the YouTube API, you will need to register for access to its developer program. You can do this at `www.youtube.com`. You will be assigned a developer ID that should be included in all calls to YouTube.

Try It Out   Building Getdata.aspx

To build the data provider, follow these steps:

1. Create a new page named `getdata.aspx`. Make sure you click the checkbox labeled "Place code in a separate file" when you create the page.

2. The user interface (`aspx`) for this page will never be used, so you can completely ignore it. Turn your attention to the code-beside for the page. This is where the data retrieval code is placed.

3. The page will be sent a parameter named `api` in the querystring. This will indicate whether the page should query Amazon or YouTube. In the `page_load` event for the page, place the following `if` statement:

```
// Is this a Youtube api call or an Amazon call?
if (Request.Params["api"] == "youtube")
{
    // a YouTube URI
    strURI =
"http://www.youtube.com/api2_rest?method=youtube.videos.list_by_tag&dev_id=[YOUR
ID]&tag=" + Request.Params["tag"];
}
else
{
    // Build an Amazon URI
    strURI = amazonUtility.BuildAmazonURI(Request.QueryString);
}
```

This code decides (based on the `api` parameter expected in the querystring) whether to obtain data from Amazon or YouTube.

4. In the case of YouTube, a simple REST URL is constructed:

```
strURI =
"http://www.youtube.com/api2_rest?method=youtube.videos.list_by_tag&dev_id=[YOUR ID
HERE]&tag=" + Request.Params["tag"];
```

5. In the case of Amazon, a number of potential operations are supported, including ItemLookup, ItemSearch, and so on. To help with all the permuations, a dedicated function has been created in the amazonUtility class:

```
strURI = amazonUtility.BuildAmazonURI(Request.QueryString);
```

6. The remainder of the getdata.aspx.cs page_load event is code to execute an HTTP GET query using the URL you just constructed. This is similar to code you have seen in earlier chapters and looks like this:

```
    // Obtain the data
    XmlDocument myDoc = webUtility.GetUri(strURI);

    // If the data passed back is ok
    if (myDoc != null)
    {
        Response.Clear();
        string strResults =
            webUtility.DoXSLTransformation(myDoc, "AmazonYouTube.xsl");
        Response.Write(strResults);
    } else {

        Response.Write("No data returned");
    }
```

In this code, I clear the Response (highlighted) before attempting to send back the XML data. This is because ASP.NET has already begun adding headers and information to the Response. Because I want to override the default response, I clear all of that out before writing the XML to the Response stream.

In this case, the data is transformed on the server using a combination of the webUtility class you created in Chapter 8 and an XSL file named AmazonYouTube.xsl.

There are a few more pieces that need to be built before you can test getdata.aspx.

How It Works

The getdata.aspx page accepts a number of parameters pertaining to either the Amazon ECS or the YouTube developer API. Based on the api parameter sent, the page decides whether to query Amazon or YouTube.

In the case of Amazon, a number of queries are supported, including ItemSearch, ItemLookup, and so on. In the case of YouTube, only one operation makes sense, that of looking up videos and their respective URLs.

The page retrieves data from either API in the form of an XML document. This document is transformed on the server using XSL into HTML. The resulting HTML is then sent down to the browser.

The Web server just sends HTML, hence the name "JAH."

Validating the Amazon REST URI

With all the permutations of parameters and operations available for the Amazon API, it becomes cumbersome to try to manage all of these with simple string concatenations.

There is also the issue of security. In any publicly available application, you always want to implement some form of validation on user input. To avoid a malicious user injecting database queries or dangerous text into the `getdata.aspx` querystring, and having this text being passed to Amazon, the parameters must be validated as part of the process.

As a result, this example includes a dedicated function to create valid URIs that can be used with the Amazon API, as shown in Listing 9-1.

Listing 9-1: The `BuildAmazonURI` **Function**

```
public static string BuildAmazonURI(NameValueCollection myQueryString)
{
    string strURI = "";
    string strRoot =
"http://webservices.amazon.com/onca/xml?Service=AWSECommerceService&";
    string strAccessKeyId = "AWSAccessKeyId=" +
ConfigurationManager.AppSettings["AWSAccessKeyId"] + "&";
    string strAssociateTag = "AssociateTag=" +
ConfigurationManager.AppSettings["AssociateTag"] + "&";

    string strOperation = CheckNull(myQueryString, "Operation", "ItemSearch");
    string strResponseGroup = CheckNull(myQueryString, "ResponseGroup", "Medium");
    string strItemId = CheckNull(myQueryString, "ItemId", "");
    string strKeywords = CheckNull(myQueryString, "Keywords", "");
    string strSearchIndex = CheckNull(myQueryString, "SearchIndex", "");
    string strDirector = CheckNull(myQueryString, "Director", "");
    string strAuthor = CheckNull(myQueryString, "Author", "");
    string strArtist = CheckNull(myQueryString, "Artist", "");
    string strActor = CheckNull(myQueryString, "Actor", "");

    // Return the concatenated URI
    strURI = strRoot + strAccessKeyId +
        strOperation + strResponseGroup +
        strItemId + strKeywords +
        strSearchIndex + strDirector +
        strAuthor + strArtist + strActor
        ;
    return strURI;
}
```

How It Works

`BuildAmazonURI` works like this:

1. The `BuildAmazonURI` function accepts the original request `querystring` in the form of a specialized name-value collection (part of the `System.Collections.Specialized` namespace).

2. The function knows or anticipates a certain set of parameters as specified in the Amazon documentation (things like `keywords`, `searchIndex`, or `operation`).

3. For each valid parameter, the code checks to see if it's null. If so, in certain cases, a default value is specified.

```
string strResponseGroup = CheckNull(myQueryString, "ResponseGroup", "Medium");
```

In most cases, empty or null parameters are simply omitted from the final string.

4. Lastly, the various components of the URI, the root, the `AWSAccessKeyId` and `AssociateTag`, and so on, are concatenated together to form the final URI.

You could clearly go a step further in making this function more sophisticated. For example, you might consider removing angle brackets or single quotes to further validate the input. I have omitted this code for clarity.

Dealing with a Network Proxy

Once the correct URI for either Amazon or YouTube is created, the URI is obtained using the same techniques from Chapter 8:

```
XmlDocument myDoc = webUtility.GetUri(strURI);
```

Sometimes you might find you are behind a corporate firewall and traffic is limited to traveling through a network proxy. A *network proxy* is nothing more than a gateway through which traffic must pass. If you're on a corporate network, your browser might already be using a proxy to communicate with the Internet.

If you do find yourself behind a proxy, the `GetUri` function will fail because it has no knowledge of the proxy or how to route through it. You may experience problems issuing `HttpWebRequests` to obtain REST URIs.

There are two options here. The first solution is to provide your proxy information to the `HttpWebRequest` object inside `GetUri`, as follows:

```
// Create a request object
HttpWebRequest myRequest = (HttpWebRequest)WebRequest.Create(strURI);
myRequest.Proxy = new WebProxy("myWeb.Proxy.com", 8080);
```

This code sets the proxy information on the `WebRequest` so that all calls are routed through the proxy, just as your browser is routing them.

An alternative is to provide a configurable solution by specifying the proxy in the `web.config` file. This setting looks like this:

```
<system.net>
    <defaultProxy>
        <proxy usesystemdefault="False"
            proxyaddress="http://myWeb.Proxy.com:8080" bypassonlocal="True"/>
    </defaultProxy>
</system.net>
```

Consider adding this code to your specific implementation, if necessary.

More XSL Tools

Once the data comes back from the partner site in the form of an XML document, it must be transformed into HTML. In Chapter 8, you accomplished a number of things in XSL. You learned how to structure an XSL document using templates. You also learned how to produce output using the `<xsl:value-of>` elements and also the `<xsl:output>` node.

In this chapter, you take things a little further by introducing the XSL equivalent of `if-then-else` and learn how to implement recursion in XSL using named templates.

XSL If-Then-Else

Decisions in XSL are somewhat similar to other languages in that you have a condition or expression that must be tested. Based on the result of the expression, the code will follow a specific path:

```
<xsl:choose>
    <xsl:when test="SOME CONDITION">
        <!-- Do something -->
    </xsl:when>
    <xsl:otherwise>
        <!-- Do something else -->
    </xsl:otherwise>
</xsl:choose>
```

Matching a Template to More than One Element

When you perform an `ItemSearch` query against Amazon, the API returns an XML document with a root node named `ItemSearchResponse`. When you perform an `ItemLookup` query against Amazon, the API returns an XML document with a root node named `ItemSearchResponse`.

Regardless of the root node (`ItemLookupResponse` or `ItemSearchResponse`), the document still contains `Items` and `Item` nodes with a consistent structure. In this instance it makes sense to process these with a single set of XSL templates.

To reuse the XSL you have created, you must define a template that can match on *either* of the `ItemLookupResponse` or `ItemSearchResponse` nodes:

```
<xsl:template match="a:ItemLookupResponse|a:ItemSearchResponse">
    <h2>Related results from Amazon</h2>
    <xsl:apply-templates select="a:Items"/>
</xsl:template>
```

This template matches on both types of response by combining `ItemLookupResponse` and `ItemSearchResponse` in the `match` attribute of the the template definition.

Transforming the YouTube Response

The best way to figure out an XSL transformation template is to look at the sample data. The next section walks you through obtaining sample YouTube data using the code you've built so far.

A Sample YouTube Response

You have not yet built the XSL template to transform the content. You can still test `getdata.aspx` with your browser. To do this, temporarily comment-out the call to `DoXslTransformation` and add code to print out the raw XML response from either Amazon or YouTube using your browser:

```
Response.Clear();
// Uncomment these line if you need to debug the transformed xml
Response.ContentType = "text/xml";
Response.Write(myDoc.InnerXml);
Response.End();
// string strResults = webUtility.DoXSLTransformation(myDoc, "AmazonYouTube.xsl");
// Response.Write(strResults);
```

To obtain a sample YouTube XML response, try running the application and entering the following URL into the browser:

```
http://localhost:1356/09_01_MovieMogul/getdata.aspx?api=youtube&tag=timetravel
```

Be sure to modify the port information to match your own application. Visual Studio dynamically assigns a port to every Web application. Here, the port is 1356; yours might be different, however, so be sure you modify the URL to match.

To find the port, look at the properties of the Web project in Visual Studio. The section named "Developer Web Server" has a property named `port number`.

Here's a sample response as generated by `getdata.aspx`:

```
<?xml version="1.0" encoding="utf-8" ?>
<ut_response status="ok">
  <video_list>
    <video>
      <author/>
      <id>Fat1NH8-VhE</id>
      <title>Many Martys</title>
      <length_seconds>186</length_seconds>
      <rating_avg>5.00</rating_avg>
      <rating_count>1</rating_count>
      <description>I made this as an 'intro video' for school</description>
      <view_count>204</view_count>
      <upload_time>1142107967</upload_time>
      <comment_count>1</comment_count>
      <tags>timetravel</tags>
      <url>http://www.youtube.com/?v=Fat1NH8-VhE</url>
      <thumbnail_url>
        http://sjl-static2.sjl.youtube.com/vi/Fat1NH8-VhE/2.jpg
      </thumbnail_url>
    </video>
  </video_list>
</ut_response>
```

YouTube returns a number of video details, most of which are self-explanatory. The main ones highlighted here are the URL that is a link to the video on YouTube's site itself and a link to a representative thumbnail image of the video. These will both be handy in building the HTML output for the content page.

The YouTube XSL Template

As you have seen, YouTube results are extremely simple to process, containing straight XML based entirely in the default namespace. Listing 9-2 shows the code for a simple template that displays each video node in a table row.

Listing 9-2: The YouTube XSL Template

```
<xsl:template match="video">
  <tr><td>
    <a target="_blank">
        <xsl:attribute name="href">
            <xsl:value-of select="url" />
        </xsl:attribute>
        <img border="0" width="130" height="97" align="left">
            <xsl:attribute name="src">
                <xsl:value-of select="thumbnail_url" />
            </xsl:attribute>
            <xsl:attribute name="alt">
                <xsl:value-of select="title" />
            </xsl:attribute>
            <xsl:attribute name="title">
                <xsl:value-of select="title" />
            </xsl:attribute>
        </img>
    </a>
   </td><td>
     <a target="_blank">
        <xsl:attribute name="href">
            <xsl:value-of select="url" />
        </xsl:attribute>
        <xsl:value-of select="title" />
    </a><br/>
  Average Rating: <xsl:value-of select="rating_avg" /> |
  Length: <xsl:value-of select="length_seconds" /> secs<br/>
    <xsl:value-of select="description" />
    </td>
    </tr>
</xsl:template>
```

This template will be matched to all video nodes. The template contains basic XSL instructions to display the various properties of a video (such as description, URL, and thumbnail image).

The sample code associated with this chapter contains the full-blown XSL transformation. Figure 9-5 shows the resulting HTML in the browser.

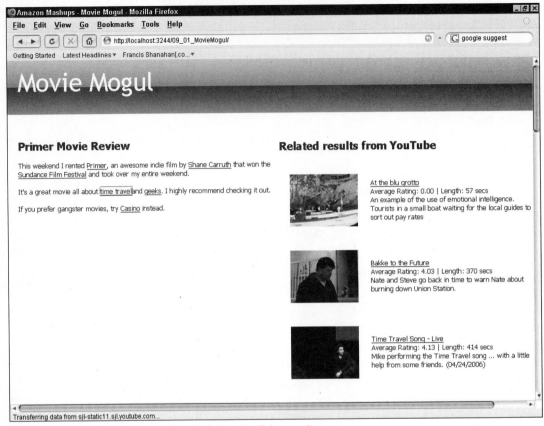

Figure 9-5: The finished application displaying YouTube results

The XmlHttpRequest Object

The `XmlHttpRequest` is the main object that powers this example. The `XmlHttpRequest` object is available to JavaScript without requiring any additional security privileges. The following table shows a breakdown of that object's methods.

Method Name	Description
`abort ()`	This method aborts an in-flight request.
`addEventListener ()`	Registers an event handler to the object.
`dispatchEvent ()`	Fires off an event that, in turn, triggers any handlers listening on that event.
`getAllResponseHeaders ()`	Returns all HTTP headers associated as with the response.

Method Name	Description
getResponseHeader ()	Gets a specific HTTP header from the response.
open ()	Creates a new request, using a target URL and HTTP method (GET or POST).Initiates a new request. Note the request is not sent until "send" is called.
overrideMimeType ()	Overrides the MimeType sent back from the server. This is useful if you wanted to treat an XML stream as plain text, for example.
removeEventListener ()	Removes an event handler from an event target.
send()	Sends the constructed HTTP request.
setRequestHeader ()	Allows you to set an HTTP header in the request.

You will need to make use of the open() and send() methods, as detailed in the following section.

Making the Request

To partially update a page, the user clicks a link containing a javascript function call:

```
<a href='javascript:void(0)' onclick='Lookup("B0007N1JC8")'>Primer</a>
```

This is a fake link that goes nowhere. The onclick event contains a call to the Lookup() function that is defined in the request.js script file:

```
function Lookup(ItemId){
    GetData("operation=ItemLookup&ItemId=" + ItemId);
}
```

As you can see, Lookup() does nothing more than call GetData(). It passes a string that will become a querystring. The parameters here are directly out of the Amazon ECS. Lookup() sends GetData the required parameters to perform an Amazon ItemLookup operation, including the ItemId.

There are a number of such *helper* functions, as listed here:

```
function DirectorSearch(keywords){
    GetData("operation=ItemSearch&Director=" + keywords + "&SearchIndex=DVD");
}

function YouTube(keywords){
    GetData("api=youtube&tag=" + keywords );
}

function ActorSearch(keywords){
    GetData("operation=ItemSearch&Actor=" + keywords + "&SearchIndex=DVD");
}
```

Each function simply creates a string and passes it on to GetData. GetData is another JavaScript function that also resides in request.js. GetData is the code that actually calls the getdata.aspx page you created earlier to obtain the transformed HTML (Listing 9-3).

Listing 9-3: Creating an Asynchronous Request

```
function GetData(myOperation) {

    myUrl="getdata.aspx?" + myOperation;

    // Is this a Microsoft browser?
    if (window.ActiveXObject) {
        // Create a new request
        myRequest = new ActiveXObject("Microsoft.XMLHTTP");
        if (myRequest) {
            myRequest.onreadystatechange = HandleResponse;
            myRequest.open("GET", myUrl, true);
            myRequest.send();
        }
    } else if (window.XMLHttpRequest) {
        // This is Firefox or Safari...
        myRequest = new XMLHttpRequest();
        myRequest.onreadystatechange = HandleResponse;
        myRequest.open("GET", myUrl, true);
        myRequest.send(null);
    }
}
```

How It Works

1. The first thing that happens is an XmlHttpRequest object is created. In this example, the JavaScript branches to support either Internet Explorer–specific implementation of XmlHttpRequest, or the Mozilla/Firefox/Safari implementation.

2. GetData has been passed in a portion of the desired URL, which it concatenates as a querystring onto the address of getdata.aspx. The result is a URL that might look something like this:

   getdata.aspx?api=youtube&tags=Zeppelin

3. As part of preparations before the request is sent, a javascript function is assigned to handle the response. This is essentially a callback mechanism because the JavaScript code will continue once the request is made. It will not wait and block until the response is received. In this case, the callback function is named HandleResponse.

4. Finally, the request is sent and the function exits.

This all happens behind the scenes, and the user is typically unaware that anything has happened at all.

Handling the Response

Once the Web server receives the request and obtains the data from the partner site, it begins sending back the response. This might take a number of interactions between browser and server, depending on the size of the data. Again, this happens behind the scenes with no additional coding necessary.

Before accessing the response data, you must check the `readyState` property of the request object to see if the entire response has been received. As per the following table, there are five possible `readyStates`; the one you're interested in is "4" or *complete*.

readyState	Description
0	The request has not yet been initialized.
1	The request is loading data.
2	The object has loaded the data.
3	The object is still parsing and scanning through the data.
4	The object's parsing has completed and the data is ready for consumption.

Listing 9-4 is the callback function assigned to handle the Web server response.

Listing 9-4: Handling the Web Server Response

```
function HandleResponse() {

    // Find the results div
    var myDiv = document.getElementById('results');

    // Readystate 4 means we're done
    if (myRequest.readyState == 4) {

        // If the server returned OK
        if (myRequest.status == 200) {

            myDiv.innerHTML = myRequest.responseText;
        } else {
            myDiv.innerHTML = "Oops there was a problem, " + myRequest.statusText;
            myDiv.innerHTML = "<br/>Try again later";
        }
    }
}
```

How It Works

1. First, the code obtains a reference to the results `<div>` element on the page. This is where the success or failure output will be rendered.

```
var myDiv = document.getElementById('results');
```

2. Next, the code checks to ensure that the entire response has been received and the status is set to "complete":

```
if (myRequest.readyState == 4) {
```

3. The code then checks that this was a successful response from the Web server. The error code 200 here denotes a successful response from the Web server (just as 404 denotes a page not found):

```
if (myRequest.status == 200) {
```

4. Finally, the `responseText` property is accessed to display the results. In the event of an error, an appropriate message is written out in place of the results:

```
myDiv.innerHTML = myRequest.responseText;
```

Try It Out   **Simple Asynchronous Communication**

To familiarize yourself with how this JavaScript communication works, try this simple experiment:

1. Open the `getdata.aspx` page.

2. Insert the following code in the first few lines of the `page_load` event:

```
Response.Clear();
Response.Write ("Someone told me to print " + Request.Querystring["args"]);
Response.End();
return;
```

3. Assuming you have already implemented the `request.js` JavaScript detailed earlier, and have linked this into your `default.aspx` page, add a new `href` to `default.aspx` that looks like this:

```
<a href="javascript:void()" onclick="GetData('args=Hello World')">click me</a>
```

4. Compile and run this example. Navigate to `default.aspx`. Clicking the link calls back to the `getdata.aspx` and prints out the results.

Try the following. Insert some markup onto the page. Remove the `Response.End()` statement from the code-beside. Run the application.

The Web server writes out the requested string but, because you did not end the HTTP stream, the server appends whatever content was contained in the ASPX page.

In this example, the server is sending an HTML snippet down to the browser. Coming up in Chapter 10, I'll show you how to send down XML to the browser and how to transform that XML into HTML locally.

Dealing with Amazon Errors

Over the course of your interactions with the Amazon ECS, I'm sure by now you have encountered instances whereby Amazon has responded with error information. Amazon has done an excellent job of providing status, error code, and verbose descriptions of any errors that occur. To handle these, you simply need to know where to look. Add the following templates to your Amazon transformation to handle and display error information, along with your results (Figure 9-6):

```xsl
<xsl:template match="a:Items">
    <xsl:apply-templates select="a:Request/a:Errors/a:Error"/>
    <xsl:apply-templates select="a:Item"/>
</xsl:template>

<xsl:template match="a:Error">
  <div class="errors">Errors from Amazon</div>
  <xsl:value-of select="a:Message"/>
</xsl:template>
```

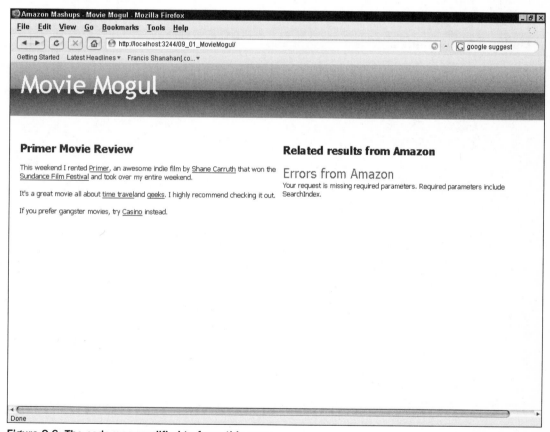

Figure 9-6: The code was modified to force this error

Parsing the Amazon BrowseNode Structure

As mentioned in Chapter 2, Amazon classifies data into various categories. These categories are known as `BrowseNodes`. A product can be classified according to a number of categories (for example, a DVD might be classified by Director, by Genre, and so on).

The `BrowseNode` structure itself is hierarchical, which makes sense. Take as an example "Casino." This is a Robert DeNiro film. "Robert" starts with "R," which falls into the Actors `BrowseNode`, which is a part of the DVD node, and so on.

`BrowseNodes` typically get more general the higher up the node structure you go. The lower down you go, the more specific the classification.

By specifying the `ResponseGroup=BrowseNode` parameter in a typical REST request, you can obtain the `BrowseNodes` along with your results.

Listing 9-5 shows a sample `BrowseNode` response. Notice that each node is contained within the other as the nodes become more and more general.

Listing 9-5: A Sample `BrowseNode` **Response**

```
<BrowseNodes>
  <BrowseNode>
    <BrowseNodeId>163451</BrowseNodeId>
    <Name>Biography</Name>
    <Ancestors>
     <BrowseNode>
        <BrowseNodeId>508532</BrowseNodeId>
        <Name>Documentary</Name>
        <Ancestors>
          <BrowseNode>
            <BrowseNodeId>404276</BrowseNodeId>
            <Name>Genres</Name>
            <Ancestors>
              <BrowseNode>
                <BrowseNodeId>130</BrowseNodeId>
                <Name>DVD</Name>
                <Ancestors>
                  <BrowseNode>
                    <BrowseNodeId>139452</BrowseNodeId>
                    <Name>Video</Name>
                  </BrowseNode>
                </Ancestors>
              </BrowseNode>
            </Ancestors>
          </BrowseNode>
        </Ancestors>
      </BrowseNode>
    </Ancestors>
  </BrowseNode>
  <BrowseNode>
    <BrowseNodeId>163452</BrowseNodeId>
    <Name>General</Name>
```

```
      <Ancestors>
        <BrowseNode>
          <BrowseNodeId>508532</BrowseNodeId>
          <Name>Documentary</Name>
          <Ancestors>
            <BrowseNode>
              <BrowseNodeId>404276</BrowseNodeId>
              <Name>Genres</Name>
              <Ancestors>
                <BrowseNode>
                  <BrowseNodeId>130</BrowseNodeId>
                  <Name>DVD</Name>
                  <Ancestors>
                    <BrowseNode>
                      <BrowseNodeId>139452</BrowseNodeId>
                      <Name>Video</Name>
                    </BrowseNode>
                  </Ancestors>
                </BrowseNode>
              </Ancestors>
            </BrowseNode>
          </Ancestors>
        </BrowseNode>
      </Ancestors>
    </BrowseNode>
  </BrowseNodes>
```

Recursive XSL Templates

As you can see from Listing 9-5, the structure of the BrowseNodes is a tree structure. The only effective way of parsing a tree structure is through recursion. This is something that's relatively easy in XSL using a concept called *named templates*.

The basic pseudo-code is as follows:

1. Take a node and check if that node has parents (ancestors).

2. If ancestors are present, iterate through them.

3. For each ancestor, go to Step 1 and repeat the process.

4. At the top-most node, no ancestors are present, so print out this node's value and return.

By doing things in this manner, the nodes will print out from left to right in the order of highest to lowest. For example, grandfather → father → son, and so on.

The following template assigns a name to the template myBranch. The template executes according the to pseudo-code described earlier. It calls itself using the <xsl:call-template> statement for all ancestors found:

```
<xsl:template match="a:BrowseNode" name="myBranch">
    <xsl:choose>
      <xsl:when test="a:Ancestors/a:BrowseNode">
        <xsl:for-each select="a:Ancestors/a:BrowseNode">
```

```
            <xsl:call-template name="myBranch" />
        </xsl:for-each>
    </xsl:when>
    <xsl:otherwise>
      <br/>
    </xsl:otherwise>
  </xsl:choose>
  &gt;&gt; <xsl:value-of select="a:Name" />
</xsl:template>
```

The following is the output of this template when provided with a valid `BrowseNode` response:

```
>> Video >> DVD >> Genres >> Drama >> General
>> Video >> DVD >> Genres >> Mystery & Suspense >> Suspense
>> Video >> DVD >> Genres >> Mystery & Suspense >> Mystery
>> Video >> DVD >> Stores >> Actors & Actresses >> ( D ) >> DeNiro, Robert
>> Video >> DVD >> Stores >> Actors & Actresses >> ( P ) >> Pesci, Joe
>> Video >> DVD >> Stores >> Actors & Actresses >> ( R ) >> Rickles, Don
>> Video >> DVD >> Stores >> Actors & Actresses >> ( S ) >> Stone, Sharon
>> Video >> DVD >> Stores >> Actors & Actresses >> ( W ) >> Woods, James
>> Video >> DVD >> Stores >> Directors >> ( S ) >> Scorsese, Martin
>> Video >> DVD >> Genres >> Mystery & Suspense >> Crime >> Gangsters
>> Video >> DVD >> Features >> Titles >> ( C )
>> Video >> DVD >> Genres >> Mystery & Suspense >> Crime >> General
>> Video >> DVD >> Genres >> Mystery & Suspense >> General
>> Video >> DVD >> Stores >> Studio Specials >> Universal Studios Home
Entertainment >> All Universal Studios Titles
>> Video >> DVD >> Stores >> Studio Specials >> Universal Studios Home
Entertainment >> Drama
```

Running the Application

If you've been following along, you should by now be done with the coding. You should have a `default` `.aspx` page containing some content. The content has a set of JavaScript-enabled links, and each link is coded to invoke a `javascript` function. The JavaScript will issue an `XmlHttpRequest` to the server. The server will process this request using `getdata.aspx` and retrieve some XML. That XML is then transformed and streamed back down to the browser. The browser has another `javascript` function poised and ready to handle the response. Go ahead and run the application and play around with it.

Resolving Namespace Issues in C#

From time to time when working with the .NET Framework, you may find you've added a piece of code, but neglected to add a `using` statement for all the right namespaces. In such cases, you get an `Error` when the project is built, similar to the following:

```
The type or namespace name 'XmlDocument' could not be found (are
you missing a using directive or an assembly reference?)
```

Starting in Visual Studio 2005, you can easily rectify this by right-clicking the offending type and choosing Resolve from the menu. This menu item will automatically add a `using` statement for the correct namespace, in this case `System.Xml`.

Benefits of this Approach

So, you might ask, "Why put the onus on the browser to do all this extra work?" The answer is twofold.

The first reason is scalability. When you shift the workload from the server to the client, you now have an application that scales relative to the number of users visiting the site.

The second reason is, by enhancing the functionality carried out on the browser, you end up with a much more interactive application than if you were just serving up static content from the Web server. In a traditional Web site, the Web server serves a page, the user clicks a link, and the server sends down a new page. In the new world, the browser gets a page from the server and, depending on what the user chooses to do, that page might refresh a small portion of itself asynchronously over time.

Summary

In this chapter, you implemented another mashup that combined Amazon movies and YouTube movies. This is an interesting mashup using asynchronous techniques that should be easily customizable to suit your own content needs. You also did the following:

❑   Implemented a generic JavaScript library for issuing asynchronous requests

❑   Implemented a generic data-retrieval page for querying Amazon and YouTube

❑   Used recursion in XSL to transform the Amazon `BrowseNode` structure

In Chapter 10, you implement a full-blown Ajax example using eBay and Amazon. You implement a search interface to query Amazon WishLists and comparison-shop with eBay. You also learn how to translate XML in the browser and remove this burden from the server.

Before going on, try the following exercises to test your knowledge of the content covered in this chapter.

Exercises

1.   How can you use XSL to parse a hierarchical tree structure?

2.   How can you issue asynchronous HTTP requests using JavaScript?

3.   What facilities does Amazon provide for handling errors in the ECS API?

4.   What port does Visual Studio typically assign to a Web application?

5.   Why should you validate the Amazon REST URL?

6.   Why should you use `Response.Clear()` and `Response.End()` when outputting XML from ASP.NET?

An Ajax-Powered Wish List

Mention mashups in most technology communities and the topic inevitably turns toward Ajax (Asynchronous JavaScript and XML). This technique has powered some of the most popular mashups on the Internet today, including many of Google's and Microsoft's own sites.

In this chapter, you learn how to use Ajax to consume a wide range of data with very little code. Specifically, you learn how to do the following:

❑ Build an Ajax-powered site from the ground up

❑ Transform XML data within the browser

❑ Search eBay auction listings for comparison shopping

❑ Use the Amazon list search/lookup interface

❑ Use the Amazon remote shopping cart

The Battle Plan: eBay Plus Amazon Using REST and AJAX

As well as purchasing and reviewing thousands of products, Amazon allows customers to define personal lists of products. These lists can be shared with others in the form of baby registries, wedding registries, or good old-fashioned wish lists.

The goal in this chapter is to convey an understanding of Ajax and to create a working application in the process.

What Is AJAX?

Ajax provides a way for a Web page to communicate from a browser with the Web server that served it. For a more detailed explanation, see Chapter 6, "Mashup Techniques."

Chapter 10

Understanding the Architecture

In this chapter, you build a WishList Browser. This is a Web site that can be used to search Amazon for wish lists. Once users have found the wish list they're looking for, they can view the details of that list, along with the price of each item. They can also add these items to a remote shopping cart stored on Amazon, but presented within the context of the mashup. This cart can then be used to complete the transaction during checkout and purchase the items.

As an added bonus, users are able to seamlessly search eBay for specific products to see if there's a cheaper buying opportunity elsewhere.

Figure 10-1 shows the architecture of this specific Ajax solution.

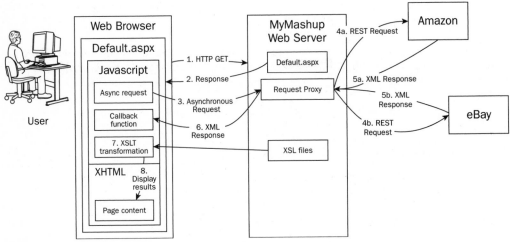

Figure 10-1: The WishList Browser solution architecture

How It Works

There are many variations on the Ajax theme, but this particular sample application implements the most common:

1. The user navigates to a page (default.aspx) with a typical HTTP GET request.

2. The page is served. The page includes a small JavaScript library.

3. When the user performs a specific action (performing a search, for example), a javascript function is called that initiates an HTTP GET request using XmlHttpRequest.

4. This request is received by a proxy (a pass-through) on the server, which then reaches out to either Amazon (Step 4a) or eBay (Step 4b) for additional data.

5. The partner sites respond with XML (either Step 5a or Step 5b) and send it back to the server.

6.   The server then passes this data back to the browser without transformation.

7.   The browser receives the XML data back from the server. The browser then processes this response using JavaScript and XSL.

8.   The data is transformed into HTML or XHTML, and then displayed in the page typically by being inserted into a `<div>` tag.

How Is this Different from the Last Example?

This is a non-trivial application with a number of moving parts. To reduce the slope of the learning curve, a lot of the code used in Chapter 9 will be reused. However, there is a subtle difference that distinguishes this application from the last. In Chapter 9, the transformation of data was done on the Web server. In this application, the data transformation is done at the browser. The server data access layer (`getdata.aspx`) is a pure pass-through. No mashing occurs on the server. Figure 10-2 shows a screenshot of the finished WishList Browser application.

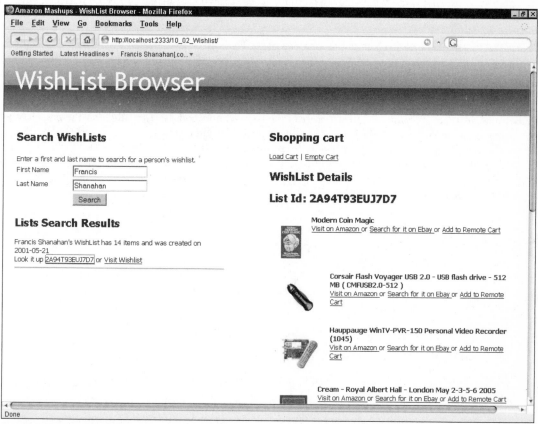

Figure 10-2: The finished application in action

Pros and Cons of Ajax

As a technique, Ajax has a lot of benefits, including the following:

❑ It provides a perceived performance increase. When it comes to usability, seeing is believing. From the user's perspective the page is refreshing content without an entire page load. The browser is not constantly refreshing and, overall, this has the effect that the application just *feels* faster.

❑ The application can shift the processing load to the browser, giving the overall application better scalability and potentially higher throughput.

❑ The application can behave in a manner that is typically not associated with or possible in a browser environment. By utilizing JavaScript and disparate data sources, the Web site behaves more interactively, and the users feel like they are participating in an experience, rather than just clicking from page to page.

There are, however, some things to watch out for. These drawbacks are easy to avoid if given some thought early on in the design.

Try not to use Ajax to refresh an entire area of a page. This can be unexpected by the user and leads to a disjointed experience. Rather, try to use Ajax judiciously to update smaller areas that may not be the primary focus of the user. Admittedly, I am breaking my own rule in the sample application but this is allowable given that the goal is to convey how the technique works.

Because the markup, content, and structure of the page is modified dynamically after the page has been rendered by the Web server, the browser has no chance of using its built-in history and bookmarking capabilities. If a user is four steps into a five-step process implemented using Ajax and the user instinctively selects the Back button, the user will be brought to the page he or she visited before the five-step process began — effectively, kicked back to the beginning. Be aware of this when designing your Ajax application to avoid a lot of frustrated users.

Setting Up the Project

As stated, a lot of the code will be reused and modified from Chapter 9. If you have not already read through Chapter 9, it might be worth a review to ensure that you are up to speed on the various components used in the solution.

1. Create a new project or reuse the application from Chapter 4.

2. Add in the existing getdata.aspx from Chapter 9.

3. Create a new folder for JavaScript named js. Add in the request.js script from Chapter 9.

4. Add in the amazonUtility.cs and webUtility.cs classes from Chapter 9.

5. Create a new folder named xml. This is where the numerous XSL files used in this chapter will be placed.

6. Create a new form on default.aspx that contains two standard HTML text inputs and a Submit button. These are non-ASP.NET controls that will be used to capture search criteria for

the Amazon list search API. The Design view of the `default.aspx` is shown in Figure 10-3. Feel free to create a look and feel that matches your tastes.

7. Add four `div` tags to the `default.aspx` page. These will be used as content placeholder areas for content retrieved from the partner sites. The first `div` is assigned an `id ="results"` as in Chapter 9. The second is identified as `"lists"`, the third is assigned an ID of `"cart"`, and the fourth will be used to store any debug messages generated by the application. Feel free to arrange these however you see fit:

```
<div id="results">Results go here</div>
<div id="lists"></div>
<div id="cart"></div>
<div id="debug"></div>
```

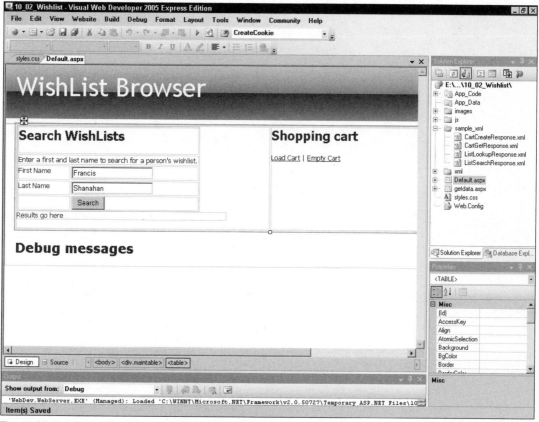

Figure 10-3: The design time view of the client interface

This completes the design of the client interface and the setup of the project. The remainder of this chapter focuses on modifications to code reused from Chapter 9, as well as the creation of new code to implement the application.

Searching Amazon for Wish Lists

The Amazon ECS supports three types of lists: wish lists, baby registries, or wedding registries. Amazon customers typically define a list with the objective of sharing it. You can search Amazon lists by a number of parameters described in the following table.

Parameter	Description
Operation	Setting the operation to `ListSearch` indicates that this is a request for lists.
Name	Specifies the name of the owner of the list. For example, `Francis Shanahan` would find my lists.
ListType	Valid values are `WishList`, `BabyRegistry`, `WeddingRegistry`, or `ListMania`. The first three are self-explanatory. The last, `ListMania`, is a random list created by an Amazon customer typically formed around a topic such as "camcorder accessories" or "Xbox essentials."
ResponseGroup	Should be set to `ListInfo` as a specific response group dedicated to lists.

The `ListSearch` will provide a group of `List` nodes. Each list has a `ListId` that can be used with a `ListLookup` operation to obtain the list details.

The following table describes the required parameters to perform a `ListLookup`.

Parameter	Description
Operation	The value of `ListLookup` indicates a request for a specific list.
ListId	The identifier of this list obtained from a `ListSearch` operation.
ListType	`ListIds` are not unique, so you need to specify this parameter as before.

Following is a sample response from the Amazon `ListSearch` API. This search looked for `Lists` of type `WishList`, including the `FirstName` of Francis:

```
<Lists>
  <Request>
    <IsValid>True</IsValid>
    <ListSearchRequest>
      <FirstName>Francis</FirstName>
      <ListType>WishList</ListType>
    </ListSearchRequest>
  </Request>
  <TotalResults>7011</TotalResults>
  <TotalPages>702</TotalPages>
  <List>
    <ListId>23NU55551F2</ListId>
    <ListURL>http://www.amazon.com/gp/registry/555RKICR1F2</ListURL>
```

```
      <ListName>Wish List</ListName>
      <ListType>WishList</ListType>
      <TotalItems>22</TotalItems>
      <TotalPages>3</TotalPages>
      <DateCreated>2006-02-07</DateCreated>
      <CustomerName>Francis Farmer</CustomerName>
    </List>
    <List>
      <ListId>13S554ODVDG</ListId>
      <ListURL>http://www.amazon.com/gp/registry/555HX4ODVDG</ListURL>
      <ListName>Wishlist</ListName>
      <ListType>WishList</ListType>
      <TotalItems>55</TotalItems>
      <TotalPages>6</TotalPages>
      <DateCreated>2001-05-26</DateCreated>
      <CustomerName>Francis Bacon</CustomerName>
    </List>
  </Lists>
```

All that's required is the ListID and the ListType to look up that list. Here's the response from the ListLookup query. A single list item has been highlighted. You must specify the ResponseGroup as ListInfo and ListItems to get the full set of data back:

```
<?xml version="1.0" encoding="utf-8" ?>
<Lists>
  <Request>
    <IsValid>True</IsValid>
    <ListLookupRequest>
      <ListId>2A94T93EUJ7D7</ListId>
      <ListType>WishList</ListType>
      <ResponseGroup>ListItems</ResponseGroup>
      <ResponseGroup>ListInfo</ResponseGroup>
    </ListLookupRequest>
  </Request>
  <List>
    <ListId>2A94T93EUJ7D7</ListId>
    <ListURL>http://www.amazon.com/gp/registry/2A94T93EUJ7D7</ListURL>
    <ListName>Wishlist</ListName>
    <ListType>WishList</ListType>
    <TotalItems>16</TotalItems>
    <TotalPages>2</TotalPages>
    <DateCreated>2001-05-21</DateCreated>
    <CustomerName>Francis Shanahan</CustomerName>
    <ListItem>
      <ListItemId>I28EY4RD7VZ1ND</ListItemId>
      <DateAdded>2005-11-22</DateAdded>
      <QuantityDesired>1</QuantityDesired>
      <QuantityReceived>1</QuantityReceived>
      <Item>
        <ASIN>0486242587</ASIN>
        <ItemAttributes>
          <Title>Modern Coin Magic</Title>
        </ItemAttributes>
      </Item>
    </ListItem>
```

```
    <ListItem>
      <ListItemId>I1ZKK7M8WZ2GJH</ListItemId>
      <DateAdded>2005-11-13</DateAdded>
      <QuantityDesired>1</QuantityDesired>
      <QuantityReceived>0</QuantityReceived>
      <Item>
        <ASIN>B0007LBNFI</ASIN>
        <ItemAttributes>
          <Title>Corsair Flash Voyager USB 2.0 USB flash drive 512 MB (
CMFUSB2.0-512 )</Title>
        </ItemAttributes>
      </Item>
    </ListItem>
    <ListItem>
      <ListItemId>IVIH1TNKPVHSX</ListItemId>
      <DateAdded>2005-11-12</DateAdded>
      <QuantityDesired>1</QuantityDesired>
      <QuantityReceived>1</QuantityReceived>
      <Item>
        <ASIN>B000AARKW6</ASIN>
        <ItemAttributes>
          <Title>Carlito's Way</Title>
        </ItemAttributes>
      </Item>
    </ListItem>
  </List>
</Lists>
```

Modifications to the Data Provider

In Chapter 9, you used a page named getdata.aspx to retrieve and transform data on the Web server. This page will be reused in this chapter. The code will be re-factored to act as a straight pass-through for the XML it receives.

Sending XML from getdata.aspx

To send XML back from the getdata.aspx page (as opposed to the normal HTML stream), follow these steps:

1. Once you have a valid XML document and are ready to send it to the browser, clear the Response stream:

```
Response.Clear();
```

2. Set the content type on the Response stream to XML. This is to ensure that the browser will not attempt to process this response as HTML:

```
Response.ContentType = "text/xml";
```

3. Write out the XML data:

```
Response.Write(myDoc.InnerXml);
```

You could also consider converting the XML to a string, but this is not necessary.

4. End the response. If you don't end the response, the Web page will append whatever markup is present in the ASPX presentation tier:

```
Response.End();
```

That's it! Your page will now respond purely with XML as opposed to traditional HTML.

How It Works

The `getdata.aspx` page is now a generic XML proxy. Any data it's asked for (be it Amazon, or YouTube, eBay, and so on) it will acquire in the form of an `XmlDocument` using REST. It works like this:

1. The page is currently set up to accept a number of parameters. The page examines the `querystring`, specifically the `api` parameter to determine which API to call.

2. Based on this information, a URL is built. This URL is then used to issue an HTTP `GET`.

3. This, in turn, responds with an XML document (not HTML), which is then sent down to the browser.

When `getdata.aspx` is used to query Amazon, it's sent purely Amazon-specific parameters. Here's an example:

```
http://localhost:1129/10_02_Wishlist/getdata.aspx?api=amazon&operation=ItemLookup&I
temId=6305168857
```

When used to query YouTube, as in the last example, the parameters look like this:

```
http://localhost:1129/10_02_Wishlist/getdata.aspx?api=youtube&tag=Zeppelin
```

As you'll see later in this chapter, the eBay API will also be incorporated into this model.

This model makes no assumptions as to the validity of the parameters being sent in. In the case of Amazon, some validation is done in the `BuildAmazonURI` *function.*

This function must be modified, as described in the next section.

Modifying the BuildAmazonURI Function

In Chapter 9, you created a special function to parse out Amazon parameters from the `getdata.aspx` querystring and create a valid Amazon URL.

The suite of parameters allowed in Chapter 9 was limited to product searches and lookups only. In this example, the code includes operations on the Amazon remote shopping cart, as well as wish list searches and lookups. As a result, the `BuildAmazonURI` function must be modified to include these additional parameters, as shown in Listing 10-1.

Listing 10-1: The Modified `BuildAmazonURI` **Function**

```
public static string BuildAmazonURI(NameValueCollection myQueryString)
    {
        string strURI = "";
        string strRoot =
"http://webservices.amazon.com/onca/xml?Service=AWSECommerceService&";
        string strAccessKeyId = "AWSAccessKeyId=" +
ConfigurationManager.AppSettings["AWSAccessKeyId"] + "&";
        string strAssociateTag = "AssociateTag=" +
ConfigurationManager.AppSettings["AssociateTag"] + "&";

        string strOperation = CheckNull(myQueryString, "Operation", "ItemSearch");
        string strResponseGroup = CheckNull(myQueryString, "ResponseGroup", "");
        string strItemId = CheckNull(myQueryString, "ItemId", "");
        string strKeywords = CheckNull(myQueryString, "Keywords", "");
        string strSearchIndex = CheckNull(myQueryString, "SearchIndex", "");
        string strDirector = CheckNull(myQueryString, "Director", "");
        string strAuthor = CheckNull(myQueryString, "Author", "");
        string strArtist = CheckNull(myQueryString, "Artist", "");
        string strActor = CheckNull(myQueryString, "Actor", "");
        string strListType = CheckNull(myQueryString, "ListType", "");
        string strName = CheckNull(myQueryString, "Name", "");
        string strFirstName = CheckNull(myQueryString, "FirstName", "");
        string strLastName = CheckNull(myQueryString, "LastName", "");
        string strEmail = CheckNull(myQueryString, "Email", "");
        string strListId = CheckNull(myQueryString, "ListId", "");
        string strItem1ASIN = CheckNull(myQueryString, "Item.1.ASIN", "");
        string strItem1Quantity = CheckNull(myQueryString, "Item.1.Quantity", "");
        string strMergeCart = CheckNull(myQueryString, "MergeCart", "");
        string strCartID = CheckNull(myQueryString, "CartId", "");
        string strItem1CartItemId = CheckNull(myQueryString, "Item.1.CartItemId",
"");

        string strHMAC = CheckNull(myQueryString, "HMAC", "");

        // Return the concatenated URI
        strURI = strRoot + strAccessKeyId +
            strOperation + strResponseGroup +
            strItemId + strKeywords +
            strSearchIndex + strDirector +
            strAuthor + strArtist +
            strActor + strListType +
            strName + strFirstName +
            strLastName + strEmail + strListId +
            strItem1ASIN + strItem1Quantity +
            strMergeCart + strCartID +
            strHMAC + strItem1CartItemId;

        return strURI;
    }
```

It's unlikely that all parameters included in the function would ever be specified. The result would be the longest Amazon URI ever in existence. It would only come about if someone hacked your code, or if you misused your own application. In any event, any invalid combination of parameters sent in will be handily dismissed by the Amazon REST interface.

The eBay API

In this application, you combine Amazon data with the ability to search eBay for the same item. If a cheaper price exists on eBay, then, of course, your users might be interested in hopping over there to place a bid on the item instead of paying the Amazon price.

Amazon has done a tremendous job of making its data and services available through community-driven developer programs. eBay has an equally rich set of data, and is not far behind Amazon in terms of making this data available to the programmer.

You can sign up for free access to the eBay developer program at the following Web site:

```
http://developer.ebay.com
```

eBay supports a wide range of access methods to its platform including software development kits for Java, PHP, .NET, and SOAP. I will make use of the REST interface for the sake of simplicity.

The eBay Registration Process

When you register with the eBay developer program you will be assigned a set of *sandbox keys*. These keys entitle you to use the non-production instance of the eBay API. This is a special area, known as the *sandbox*, that you can use to develop and test your application. This is a safer mechanism than having you test against production auction data.

The next step in the process is to create a sandbox test account, sometimes known as a *sandbox test user account*.

With both the sandbox keys and the sandbox user account, you can generate a sandbox REST token using the tool located at this URL:

```
http://developer.ebay.com/tokentool
```

Once you have tested your application against the sandbox and are happy with it, the next step is to move out of the sandbox and into production. "Production" here refers to the live production instance of the eBay data repository. This is where people's auctions are live and in-flight.

To register for production access, your application must be submitted for certification. You can do this at the following location:

```
http://developer.ebay.com
```

Once you perform this step, you will be assigned a set of *production keys*, similar to the sandbox keys you obtained earlier. You can use these production keys in the same fashion as before to obtain a production REST token for use in your application code.

This is a complicated process, but as you have seen, every vendor is approaching the notion of a Web service platform from a new perspective. As a mashup developer, it's a fact of life that to use a company's data, there will be a slight learning curve to get up to speed on its platform.

The eBay REST Interface

All eBay REST API calls are sent to the following address:

```
http://rest.api.ebay.com/restapi
```

What follows is all the data required by eBay to perform the operation. The following table describes some of the required and optional elements of a typical eBay REST call. For more information, refer to the eBay developer documentation available at `http://developer.ebay.com`.

Parameter	Required?	Description
CallName	Required	The method name to invoke. For example, `GetSearchResults`.
RequestToken	Required	The token you generated as part of the registration process.
SearchInDescription	Optional	Specifies whether the search item should be matched to strings in the title, description, or subtitles of the item. Defaults to `false`.
Query	Required	The keywords or expression to search for.

As of this writing, only the `GetSearchResults` API is supported through eBay's REST API. All other eBay operations are available through the eBay SOAP interface.

Transforming XML within the Browser

Just as there is an Internet Explorer (IE) and a Mozilla standard mechanism to implement `XmlHttpRequest`, the same applies to the XSL transformation.

The following "Try It Out" transforms a document using Internet Explorer's built-in XML objects.

Try It Out   Transforming a Document

1. Create a new project that includes a new page named `default.aspx`.

2. Add a new XML file to the project. Name this file `zeppelin.xml`. This will be the sample data for the transformation:

```xml
<?xml version="1.0" encoding="utf-8" ?>
<zeppelin>
  <album name="Led Zeppelin II">
    <song title="Black Dog"></song>
  </album>
  <album name="Walking Into Clarksdale">
    <song title="Gallows Pole" ></song>
    <song title="Bring It Home"></song>
  </album>
  <album name="UnLedded">
    <song title="The Rain Song"/>
```

```
        <song title="The Ocean" />
      </album>
  </zeppelin>
```

3. Add a new XSL file to the project. Name this file `Simple.xsl`. This will provide the transformation templates to generate the results:

```
<?xml version="1.0" encoding="utf-8"?>

<xsl:stylesheet version="1.0"
    xmlns:xsl="http://www.w3.org/1999/XSL/Transform">
  <xsl:output method="html" />
  <xsl:template match="/">
    <xsl:apply-templates select="zeppelin/album" />
  </xsl:template>

  <xsl:template match="album">
    <h2>
      Album Name:<xsl:value-of select="@name" />
    </h2>
    <xsl:apply-templates select="song" />
  </xsl:template>

  <xsl:template match="song">
    Track Name:<b>
      <xsl:value-of select="@title" />
    </b><br/>
  </xsl:template>

</xsl:stylesheet>
```

4. Create a new JavaScript script block and define some global variables:

```
<script language="javascript">
    var myXml ;
    var myXsl ;
</script>
```

5. Add a function to initialize the global variables. This will be invoked when the page is loaded:

```
function Init(){
        if (window.ActiveXObject){
        // Create an Xml object
        myXml = new ActiveXObject("Msxml2.DomDocument");
        // Create an Xsl object
        myXsl = new ActiveXObject("Msxml2.DomDocument");
        } else {
           myXml = document.implementation.createDocument("","xsl",null);
           myXsl = document.implementation.createDocument("","xsl",null);
        }

        // Set both documents to be synchronous
        myXml.async=false;
        myXsl.async=false;

        // load the sample file
```

```
    myXml.load('zeppelin.xml');

  // Load the sample transformation
  myXsl.load('Simple.xsl');
}
```

6. Add one more function to the JavaScript block. This is what actually performs the transformation using the browser's built-in XML/XSL processors:

```
function DoTransform(){

    if (window.ActiveXObject){
        // Transform the data.
        var strTmp = myXml.transformNode(myXsl);

        // Print out the results
        document.getElementById('results').innerHTML = strTmp;
    } else {
        // Create Processor
        var myProcessor = new XSLTProcessor();
        myProcessor.importStylesheet(myXsl);

        var myResults = myProcessor.transformToFragment(myXml, document);
        var target = document.getElementById('results');
        // display the response
        target.appendChild(myResults);
    }
}
```

7. When the page loads, it must invoke the `Init` function. Add the following attribute to the body tag of `default.aspx`:

```
</head>
<body onload="Init()">
    <form id="form1" runat="server">
```

8. Add the following `div` tag to the page to store the results:

```
<div id="results">
            Results go here.
        </div>
```

9. Add the following `input` tag to actually trigger the transformation:

```
<input type="button" onclick="DoTransform()" value="Click Me" />
```

10. Launch the application and click the Input button.

The application should load the XML and XSL documents, transform the data, and display the results. The screen should look similar to Figure 10-4.

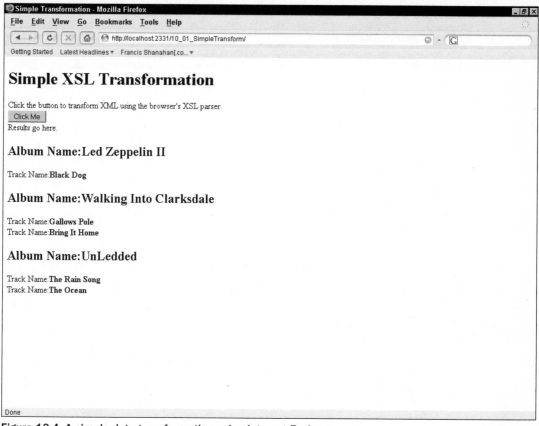

Figure 10-4: A simple data transformation using Internet Explorer

To achieve the same result in Mozilla/Firefox/Safari, you must use a different set of classes to perform the translation, as follows:

```
// Create Processor
myProcessor = new XSLTProcessor();
myProcessor.importStylesheet(myXsl);

myResults = myProcessor.transformToFragment(myXml, document);

// Finally display the response
myTarget.innerHTML = "";
myTarget.appendChild(myResults);
```

The JavaScript Requester

Now that you can transform data in JavaScript, it's time to turn your attention back to the WishList Browser application. The following listing displays the JavaScript GetData() function. It has been modified from Chapter 9 to be slightly more versatile. GetData now uses an array of XSL sheets to transform the data, as explained in the next section.

```
// this function actually performs the request for data.
function GetData(myXslIndex, myTarget, myOperation) {

    // Set some variables used in the response handler
    gCurrentXsl = myXslIndex;
    gTargetDiv = myTarget;

    // Show progress
    document.getElementById(gTargetDiv).innerHTML = "<h2>Loading...</h2>";

    var myCacheBreaker =Math.floor(Math.random()*10000);
    // Break the caching by attaching a random number.
     var myUrl="getdata.aspx?" + myOperation + "&cacheBreaker=" + myCacheBreaker;

    // Is this a Microsoft browser?
    if (window.ActiveXObject) {
        // Create a new request
        myRequest = new ActiveXObject("Microsoft.XMLHTTP");
        if (myRequest) {
            myRequest.onreadystatechange = HandleResponse;
            myRequest.open("GET", myUrl, true);
            myRequest.send();

        }
    } else if (window.XMLHttpRequest) {
        // If this is Firefox or Safari...
        myRequest = new XMLHttpRequest();
        myRequest.onreadystatechange = HandleResponse;
        myRequest.open("GET", myUrl, true);
        myRequest.send(null);
    }
    myPrint(myUrl);
}
```

Setting Up the XSL Array

This application performs a lot of transformations with six different XSL files. Because the application performs so many transformations, rather than load each XSL file in the browser as needed, it makes more sense to load each right when the page is loaded. The XSL files are then stored for the life of the page, and ready when needed. A JavaScript array is used to store the XSL files:

```
var gXsl = new Array;
```

When the page loads, an array of JavaScript XML objects is built up inside this array (remember XSL is also XML). Unfortunately, two browser-specific versions of this code must be implemented because of differences in Firefox/Mozilla and Internet Explorer's implementation of the XML javascript object model.

The `Init` function is called when the page loads:

```
function Init(){
    // Branch the code to support either IE or Firefox
    if (window.ActiveXObject)
    {
        InitXslIE();
    }
    else
    {
        InitXslFF();
    }
    // Load all the stylesheets.
    LoadXsl();
}
```

This is the code to instantiate the IE-specific XML objects:

```
// Initialize the XSL in IE
function InitXslIE() {
    for (var i = 0; i< 6 ; i++ ){
        gXsl[i] = new ActiveXObject("Msxml2.DomDocument");
    }
    // setup the xml object.
    gXml = new ActiveXObject("Msxml2.DomDocument");
    gXml.async=false;
}
```

Here is the code to instantiate the Firefox-specific XML objects. This code also works in Safari on a Macintosh, and some other variants of Mozilla:

```
// Initialize the XSL objects in Firefox
function InitXslFF() {
    for (var i = 0; i< 6 ; i++ ){
        gXsl[i] = document.implementation.createDocument("","xsl",null);
    }

    // Finally the XML object
    gXml = document.implementation.createDocument("","xml",null);
    gXml.async=false;
}
```

The main difference between the browsers is in how the objects are instantiated.

Lastly, the actual XSL files are loaded down from the server:

```
// Load an array of XSL sheets
function LoadXsl(){
    gXsl[0].load('xml/AmazonListSearch.xsl');
    gXsl[1].load('xml/AmazonListLookup.xsl');
    gXsl[2].load('xml/AmazonYouTube.xsl');
    gXsl[3].load('xml/AmazonCartCreate.xsl');
    gXsl[4].load('xml/AmazonCartGet.xsl');
    gXsl[5].load('xml/ebaySearch.xsl');
}
```

The Response Handler

The function to handle the JavaScript response is similar to Chapter 9, but it, too, has been modified. In this Ajax application, the response handler must hand off the received XML document object to a transformation function, as follows:

```
function HandleResponse() {

    // Readystate 4 means we're done
    if (myRequest.readyState == 4) {

        // If the server returned OK
        if (myRequest.status == 200) {
            gXml = myRequest.responseXML;
            TransformResponse();
        } else {
            myDiv.innerHTML =
                "<br/>Oops there was a problem, " + myRequest.statusText;
            myDiv.innerHTML += "<br/>Try again later";
        }
    }
}
```

The Transformation Function

The last piece in the client-side puzzle is the transformation function. This function uses the array of XSL objects defined earlier to perform the actual transformation:

```
// Transform the XML data
function TransformResponse()
{
    var myXsl = gXsl[gCurrentXsl];
    var myXml=gXml;
    var myResults;
    var myProcessor;
    var myTarget = document.getElementById(gTargetDiv);

    if (window.ActiveXObject)
    {
        // IE specific transformation.
        myResults = myXml.transformNode(myXsl);
        myTarget.innerHTML = myResults;
    }
    else
    {
        // Create Processor
        myProcessor = new XSLTProcessor();
        myProcessor.importStylesheet(myXsl);

        myResults = myProcessor.transformToFragment(myXml, document);

        // Finally display the response
```

```
        myTarget.innerHTML = "";
        myTarget.appendChild(myResults);
    }
}
```

Again, this code needs to branch depending on the browser executing it. The Mozilla branch in this case is slightly more complex, but achieves a similar result to the IE section.

Transforming the List XML Structure

The desired output from the List transformation is a set of search results. When you click a list item in the results, the idea is that another Ajax call will be made to obtain the list details. To achieve this, each result contains a link that includes a `javascript` function call tied to the `onclick` event. It looks like this:

```
<a href="javascript:void(0)" onclick="ListLookup('[SOME LIST ID]')">Bob's List</a>
```

To create this link using XSL, the following template is used:

```
<!-- The List template -->
  <xsl:template match="a:List">
    <xsl:value-of select="a:CustomerName"/>'s
      <xsl:value-of select="a:ListType"/> has
    <xsl:value-of select="a:TotalItems"/> items and was
    created on <xsl:value-of select="a:DateCreated"/><br/>
    Look it up <a href="javascript:void(0)">
      <xsl:attribute name="onclick">ListLookup('<xsl:value-of
select="a:ListId"/>');</xsl:attribute>
      <xsl:value-of select="a:ListId"/>
    </a> or
    <a>
      <xsl:attribute name="href">
        <xsl:value-of select="a:ListURL"/>
      </xsl:attribute>
      Visit <xsl:value-of select="a:ListName"/>
    </a><br/>
    <hr/>
  </xsl:template>
```

This template generates a single list-item HTML result. The highlighted rows generate the `javascript` link you need to trigger a new Ajax call and look up the list details.

Working with the Remote Shopping Cart

Let's face it. The main purpose of allowing access to all this Amazon data is to drive purchases and sales of Amazon product information. Most people building applications against Amazon's Web service API are interested in their users making purchases.

Part of any purchasing process is browsing products and setting them aside for purchase during checkout — essentially implementing a shopping cart.

You could implement your own shopping cart that stores the Amazon Standard Identification Numbers (ASINs) in the users' sessions. When users try to check out, they would have to enter credit card information into your site. This is unreasonable for a number of reasons:

❑ Most users, of course, are concerned about the privacy of their information.

❑ There would be no way to submit the items for delivery to Amazon once the items had been paid for.

❑ The process of accepting credit card transactions is non-trivial, and involves acquiring a merchant ID and going through a certification process.

These all represent a significant barrier to entry for a humble developer. It's a far more attractive notion to maintain a shopping cart on Amazon's Web site, and let Amazon manage the checkout process.

To facilitate this, Amazon provides a remote shopping cart capability. Rather than leaving your site and going to Amazon to maintain a shopping cart, you can define a remote shopping cart that is actually maintained on Amazon's platform, but accessible using the same mechanism you use for all other data access.

Shopping Cart Operations

There are five dedicated Cart operations supported by the ECS. The following table describes the APIs at a high level.

Operation	Description
CartGet	Provides a means for your site to retrieve the shopping cart information that is maintained on Amazon.
CartAdd	Adds an item to the cart.
CartModify	Modifies an item contained in the cart (for example, to change the quantity or remove an item from the cart).
CartClear	Empties a cart.
CartCreate	Creates a new shopping cart and adds an item to the cart. Use this API to obtain an HMAC and CartID.

The typical sequence of events when using the remote shopping cart is as follows:

1. A user browses or searches your site until locating a product for purchase.
2. The user chooses Add to Cart and a new cart is created with CartCreate.
3. The user continues to shop and add items to the cart. This is done with CartAdd.
4. The user views the items in the cart with CartGet.
5. The user changes item quantities, or removes items from the cart using CartModify.
6. The user completes all shopping and then wants to check out. The CartGet response includes a specially encoded URL that directs the user to a page on Amazon that facilitates the checkout process.

The following sections cover these steps.

Creating a New Shopping Cart

A new shopping cart is created by issuing a `CartCreate` operation call with an item `ASIN`. Amazon identifies each shopping cart using a compound key comprised of a `CartId` and a code called an `HMAC`. When you create a new cart, Amazon assigns a `CartId` and `HMAC` to the cart.

The item is added to the cart, and the `CartId` and `HMAC` are returned in the response. Your site must make a note of these identifiers for use in future `Cart` API calls.

If either the `CartId` or the `HMAC` are lost, then the cart will be lost. You cannot retrieve a cart by searching; you must have the assigned `CartId` and `HMAC`.

A new cart can be created using `getdata.aspx` and the following URL:

```
http://yourHostHere/getdata.aspx?Operation=CartCreate&Item.1.ASIN=0486242587&Item.1
.Quantity=1&MergeCart=True&cacheBreaker=6488
```

Listing 10-2 shows the response generated from this URL. Take note of the `CartId`, `HMAC`, and a special URL-encoded version of the `HMAC`. The `HMAC` can contain special characters such as an equals (=) or plus (+). Including these in a REST URL natively would cause problems with the URL. Amazon has provided the added convenience of encoding the `HMAC` value so that it can easily be passed back into subsequent API calls.

Listing 10-2: The `CreateCart` **XML Response**

```
<CartCreateResponse>
  <OperationRequest>
    ...
    <RequestId>0XC689PV4PGVYR5A89Q8</RequestId>
    <Arguments>
      <Argument Name="MergeCart" Value="True"/>
      <Argument Name="Service" Value="AWSECommerceService"/>
      <Argument Name="AWSAccessKeyId" Value="[YOUR ID HERE]"/>
      <Argument Name="Item.1.ASIN" Value="0486242587"/>
      <Argument Name="Item.1.Quantity" Value="1"/>
      <Argument Name="ResponseGroup" Value="Cart"/>
      <Argument Name="Operation" Value="CartCreate"/>
    </Arguments>
    <RequestProcessingTime>0.360120058059692</RequestProcessingTime>
  </OperationRequest>
  <Cart>
    <Request>
  ...
    </Request>
    <CartId>103-3227000-0146266</CartId>
    <HMAC>jjoOStUoD/aMKewif9Ct9P4wZVY=</HMAC>
    <URLEncodedHMAC>jjoOStUoD%2FaMKewif9Ct9P4wZVY%3D</URLEncodedHMAC>
    <PurchaseURL>
      https://...
    </PurchaseURL>
```

Remote shopping carts stay active for 90 days! This means your users can create a cart on your site and, as long as you maintain the HMAC *and* CartId, *they can come back and view it again and potentially buy something.*

Empty carts are valid for five days, after which they get cleaned up on the Amazon side.

Obtaining the Contents of a Shopping Cart

A shopping cart's contents can be displayed through the following URL, provided you have the CartId and HMAC. Note, for testing purposes, you'll need to obtain these from the CartCreate API.

```
http://yourHostHere/10_02_Wishlist/getdata.aspx?Operation=CartGet&CartId=002-308179
3-6416056&HMAC=NQ7475J20uLafBdbQ4JF7j%2FHkcI%3D&cacheBreaker=8300
```

Listing 10-3 shows the abridged XML response from the CartGet.

Listing 10-3: The CartGet **XML Response**

```
<CartGetResponse>
  <OperationRequest>
    ...
  </OperationRequest>

  <Cart>
    <Request>
    ...
    </Request>
    <CartId>002-3081793-6416056</CartId>
    <HMAC>NQ7475J20uLafBdbQ4JF7j/HkcI=</HMAC>
    <URLEncodedHMAC>NQ7475J20uLafBdbQ4JF7j%2FHkcI%3D</URLEncodedHMAC>
    <PurchaseURL>
      https://www.amazon.com/gp/cart/...
    </PurchaseURL>

    <SubTotal>
      <Amount>995</Amount>
      <CurrencyCode>USD</CurrencyCode>
      <FormattedPrice>$9.95</FormattedPrice>
    </SubTotal>

    <CartItems>
      ...
      <CartItem>
        <CartItemId>U37BQWEOWW17T3</CartItemId>
        <ASIN>0486242587</ASIN>
        ...
        <Title>Modern Coin Magic</Title>
        <ProductGroup>Book</ProductGroup>
        ...
        <ItemTotal>
          <Amount>995</Amount>
          <CurrencyCode>USD</CurrencyCode>
```

```
            <FormattedPrice>$9.95</FormattedPrice>
          </ItemTotal>
        </CartItem>
      </CartItems>
    </Cart>
  </CartGetResponse>
```

Adding Items to a Cart

To add an item to the cart, you must know the item's ASIN. If you are adding multiple items to a cart in a single API call, then each one should be indexed using the Item parameter. For example, the first item to be added to the cart will be specified by the following:

```
Item.1.ASIN=[SOME ASIN]&Item.1.Quantity=1
```

If you are adding two items, index them as follows:

```
Item.1.ASIN=[ASIN 1]&Item.1.Quantity=1&Item.2.ASIN=[ASIN 2]&Item.2.Quantity=1
```

All available items will be added to the cart.

When adding items to a cart, you will find that anything out of stock or unavailable will be added to a special section of the cart known as "Saved for later." This is not immediately apparent from the Amazon response because the ECS reports no errors for out-of-stock items. If you are having trouble with particular items not ending up in your cart, this might be the reason.

Emptying the Cart

Clearing out all entries from the cart is easy. Simply call CartClear and pass in the CartId and HMAC.

Note that CartClear does not destroy the cart; it simply empties it. You can still continue to use the CartId and HMAC combination because the cart is still valid. In fact, there is no way to programmatically destroy a remote cart. Remember, carts can remain empty for up to five days; thereafter, they will be removed from Amazon's system.

Storing the HMAC and CartId

The user's cart is not really confidential. (Do you cover up your basket while browsing the grocery store?) However, you might want to keep access to it secure. Anyone who gets the CartId and HMAC can, in theory, look up the contents of the cart.

Ideally, you would store the HMAC and CartId along with other user profile information in a database. Users would need to log in to retrieve their carts. This provides an extra layer of security, but a minor inconvenience before access to the cart is granted.

With the sample code, I have kept things simple and stored the HMAC and CartId in cookies on the browser. To accomplish this, you'll need a couple of generic JavaScript functions, all stored in a JavaScript file called cart.js.

Writing a Cookie Using JavaScript

Cookies are little bits of information that are stored either in memory or as a tiny file associated with the browser. Cookies are not that secure, although they are typically only accessible from the site that sent them.

Cookies are typically sent down to the browser by the Web server. You can also write a cookie using just JavaScript. To write a cookie using purely JavaScript, you must specify the name of the cookie, the value it should have, and when it should expire.

The following function encapsulates the logic to write a cookie that will expire in a specific number of days:

```
function CreateCookie(myName, myValue, numDays)
{
        var myDate = new Date();

        // Define expiration as a number of milliseconds;
        var myTimeToLive = numDays * 24 * 60 * 60 * 1000;

        // set the time to the expiration time
        myDate.setTime(myDate.getTime() + myTimeToLive);

        // Convert to a string
        var myExpiration = "; expires=" + myDate.toGMTString();

        // Write out the cookie
        document.cookie = myName + "=" + myValue + myExpiration + "; path=/";
}
```

That takes care of storing the cookies. You also need a corresponding function to read the cookies:

```
function ReadCookie(myName)
{
        // Obtain an array of cookie name-values
        var objCookies = document.cookie.split(';');

        var myNameTag = myName + "=";

        // Search the cookie array for the one you're looking for.
        for(var i=0 ; i < objCookies.length; i++)
        {
                var myCookie = objCookies[i];

                // Need to trim the cookie of any leading spaces
                while (myCookie.charAt(0)==' ') myCookie = myCookie.substring(1,
myCookie.length);
                // Does this match?
                if (myCookie.indexOf(myNameTag) == 0) {
                        return myCookie.substring( myNameTag.length, myCookie.length);
                }
        }
        return null;
}
```

`ReadCookie` takes a single parameter that is the name of the cookie to obtain. Because cookies are stored as a concatenated string by the browser, the browser then iterates through this string, looking for key-names to match. Once it finds one, it returns the value.

The WishList application uses Ajax to retrieve the shopping cart information, which, in turn, contains the `CartId` and `HMAC`. The `CartId`/`HMAC` information is not available in a usable form until after the browser has transformed the data. As a result, it's easiest to just use JavaScript to store the cookies, rather than try to have the Web server do it. The Web server has no knowledge of `CartId` or `HMAC`. The browser, on the other hand, can use a nifty trick involving dynamic JavaScript to store these values in cookies.

When the `CartCreate` API is called, the response from Amazon is transformed using an XSL file named `AmazonCartCreate.xsl`.

The `HMAC` and `CartId` values are contained in the response under the following nodes:

```
CartCreateResponse/Cart/CartId
CartCreateResponse/Cart/HMAC
CartCreateResponse/Cart/URLEncodedHMAC
```

The following template is included in the transformation to produce dynamic JavaScript and execute it:

```
<xsl:template match="n:Cart">
<a>
  <xsl:attribute name="href">
    <xsl:value-of select="n:PurchaseURL"></xsl:value-of>
  </xsl:attribute>
  <xsl:attribute name="target">_blank</xsl:attribute>
  <b>Cart Total: </b>
<xsl:value-of select="n:SubTotal/n:FormattedPrice" />
  Click Here to Checkout now</a>
  <br/>
  <script defer="">
  CreateCookie('myCartId','<xsl:value-of select="n:CartId"/>', 7);
  CreateCookie('myHMAC','<xsl:value-of select="n:URLEncodedHMAC"/>', 7);
  LoadCart();
  </script>
</xsl:template>
```

When the Ajax engine transforms this, a piece of JavaScript is injected into the HTML of the page. The JavaScript looks similar to this:

```
<script defer="">
    CreateCookie('myCartId','ABCDEFG', 7);
    CreateCookie('myHMAC','HIJKLMNOP', 7);
    LoadCart();
</script>
```

This JavaScript is executed immediately and, thus, the actual act of transforming and rendering the content onto the page is what stores the cookie values in the browser.

Breaking Browser Caching

Browser caching works slightly differently in every browser, and is an important notion to be aware of. If you are not cognizant of caching, you may find yourself scratching your head for hours wondering why your code is not executing as anticipated.

When browser caching is turned on, and the browser makes a request for a URI, the response is stored along with the URI that generated it. The browser does this as a convenience and as a performance improvement. When the same URI is queried again later, instead of making a new network call out to retrieve the fresh data, the browser will check its cache for a matching URI/response pair. In the event it finds a match, the cached response is presented.

What this means for you is that when your code issues an `XmlHttpRequest` in JavaScript for a URL, the response you are seeing may not be a fresh one. Normally, for searches and item lookups, this is not an issue. In fact, this is sometimes a benefit. However, when programming something like the Amazon remote shopping cart, browser caching becomes a problem.

The typical scenario is that the user visits your site and a remote cart is created by adding a new item to the cart using `CartCreate`. This is followed by a call to `CartGet` and the initial cart is displayed containing one item.

The user then might delete an item, which uses `CartModify`, followed by `CartGet`. Unfortunately, although the item has indeed been removed, because the response for `CartGet` is cached, the cart still appears to be holding one item.

To break browser caching, you simply need to modify every URL so that it's unique. This is as simple as tacking on an additional random number to the end of the URL. The following JavaScript is added to the `GetData` JavaScript function:

```
var myCacheBreaker =Math.floor(Math.random()*10000);
    // Break the caching by attaching a random number.
var myUrl="getdata.aspx?" + myOperation + "&cacheBreaker=" + myCacheBreaker;
```

This produces a URL that looks like this:

```
http://yourPathHere/10_02_Wishlist/getdata.aspx?Operation=CartCreate&ResponseGroup=
Cart&Item.1.ASIN=0486242587&Item.1.Quantity=1&MergeCart=True&cacheBreaker=8098
```

The presence of the `cacheBreaker` parameter means that the browser will not have a URL match in its cache, and, hence, always executes the call.

Showing Progress

When you execute an asynchronous call, the user typically has no idea that it ever happened. This can be useful, but very often it's important to provide the user some indication that something is happening. This can take any form, the simplest being just displaying a message such as "Loading..." on the page. This is the route the sample code takes:

```
// Show progress
document.getElementById(gTargetDiv).innerHTML = "<h2>Loading...</h2>";
```

You might also consider using an animated GIF or a popup `<div>` to signal to the user that the page is working diligently on the request.

Debugging Tips

This example relies heavily on DHTML or JavaScript. Client-side script is notoriously troublesome to debug. Here are some tips to help navigate through the script-coding process:

❑ Use a browser that incorporates a JavaScript console (such as Firefox). You can access the console through the Tools menu item. Of course, this will only test the Mozilla branch of code, but it is helpful.

❑ Include a simple `<div id="debug">` tag in your code. Create a `Print()` function that writes to this debug `div`. Whenever you need to view a variable, insert a call to the `print` function, passing in the variable as follows:

```
function myPrint(msg){
   document.getElementById('debug').innerHTML += "<br/>" + msg;
}
```

In this manner, you can easily test the application and be aware of the variables' values. When you're finished testing, simply override the `Print()` function to return immediately, thus turning off debugging.

❑ JavaScript supports structured error handling, and it's a good idea to make use of it to catch exceptions. A typical try catch block looks like this:

```
try{
     // Do something
} catch (myException) {
     // Handle the error
     alert(e.description);
} finally {
     // Clean up
}
```

Place code in the `try` section. If that code generates an exception, the `catch` block will execute. Use this to print out the error information. The `finally` block will execute whether or not there was an error, giving you a chance to clean up any objects you need to.

Alternative Uses

There are numerous possible applications of this technique. You could track users' mouse-clicks or gestures, create an auto-complete form that fills in as the user types, perform server-side form validations without a post-back, and so on. Ensure that you are cognizant of the desired user experience before diving into coding. Try to keep the application of the Ajax technique as pinpointed and directed as possible to avoid a negative user experience.

Security Considerations

Security is always an important consideration, and there are some limitations with Ajax (Figure 10-5). JavaScript and `XmlHttpRequest` can only be used to make HTTP calls back to the server that served the original page. In other words, you cannot build a page that, when served from www.myDomain.com, uses XmlHttpRequest to obtain data directly from www.Amazon.com. The page must query back against the server from whence it came. This is the reason for the getdata.aspx page, which acts as a pass-through in this example. Chapter 11 provides a solution that tackles this issue in a secure manner using JSON and the Dynamic Scripting method.

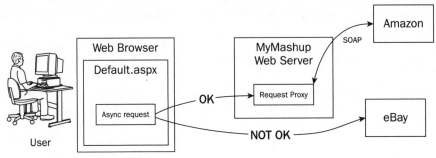

Figure 10-5: Security constraints

Browser Support

As you saw working through this chapter, Ajax doesn't have a common implementation across browsers. Luckily, by now, XMLHttpRequest has been implemented by most (if not all) of the major browsers, including Firefox, Safari, Mozilla, and Internet Explorer. Some code branching is still neces-sary, however, and you should (if at all possible) ensure that you test with as many operating system/browser combinations as you have available. You might consider using some of the virtualiza-tion technology such as VMware or Microsoft Virtual Server to accomplish this task.

Some More Ideas and Tips

Ajax has as many potential applications as you can dream up. Already it has been used to create new usage paradigms on the Internet. Here are just a few ideas:

❑ *Live Search* — Tie data retrieval to the keypress of users to provide results as they type.

❑ *Parse Large Datasets* — As you'll see in the Zollage example cited in Chapter 16, Ajax can be applied to allow a user to navigate a huge amount of data, with little to no performance decrease. By only downloading the portion of data required, and augmenting it as the dataset is navigated, you can create analysis services that previously would not have been possible in a browser.

❑ *Auto-Complete* — Provide suggestions in text-entry fields as a user types.

❑ *User tracking* — Use Ajax to snoop on your users, monitoring the links they are clicking and how long they are viewing a given page.

You might also consider using some of the publicly available Ajax libraries. Companies such as Microsoft and Tibco have released full-blown development kits built entirely around Ajax (namely Atlas and General Interface, respectively). These libraries come complete with pre-built controls and utilities ready to plug into your Web application. Underneath the covers, these libraries are using the very same techniques as described in this chapter. Now that you have written an Ajax-powered application from scratch you are not only better equipped to use a commercial library, but you might even consider creating your own. Figure 10-6 shows the finished application in action showing data from both eBay and Amazon side-by-side.

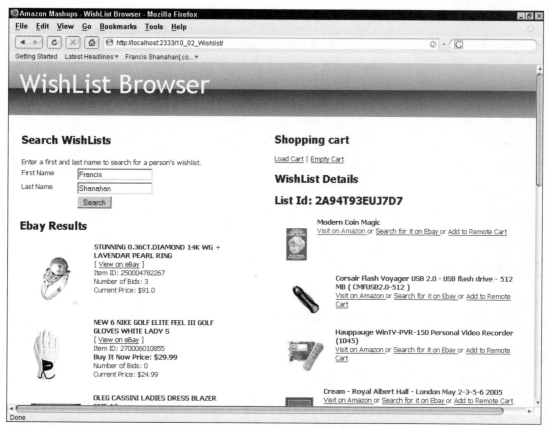

Figure 10-6: The finished application displaying data from both Amazon and eBay

Summary

With the advent of Windows Vista and Internet Explorer 7, the browser experience is going to get richer and more sophisticated. For now, Ajax and `XMLHttpRequest` is filling the void. Ajax as a technique is simple to implement, easy to use, and, if used effectively, can yield a powerful experience.

Cross-browser branching is still a requirement. However, it does not require a huge amount of code-path branching.

In this chapter, you learned the following:

❑ How Ajax can be used to power an entire user interface

❑ How to use the eBay REST API to search live auction information

❑ How to transform XML using JavaScript and XSL

❑ How to query the Amazon List structures

❑ How to use the Amazon shopping cart interface to store users' cart information remotely

❑ How to cache data within the browser

You also built a useful application that browses Amazon wish lists. Now you have no excuse for not getting that special loved one something on his or her Christmas list.

In the last few chapters, you have built a number of mashups, each one focusing on a different technique. By now, you've seen that mashups allow for a lot of creativity, both in form and function. In Chapter 11, you learn how to combine Yahoo Maps and Amazon to create an application that can be used to locate restaurants and associated customer reviews.

Before continuing on, it's worth reviewing your knowledge with the following exercises.

Exercises

1. How would you modify the WishList application to also support YouTube data?

2. How might you use this application to also support wedding or baby registries?

3. How could you implement Live Search (provide results as you type) using the techniques in this chapter?

4. How can you create a JavaScript array of XSL sheets?

5. What is the benefit of using JavaScript arrays?

6. Why is browser caching bad?

Let's Eat!

Hey, everyone needs to eat, and Amazon can help us here, too! Did you know besides books and just about every other product under the sun that Amazon also has restaurant information for a growing list of the major cities in North America?

Not only that, Amazon's outspoken customer base has eaten at these restaurants and documented their experiences through customer reviews.

This chapter shows you how to build a map mashup using the Yahoo Maps interface and Amazon data. Yahoo is slightly less publicized than Google in the map-API space, but equally capable, as you will see. Moreover, the approach and techniques are easily transferred to the Google space, should you wish to go that route.

In this chapter, you learn about the following:

❑   How Ajax-enabled Map APIs work and how to use them

❑   How to create a custom map overlay to mark positions on a map

❑   How to use GeoRSS to plot geographical locations

❑   How to query and display Amazon restaurant information

❑   How to convert restaurant addresses into points on a Yahoo Map

The Battle Plan: Yahoo Maps Plus Amazon

In this chapter, you build a number of simple pages that utilize Yahoo Maps. The ultimate goal, however, is to build a restaurant-browsing utility capable of displaying reviews and locations of restaurants on an interactive map.

You'll build on the basic map by combining the Yahoo Map presentation with custom map markers created using geographical data from Amazon. Each marker on the map will represent a restaurant from Amazon's database. Clicking a restaurant will display additional information for that location, including restaurant name, food type, and customer reviews.

Understanding the Architecture

There are a couple of moving parts in this particular application. Figure 11-1 displays the overall architecture of the final application.

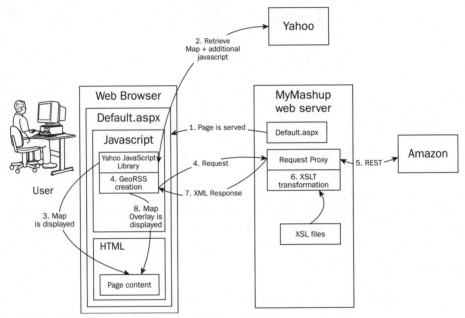

Figure 11-1: Restaurant Browser application architecture

How It Works

This is a rather complicated application with asynchronous requests going back to Yahoo, as well as your own JavaScript library communicating with Amazon.

1. When the page is first loaded, it includes a local JavaScript file for the Amazon communication along with a Yahoo JavaScript file for the maps.

2. The Yahoo library takes care of initiating the map by reaching out to Yahoo and obtaining a set of references to map tiles.

3. The map tiles are then dynamically written into a content area of the page.

4. When the users access the page, they search for restaurants to show up on the map. A URL is built and a request is made to obtain the data from Amazon.

5. The data request is forwarded on to Amazon, which responds with some data in XML format.

6. The XML is then converted on the server into GeoRSS, which is a variant of the RSS specification using a server local XSL file.

7. The link to the GeoRSS is used by the Yahoo JavaScript library to create a new map overlay. This overlay consists of a set of map markers, each with various bits of information pertaining to the restaurant.

8. The last step is to display this overlay on top of the map.

The Yahoo Maps API

Yahoo provides a number of different Map APIs, depending on your needs. These include Flash and Ajax implementations.

Just as with all Web APIs, you will need to register for access to the functionality. This is free as of this writing, although there is a (generous) limit on the number of queries you can make per day. When you register with Yahoo, you will obtain an application ID for use in its API calls.

Rather than complicate development (and the development environment), this book focuses solely on the Yahoo Ajax library. The general concepts, however, are also applicable to the Flash implementation. The Ajax implementation is discussed in detail later in this chapter.

Try It Out   Simplest Map Possible

1. Create a new HTML or ASPX page in a Visual Studio Web project.

2. In the page's `head` section, add a reference to the Yahoo Maps `javascript` library and specify your Yahoo application tag:

```
<script type="text/javascript"
src="http://api.maps.yahoo.com/ajaxymap?v=3.0&appid=[YOUR TAG HERE]"></script>
```

3. Add a new `div` to the page to contain the map:

```
<div id="mySimpleMap"></div>
```

4. Define a new style for the map `div`. This should go in the `head` section of the page:

```
<style type="text/css">
    #mySimpleMap {
        height: 600px;
        width: 600px;
    }
</style>
```

5. Create a new `javascript` function to initialize the Yahoo Map:

```
<script type="text/javascript">
var myMap ;
```

```
function InitMap() {
    myMap = new YMap(document.getElementById('mySimpleMap'));
    // Draw the map centered over New York City.
    myMap.drawZoomAndCenter("New York", 4);
}
</script>
```

This launches the map centered on New York, but you can replace this with your own location.

6. Call the `InitMap` function when the page loads:

```
<body onload="InitMap()">
```

That's it! That's all the code required to get a scrollable, zoomable, interactive map up and running. Strictly speaking, you don't even need a Web server. You could just create a static HTML page and run it from the file system.

Run the application. Figure 11-2 displays the resulting page.

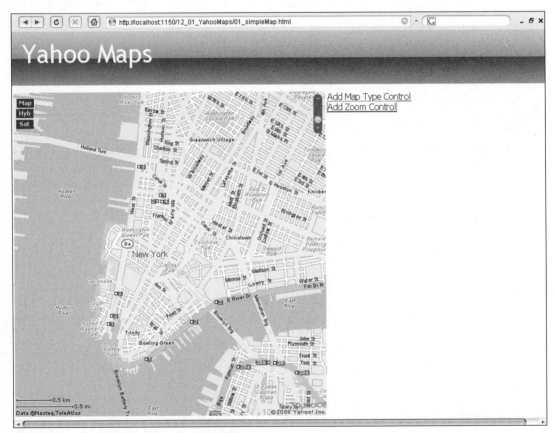

Figure 11-2: The simplest Yahoo Map possible

Yahoo Map Types

Map types refer to the nature of the graphics used to display the map. Three Yahoo map types are available for rendering. These are defined within the Yahoo API; you don't need to define these yourself.

- ❏ YAHOO_MAP_SAT — Displays satellite photography of the given location.

- ❏ YAHOO_MAP_REG — Displays a line drawing of the given location.

- ❏ YAHOO_MAP_HYB — A combination of the above. The satellite image is drawn first, and the line-drawing map information is overlaid on top.

You can set the map type displayed with the following JavaScript:

```
myMap.setMapType(YAHOO_MAP_SAT);
```

Alternatively, you can let the user set the map type by including a map Type control:

```
<a href="javascript:void(0)" onclick="myMap.addTypeControl();">Add Map Type
Control</a>
```

Zoom Levels in a Yahoo Map

Just as you'd expect, Yahoo includes the ability to display its maps at various levels of detail. You can add a zoom control to an existing map with the following JavaScript:

```
<a href="javascript:void(0)" onclick="myMap.addZoomLong();">Add Zoom Control</a>
```

Alternatively, you can specify the zoom level programmatically. For example, the following JavaScript centers a map on New York and zooms to street level:

```
myMap.drawZoomAndCenter("New York", 4);
```

The following table summarizes the more common map levels.

Map Level	Description
2	Displays maps zoomed to street level
4	Renders at the city level
8	State level view

How It Works

The application is powered primarily by Yahoo's JavaScript libraries:

```
<script type="text/javascript"
src="http://api.maps.yahoo.com/ajaxymap?v=3.0&appid=[YOUR TAG HERE]"></script>
```

When you launch the application, Yahoo's main library actually loads additional JavaScript libraries into the page that all participate in the rendering of the map. Try launching your application in Firefox and then view source. You'll find a host of additional JavaScript tags that weren't there before.

The map image can be rendered into a typical HTML `div` tag that must be assigned a width and height. If you leave out these properties, the map may not size in the browser correctly.

The map is displayed in a series of tiles. If you are quick you can probably see each one loading. As you scroll and pan the map, the page communicates back with Yahoo to load additional map tiles whenever necessary.

Try It Out   Adding Custom Markers

The default Yahoo map isn't that exciting. Let's add a few map markers to get a bit more familiar with the API. Standard map markers are just a default Yahoo icon displayed at a location. The sample code includes how to create these. In this "Try It Out" section, you create a custom marker by placing a custom image at the map location, instead of the default marker.

1. Create a new JavaScript function named `AddCustomMarker`:

```
function AddCustomMarker() {
}
```

2. Inside this new function, create a new Yahoo `YGeoPoint` object.

    The `YGeoPoint` is a class defined by the Yahoo JavaScript library. All Yahoo-specific objects are prefixed with the letter "Y".

    The `YGeoPoint` stores the latitude and longitude of the location. Note the coordinates are specified in decimals, not degrees and minutes:

```
// Create a new point
var myPoint = new YGeoPoint(40.70602, -74.00738);
```

3. Because this is going to be a custom marker, with a custom image displayed, create a `YImage` by first defining a size and then the `YImage` object itself. My image is called `myMarker.gif`:

```
// Define a size for the marker
var mySize = new YSize(100, 120);

// Create a new image for this marker
var myImage = new YImage("images/myMarker.gif", mySize);
```

4. Next, instantiate a new `YMarker` object using the `YImage` and `YGeoPoint`:

```
// Create a marker at that point with a custom Image
myCustomMarker = new YMarker(myPoint, myImage);
```

5. Add a custom message to the marker. This will be displayed whenever someone mouses over the map marker:

```
// Add auto expand
var myMessage = '<div>This is an example of a custom Image Marker</div>';
myCustomMarker.addAutoExpand(myMessage );
```

6. Finally, add the marker as an overlay on the map:

```
// Add it to the map
myMap.addOverlay(myCustomMarker);
```

7. All that remains is to call this function from your HTML code:

```
<a href="javascript:void(0)" onclick="AddCustomMarker()">Add Marker</a>
```

When you run the application and click the link, a new marker is added to the map (Figure 11-3).

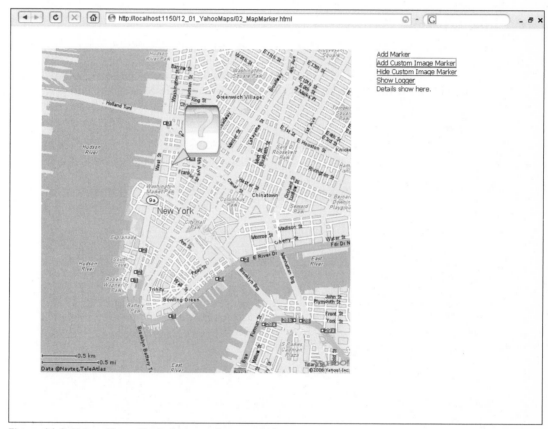

Figure 11-3: Yahoo Maps displaying a custom marker

Tying Markers to Events

Another useful feature is the ability to tie map markers to events in the browser. This lets you react to user actions (such as when the user clicks a map marker, and so on).

Using the code from the last "Try It Out" section, modify the marker creation code to include an event handler as follows:

```
// Capture the click event
YEvent.Capture(myCustomMarker,EventsList.MouseClick,
    function() { document.getElementById('details').innerHTML = "<b>You clicked
the custom marker</b>"; });
```

Of course, from this code you can see that you also need to include a new `div` named `details` to capture the output.

This time, when you run the application and click the marker, the results `div` outside the map is updated.

The YLog Utility

Yahoo provides a built-in logging/debugging utility in its implementation known as the `YLog`. The `YLog` allows you to print out any JavaScript object. The `YLog` object has a single `print` function. Output is routed to a floating window that you can drag and drop anywhere on the page. This can take the place of the typical JavaScript `alert()` function you'd use when you need to see an object's properties. Calling the `YLog.print` method looks like this:

```
YLog.print(strCityValue);
```

Figure 11-4 shows the `YLog` window in action.

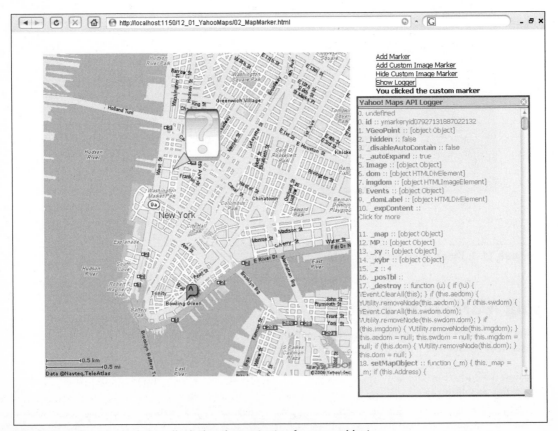

Figure 11-4: The `YLog` window displaying the contents of a `YMap` object

Adding a Border

With the default implementation of a Yahoo Map, the map sits in a `div` tag on your page. It's basically a rectangular area on the page. Depending on the situation, you may choose to integrate the map into the user interface of your page by adding a border around the map. This is easily done using a set of transparent images arranged around the map as follows:

1. Create a new folder in your project named `images` and add four new images: `top.gif`, `left.gif`, `right.gif`, and `bottom.gif`. These images will provide the graphics for the border. The easiest way to create these is to draw the entire border in a single image. Slice the image into four sections, saving each one with a transparent background.

2. Create four new `div`s and assign each one an ID such as `borderTop`, `borderLeft`, `borderBottom`, and `borderRight`. Create a CSS class for each with absolute positioning:

```
#borderRight {
    position:absolute;
}
```

3. Assign positioning to the map `div`. In the case of the example code, I know the map will be positioned at `top:40px` and `left:60px`. I also know that the map will be 590 pixels wide by 600 high:

```
#myMap
{
    position:absolute;
    z-index:1;
    top:40px;
    left:60px;
    width:590px;
    height:600px;
}
```

With the map positioning, you begin figuring out where to place your four border `div`s, as explained in the next section.

CSS Z-Index

Depending on the browser you're using, HTML is usually processed from the top down. When you have a situation with multiple images occupying the same area or overlapping, the order in which they'll be displayed can sometimes result in the wrong image ending up in the forefront.

To ensure that the images lay out in the way you'd like, you can use the CSS `z-index` attribute to specify which image or page element should end up in the foreground. If the X direction is left to right, and Y is top to bottom; then Z is from the background to the foreground. Higher values are painted further into the foreground.

Figure 11-5 gives an example of a set of `div` tags when laid out with incorrect or no `z-index`, and then again the same three `div` tags when arranged using the `z-index` attribute.

With this information and a little trial and error, you can calculate the correct positioning required to place the border, as shown in Figure 11-6. Browsers sometimes differ on their positioning of elements, so remember to test in as many browsers as possible. I typically test everything using Firefox and Internet Explorer, and find that covers most of the bases. If you have access to a Safari instance running on a Macintosh, that would be ideal.

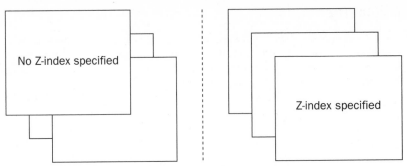

Figure 11-5: divs positioned with and without the z-index

Figure 11-6: A Yahoo Map with a custom candy border

In the case of the sample code, the required CSS styles look like this:

```
#borderRight
{
    position:absolute;
    z-index:2;
```

```
        top:15px;
        left:598px;
    }
    #borderLeft
    {
        position:absolute;
        z-index:2;
        top:0px;
        left:0px;
    }
    #borderTop
    {
        position:absolute;
        z-index:2;
        top:0px;
        left:26px;
    }
    #borderBottom
    {
        position:absolute;
        z-index:2;
        top:620px;
        left:7px;
    }
```

Building the Restaurant Browser

Now that you are familiar with the Yahoo API and its capabilities, it's time to turn your attention to building the Restaurant Browser application. For this, you'll reuse a lot of the existing code from prior chapters.

Try It Out   **Setting Up the Project**

As always, you can reuse the code from Chapter 4, or create a brand new project.

1. Start by creating a new project in Visual Studio Web Developer with a `default.aspx` page.

2. This project will reuse the `getdata.aspx` page from Chapter 10. Add it to the project using Add Existing Item.

3. Add in the `AmazonUtility.cs` and `WebUtility.cs` classes from the last example.

4. Create the user interface. In this case the UI consists of a single page with a map `div` on the left-hand side. To the right-hand side is a set of HTML controls that accept some input. These will accept Cuisine and City as search criteria. Figure 11-7 shows the client interface in design mode.

```
<strong>Choose a City:</strong>
<select id="ddCity" language="javascript" onchange="FindFood()">
    <option value="Boston">Boston</option>
    <option selected="selected" value="New%20York">New York</option>
    <option value="Chicago">Chicago</option>
    <option value="San%20Diego">San Diego</option>
    <option value="San%20Francisco">San Francisco</option>
</select>
<strong>Cuisine:</strong>
```

```
<select id="ddCuisine" language="javascript" onchange="FindFood()">
<option selected="selected" value="Steak">Steak</option>
<option value="Pizza">Pizza</option>
<option value="French">French</option>
<option value="Seafood">Seafood</option>
</select>
```

5. Add the `InitMap` JavaScript function to the page as before:

```
function InitMap(){
    myMap= new YMap(document.getElementById('myMap'));
    FindFood();
}
```

This function includes a call to a new function named `FindFood`, which you will define in a moment.

6. Add the map `div` and invoke `InitMap` from the page `onload` event:

```
<body onload="InitMap(); ">
```

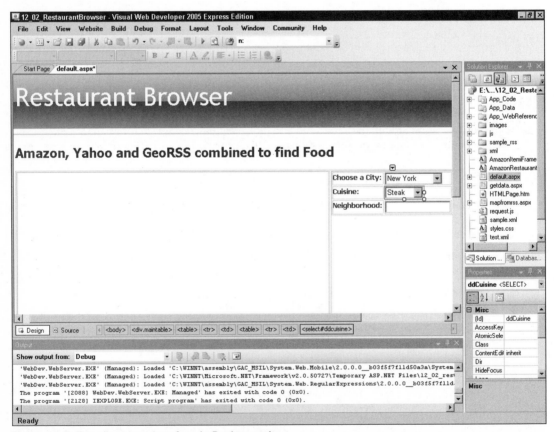

Figure 11-7: The client user interface in Design mode

All of this is fairly old-hat, based on what you've already accomplished in the beginning of this chapter.

Data Access Choices

There are two main mechanisms by which you can get GeoRSS data for use in the Yahoo Maps API. The first is to reuse `getdata.aspx`, have it retrieve the data directly from Amazon, and then transform it into GeoRSS using XSLT before returning it to the caller. This is a nice self-contained approach, but it involves deploying the ASP.NET application containing `getdata.aspx` to a publicly available Web server. You will implement this approach for the sample application.

The second mechanism involves passing an XSLT style sheet to Amazon so that the ECS can perform the transformation on its servers and send back the GeoRSS results. From a processing standpoint, this is a cleaner implementation in that no transformation is required on your side. Unfortunately it also requires that XLST file be placed in a publicly accessible site. For completeness, I will illustrate this approach, but not implement it in the sample code.

Before getting your hands dirty on the transformation, let's review how to find restaurant information in Amazon.

Finding Restaurants Using Amazon

Besides books, movies, and other products, Amazon also provides real-world restaurant information in some of the major U.S. cities. Unfortunately, as of this writing, the list of cities is quite small, but the database is constantly growing.

Of course, restaurants are not for sale, but you can get a decent amount of information on a given venue. The ECS includes customer reviews, as well as menu information in some cases, along with location addresses and the type of food served.

Amazon updates menus frequently, although it cannot guarantee the accuracy of a given menu item.

You find Amazon restaurants using the standard `ItemSearch` operation used in earlier chapters. You can limit your search to a specific geography or a specific cuisine by specifying the correct `BrowseNode` in the query.

Restaurants are searchable by the following search parameters:

❑ `City`—As of this writing, the supported cities are Seattle, Boston, New York, San Diego, San Francisco, and Chicago.

❑ `Neighborhood`—Documentation is scarce, but this seems to be a free-text match on areas within a city; for example, Little Italy (New York) or the Farmers' Market (Seattle). It also accepts non-city-specific criteria (such as downtown, east side, and so on).

❑ `Cuisine`—The type of food available. Again, this is a loosely defined criterion, but examples are Italian, Greek, French, Chinese, and so on. The `Cuisine` parameter can also be set to a type of food (for example, steak).

Here's a sample REST URL that queries Amazon for French restaurants in New York's West Side:

```
http://webservices.amazon.com/onca/xml?Service=AWSECommerceService&AWSAccessKeyId=[
YOUR KEY HERE]&Operation=ItemSearch&ResponseGroup=Large&City=New%20York&
SearchIndex=Restaurants
```

You might consider refining the search results with additional parameters such as `Cuisine` or `Neighborhood`.

Part of the response from this query will include the address of the restaurant:

```
...
<ItemAttributes>
  ...
  <Address>
     <Address1>611 E Pine St</Address1>
     <City>Seattle</City>
     <State>WA</State>
     <PostalCode>98122</PostalCode>
     <Country>US</Country>
  </Address>
  <Binding>Misc.</Binding>
....
```

You now know how to get restaurant information through Amazon. Given that you now have the restaurant address information, you would think the next logical step is to convert this into longitude and latitude for display on the map. Luckily, Yahoo's API does this for you.

The Yahoo Geo-Coding API

What do you do when you want to display a marker at a specific location on a map? You have the street address but you don't know the longitude and latitude coordinates for that location. The process of converting an address into longitude and latitude coordinates is known as *geo-coding*.

The Yahoo API provides a facility that performs the additional step of geo-coding the address information into latitude and longitude coordinates. In the old days, this would have required an additional call out to a dedicated geo-coding API:

```
http://developer.yahoo.com/maps/rest/V1/geocode.html
```

Yahoo provides a simple API. The geo-coding API accepts an address as input and spits out longitude/latitude coordinates for use within the mapping API.

The example code in this particular chapter does not need to use this API, but I have mentioned it here as something you should be aware of. The geo-coding API is great when you know the addresses in advance, or when you have one or two locations to look up. As you'll see, when you have an entire set of locations (such as a result set of restaurants), it becomes impractical to call the geo-coding API for each one, just to place it on the map.

You can easily modify `getdata.aspx` to support the geo-coding API just as you did with YouTube or eBay in earlier chapters.

The structure of the expected Yahoo URL is as follows. First comes the root of the REST API:

```
http://api.local.yahoo.com/MapsService/V1/geocode
```

This is followed by a series of parameters such as `appid`, `street`, `city`, `state`, and `zip`. These represent the application ID, used to track requests and the address parameters. Here's a sample URL:

```
http://api.local.yahoo.com/MapsService/V1/geocode?appid=[YOUR APP ID
HERE]&city=New%20York&street=10%20Church%20Street
```

This URL generates the following response.

```
<?xml version="1.0" ?>
<ResultSet
    xmlns:xsi="http://www.w3.org/2001/XMLSchema-instance"
    xmlns="urn:yahoo:maps"
    xsi:schemaLocation=
    "urn:yahoo:maps
     http://api.local.yahoo.com/MapsService/V1/GeocodeResponse.xsd">
    <Result precision="address">
      <Latitude>40.710129</Latitude>
      <Longitude>-74.011599</Longitude>
      <Address>10 CHURCH ST</Address>
      <City>NEW YORK</City>
      <State>NY</State>
      <Zip>10006</Zip>
      <Country>US</Country>
    </Result>
</ResultSet>
```

In this manner, you can easily extract the longitude and latitude for any address in the United States.

Unfortunately, locations outside the U.S. are not currently supported.

Creating a Custom Overlay Using GeoRSS

It's perfectly fine to add each individual marker to a map one by one. You could do this by parsing the Amazon XML in the browser and calling a JavaScript per marker. This could lead to a decent amount of coding, however. There is a cleaner way that Yahoo supports using something called GeoRSS and an overlay. In the following example, you add a custom overlay to the Yahoo Map using a new feed format known as GeoRSS.

What Is an Overlay?

A typical mapping application consists of a map of a specific location, combined with one or more overlays. You could think of an overlay as a plastic transparency in the real world.

The overlay consists of additional information that enriches the map, either by highlighting individual locations or by drawing a route between places.

You will use GeoRSS to create an overlay.

What Is GeoRSS?

GeoRSS is another spin on standard RSS. GeoRSS extends RSS to include geographical data such as longitude and latitude. GeoRSS contains all the base elements of RSS. Chapter 7 provides more information on RSS.

By adding a new namespace to the standard RSS XML, additional geo tags can be included in each feed item. Here's a sample GeoRSS file including some geo-specific tags:

```
<?xml version="1.0"?>
<rss version="2.0" xmlns:geo="http://www.w3.org/2003/01/geo/wgs84_pos#">
<channel>
...
<item>
    <title>Some Title</title>
    <link>http://MyDomain.com/ </link>
    <description>...</description>

    <geo:lat>22.12</geo:lat>
    <geo:long>-31.14</geo:long>

</item>
...
</channel>
</rss>
```

Yahoo Maps extends GeoRSS by including some tags of its own. These belong to the Yahoo maps namespace, which is prefixed like so:

```
xmlns:ymaps="http://api.maps.yahoo.com/Maps/V1/AnnotatedMaps.xsd
```

Here's the same sample as before, but including some ymaps-specific tags.

```
<?xml version="1.0"?>
<rss version="2.0" xmlns:geo="http://www.w3.org/2003/01/geo/wgs84_pos#"
xmlns:ymaps="http://api.maps.yahoo.com/Maps/V1/AnnotatedMaps.xsd">
<channel>
...
<item>
    <title>Some Title</title>
    <link>http://MyDomain.com/ </link>
    <description>...</description>
    <geo:lat>22.12</geo:lat>
    <geo:long>-31.14</geo:long>
    <ymaps:Address>10 Main Street</ymaps:Address>
    <ymaps:CityState>Anytown, CA
    </ymaps:CityState>
    <ymaps:Zip>12345</ymaps:Zip>
</item>
...
</channel>
</rss>
```

In this manner, the base RSS feed format has been extended to include geographical data. Because each new element is tied to its own namespace, the integrity of the original RSS feed file is maintained. A GeoRSS feed will still validate against the RSS 2.0 specification. There are various flavors of "geo" feeds, including Atom and RSS 1.0. This book focuses on the RSS 2.0 implementation.

```
http://developer.yahoo.com/maps/georss/index.html
```

The GeoRSS Transformation

To convert a typical Amazon `ItemSearch` response to GeoRSS, the following XSL file is used. This is named `AmazonRestaurants.xsl` in the sample code:

```xml
<?xml version="1.0" encoding="utf-8"?>

<xsl:stylesheet version="1.0"
    xmlns:xsl="http://www.w3.org/1999/XSL/Transform"
    xmlns:ymaps="http://api.maps.yahoo.com/Maps/V1/AnnotatedMaps.xsd"
    xmlns:a="http://webservices.amazon.com/AWSECommerceService/2005-10-05"
    xmlns:geo="http://www.w3.org/2003/01/geo/wgs84_pos#">
  <xsl:output method="xml"/>
  <xsl:template match="/">
    <rss version="2.0">
      <channel>
        <title>Amazon GeoRSS</title>
        <link>http://www.Amazon.com</link>
        <description>Sample GeoRSS file listing restaurants from
Amazon</description>
        <image>
          <url>images/food.gif</url>
        </image>
        <ymaps:Groups>
          <Group>
            <Title>Steak Restaurants</Title>
            <Id>Steak House</Id>
            <BaseIcon width="40px"
height="40px"><![CDATA[images/steak.gif]]></BaseIcon>
          </Group>
          <Group>
            <Title>French Restaurants</Title>
            <Id>French</Id>
            <BaseIcon width="40px"
height="40px"><![CDATA[images/french.gif]]></BaseIcon>
          </Group>
          <Group>
            <Title>Seafood Restaurants</Title>
            <Id>Seafood</Id>
            <BaseIcon width="40px"
height="40px"><![CDATA[images/seafood.gif]]></BaseIcon>
          </Group>
          <Group>
            <Title>Pizza</Title>
            <Id>Pizza</Id>
```

```
            <BaseIcon width="40px"
height="40px"><![CDATA[images/pizza.gif]]></BaseIcon>
            </Group>
        </ymaps:Groups>

        <xsl:apply-templates select="a:ItemSearchResponse/a:Items/a:Item" />
    </channel>
  </rss>
</xsl:template>

<xsl:template match="a:Item">
  <item>
    <title>
      <xsl:value-of select="a:ItemAttributes/a:Title"/>
    </title>
    <link>
      <xsl:value-of disable-output-escaping="yes"
select="concat('&lt;','![CDATA[')" />
      <xsl:value-of select="a:DetailPageURL" />
      <xsl:value-of disable-output-escaping="yes" select="concat(']]', '&gt;')"/>
    </link>
    <description>
      [<xsl:value-of select="a:ItemAttributes/a:Cuisine"/>]
      <xsl:value-of select="a:CustomerReviews/a:Review/a:Content"/>

    </description>
    <ymaps:Address>
      <xsl:value-of select="a:ItemAttributes/a:Address/a:Address1" />
    </ymaps:Address>
    <ymaps:CityState>
      <xsl:value-of select="a:ItemAttributes/a:Address/a:City" />, <xsl:value-of
select="a:ItemAttributes/a:Address/a:State" />
    </ymaps:CityState>
    <ymaps:Zip>
      <xsl:value-of select="a:ItemAttributes/a:Address/a:PostalCode" />
    </ymaps:Zip>
    <ymaps:Country>US</ymaps:Country>
    <ymaps:GroupId><xsl:value-of
select="a:ItemAttributes/a:Cuisine"/></ymaps:GroupId>
<ymaps:ItemUrl>http://mashups.FrancisShanahan.com/getdata.aspx?operation=ItemLookup
&amp;ResponseGroup=Large&amp;ItemId=<xsl:value-of
select="a:ASIN"/>&amp;xsl=amazonItemIframe.xsl&amp;contentType=text/html</ymaps:Ite
mUrl>
    </item>
  </xsl:template>
</xsl:stylesheet>
```

There are a few interesting things about this XSL. The first is the use of the BaseIcon Yahoo element. Map markers (RSS items) can be assigned a ymaps:GroupId, thus grouping them logically. The BaseIcon element assigns an icon to all map markers in that group. Notice how I have tied the group ID to the Amazon ItemAttributes/Cuisine element. Thus, all French restaurants will end up in a new group called French and they'll also get assigned a pre-defined icon called French.gif.

The second thing to note is something you probably already were expecting — the use of the Amazon elements for `Address` (`ItemAttributes/Address/City`, for example) directly in the `ymaps` address elements.

Converting Amazon Data to GeoRSS

When you're building software, there's usually more than one way to solve a specific problem. In previous chapters, you have transformed data on both the Web server using .NET and on the browser using JavaScript. For developers with neither the time nor inclination to implement the transformation, Amazon will perform the transformation for you.

When you call Amazon using the REST API the response is returned in XML. So far, all calls to Amazon have been through the following URI (or some variant, depending on the locale you are using):

```
http://webservices.amazon.com/onca/xml
```

By specifying an additional parameter that is the path to a publicly accessible XSL file, Amazon will perform the transformation on its server and pass back the transformed results:

```
http://webservices.amazon.com/onca/xml?
Service=AWSECommerceService&AWSAccessKeyId=[YOUR KEY HERE]
&Operation=ItemSearch&ResponseGroup=Large&City=New%20York%20&SearchIndex=Restaurant
s&Cuisine=French
&Style=http%3A%2F%2Fmashups.francisshanahan.com%2FAmazonRestaurants.xsl
```

This URL contains a `Style` parameter that specifies the location of a publicly available XSL sheet. Notice that Amazon uses a different domain to process this XSL transformation. When you specify the `Style` parameter, you will be redirected to the following URL:

```
http://xml-us.amznxslt.com/onca/xml
```

This URL is for the US locale. Of course, transformation is available for the other locales as well, including the following:

- ❏ *Canada* — `http://xml-ca.amznxslt.com/onca/xml`

- ❏ *United Kingdom* — `http://xml-uk.amznxslt.com/onca/xml`

- ❏ *France* — `http://xml-fr.amznxslt.com/onca/xml`

- ❏ *Japan* — `http://xml-jp.amznxslt.com/onca/xml`

- ❏ *Germany* — `http://xml-de.amznxslt.com/onca/xml`

Try It Out   Convert Amazon Data to GeoRSS

1. Create the `AmazonRestaurants.xsl` style sheet and upload it to a publicly accessible Internet site. Note the path to the XSL file.

2. Insert your `AWSAccessKey` in the following URL, and then test that the URL works by pasting it into a browser:

```
http://webservices.amazon.com/onca/xml?
Service=AWSECommerceService&AWSAccessKeyId=[YOUR KEY HERE]
&Operation=ItemSearch&ResponseGroup=Large&City=New%20York%20&SearchIndex=Restaurant
s&Cuisine=French
&Style=http://[YOUR PATH HERE]/AmazonRestaurants.xsl
```

Your browser should display a valid feed of GeoRSS data. In the next section, you use this to draw markers on the map.

How It Works

When you issue the vanilla API call using the standard URL, a typical `ItemSearch` response is generated. By specifying an XSL file with the `Style` parameter, Amazon loads that XSL and transforms its own response using your XSL file. The result is GeoRSS.

Making getdata.aspx More Generic

As stated earlier, I have shown you how to use Amazon to perform the transformation into GeoRSS. However, the sample code actually mimics this technique by using `getdata` to perform the transformation. This section describes how to modify `getdata` to accomplish this.

Up until now, the approach has been to hard-code any transformations done by `getdata.aspx` into the code itself. This means a code change to support a new transformation.

It would be to your advantage if `getdata` could perform transformations using whatever XSL file you tell it. This can be done with the following code change:

```
// If an XSL sheet was specified use it.
if (Request.Item["xsl"] != null)
{
    string strResults = webUtility.DoXSLTransformation(myDoc,
Request.Item["xsl"].ToString());
    Response.Write(strResults);
}
else
{
    Response.Write(myDoc.InnerXml);
}
Response.End();
```

With this change, the code will now use whatever XSL file is named by the `xsl` parameter. If none is present, of course, the code will fail.

You do need to be careful with a change like this to avoid malicious users faking out the XSL filename and potentially creating a security hole in your application.

A typical call to `getdata` will now look like this:

```
http://[YourPathHere]/getdata.aspx?operation=ItemLookup&ResponseGroup=Large&ItemId=
0393320928&xsl=amazonItemIframe.xsl
```

This would perform an `ItemLookup` and then transform the result. You've essentially replicated Amazon's functionality with very little effort. The advantage is that you now have control and can extend the functionality if needed.

Modifying BuildAmazonURI

Modify the `BuildAmazonURI` to include additional parameters. Because you'll be searching Amazon by City, Neighborhood, and Cuisine, these all need to be parsed out of the querystring. Modify the `BuildAmazonURI` function as follows:

```
...
string strCuisine = CheckNull(myQueryString, "Cuisine", "");
string strNeighborhood = CheckNull(myQueryString, "Neighborhood", "");
string strCity = CheckNull(myQueryString, "City", "");
...
strURI = strRoot + strAccessKeyId +
        ... + strCuisine + strNeighborhood + strCity;
return strURI;
```

Deploying the Solution

To make the XML produced by `getdata` accessible to the Yahoo Maps API, it must be hosted on a public Internet site. To do this, you must actually compile the ASP.NET 2.0 application into a set of binaries, and upload them to a Web site running .NET 2.0. Assuming you have a hosting provider available, you can compile the Web project using the ASP.NET compiler included in the .NET Framework.

Try It Out   **Deploy the Solution**

1. Navigate to Start → Run and type **cmd** to launch a command prompt.

2. Change directories to the Microsoft .NET Framework version 2.0:

```
cd \
cd windows\microsoft.net\Framework\v2.0.50727
```

3. Use the `aspnet_compiler.exe` to compile the application. The format of the command is as follows: `-p <Path to the Project> -v / <path to the output>`

```
aspnet_compiler.exe -p "C:\YOUR\PATH\HERE" -v / c:\temp\output
```

The instruction `-v /` tells the compiler that the project is to be found at the root of the physical path supplied.

For convenience, be sure to place these instructions in a batch file. Create a text file and rename it with a BAT extension.

These instructions may differ slightly depending on the operating system you are using. For example, if using Windows 2000, the .NET Framework will be located under `c:\winnt\Microsoft.NET`.

After executing these instructions, the compiled project output will be located under `c:\temp\output`, or whatever path you have specified. You can then deploy these files by simply sending them via FTP up to your host. With the application deployed, you should execute a test against it to ensure that it is generating the desired GeoRSS output.

Testing can be accomplished with a simple browser. Here's an example URL against my own server:

```
http://mashups.francisshanahan.com/getdata.aspx?operation=ItemSearch&ResponseGroup=
Large&SearchIndex=Restaurants&x=amazonRestaurants.xsl&City=New%20York
```

You should take a moment now and update your JavaScript code to ensure that it is pointing at the appropriate external site. Here's the JavaScript to instantiate a valid YGeoRSS object:

```
// Create the overlay
myGeoRSS = new YGeoRSS(strGeoRSSSource);

// Add the overlay
myMap.addOverlay(myGeoRSS);
```

Issues with GeoRSS

Applying a GeoRSS feed as an overlay is a nice way to add a great many locations to the map with no other geo-coding required. If you didn't use this approach, you would have to manually add each marker in isolation. Not only that, but you'd have to perform individual address lookups using the Yahoo geo-coding API to obtain longitude and latitude information for each location.

The one advantage of adding each location as an individual marker is that you can register handlers against the events generated for each marker. If you want something to happen when a user clicks a marker, the best way to do it is to capture the click-event of the marker.

The issue with GeoRSS overlays is that there is no easy way of tying events to the markers generated at each location.

The desired functionality is that users can click a marker and get additional item information. Fortunately, there is a solution. Yahoo's extensions to the GeoRSS specification provide for the inclusion of a specific URL element in a given RSS Item.

This URL is the location of a piece of content that will be displayed in an iFrame within the map marker's pop-up window. The next section describes how to accomplish this in detail.

Using an iFrame

You can also use GeoRSS and getdata.aspx combined to add an iFrame of content to every map marker.

1. Create a new style sheet to convert Amazon ItemLookup responses to HTML:

```
<?xml version="1.0" encoding="utf-8" ?>
<xsl:stylesheet version="1.0"
    xmlns:xsl="http://www.w3.org/1999/XSL/Transform"
xmlns:a="http://webservices.amazon.com/AWSECommerceService/2005-10-05">
  <xsl:output method="html" omit-xml-declaration="yes"/>
  <xsl:template match="/">
```

```
<html><body>
    <xsl:apply-templates select="a:ItemLookupResponse/a:Items/a:Item" />
</body></html>
  </xsl:template>

  <xsl:template match="a:Item">
    Title:<b><xsl:value-of select="a:ItemAttributes/a:Title"/></b><br/>
    ASIN: <xsl:value-of select="a:ASIN"/><br/>
    You could place whatever product details you'd like in here.
  </xsl:template>
</xsl:stylesheet>
```

2. Modify `getdata.aspx` to accept a `contentType` argument. This code will use the `contentType` argument to set the `Response.ContentType` of the HTTP response:

```
Response.Clear();
// If a content type was specified e.g. text/html use it.
if (Request.Params["contentType"] != null)
{
    Response.ContentType = Request.Params["contentType"].ToString();
}
else
{
    // Default to an xml response
    Response.ContentType = "text/xml";
}
```

The new call to `getdata` looks like this:

```
http://[yourPathHere]/getdata.aspx?operation=ItemLookup&ResponseGroup=Large&ItemId=
0393320928&xsl=amazonItemIframe.xsl&contentType=text/html
```

The following HTML is generated as a result:

```
<html xmlns:a="http://webservices.amazon.com/AWSECommerceService/2005-10-05">
  <body>
    Title:<b>What Do You Care What Other People Think?: Further Adventures of a
Curious Character</b><br>
    ASIN: 0393320928<br>
    You could place whatever product details you'd like in here.
  </body>
</html>
```

Now you have a link that produces HTML. This can be used in conjunction with the GeoRSS `ymaps` extension field `ymaps:ItemUrl` like this:

```
<ymaps:GroupId><xsl:value-of select="a:ItemAttributes/a:Cuisine"/></ymaps:GroupId>
<ymaps:ItemUrl>http://[yourPathHere]/getdata.aspx?operation=ItemLookup&amp;Response
Group=Large&amp;ItemId=<xsl:value-of
select="a:ASIN"/>&amp;xsl=amazonItemIframe.xsl&amp;contentType=text/html</ymaps:Ite
mUrl>
    </item>
```

By specifying a URL in the `ItemUrl`, Yahoo will include an `iFrame` in the result   map markers' pop-up windows.

How It Works

1. When you launch the application the map is displayed.

2. The user then chooses a City (or enters a type of Cuisine) to view a selection of restaurants.

3. The application makes a call to getdata, which, in turn, issues an ItemSearch for restaurants against the Amazon ECS.

4. The response is returned by Amazon to getdata, which in turn transforms the data into GeoRSS using the XSL style sheet that was designated in the querystring.

5. The GeoRSS includes a set of items that, in turn, include links back to getdata. Each link provides the right combination of parameters to Amazon to perform an ItemLookup query.

6. When a user clicks one of the markers on the map, getdata is again invoked, and this time it performs an ItemLookup to retrieve the detailed information about the restaurant.

7. The ItemLookupResponse XML is then transformed, this time into HTML, and displayed on the page in the form of an iFrame.

The final application is shown in Figure 11-8.

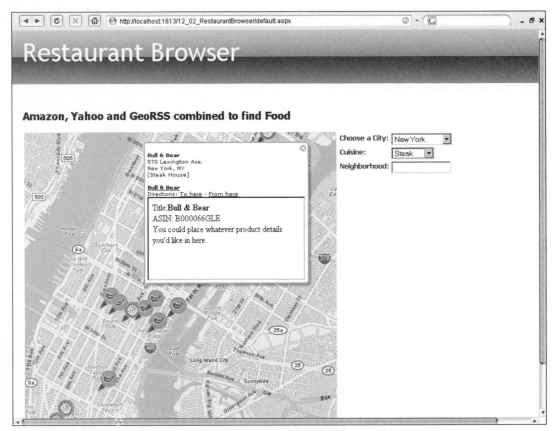

Figure 11-8: The final application displaying restaurants in downtown New York

Other Ideas

The sample code uses Yahoo Maps, which comes with a number of features. You might, however, consider using some of the other mapping APIs out there.

Alternative Mapping APIs

Google Maps was perhaps the first interactive Ajax-powered map, and gained the company a lot of press. Yahoo quickly followed, and, because the Web is flooded with examples of how to use Google Maps, I took the path less traveled in this chapter. You can find more information on Google Maps here:

```
http://www.google.com/apis/maps
```

Microsoft is never one to sit on the sidelines and it, too, has put forth a comprehensive mapping platform complete with a rich developer programming interface. The Microsoft offering is called "Virtual Earth" and is available here:

```
http://www.virtualearth.net
```

Adding Animation

One other innovation you could add to the standard map experience is the notion of animation. For example, you could create a single marker that actually moves around the screen. For this you would need some dynamic set of position or address data. This might come from a Global Positioning System (GPS) Web site, for example.

The key to making this work is to add a timer event to the page. Whenever the timer fires, the page would update the marker's position. You could accomplish this either with GeoRSS or an Ajax call as described in Chapter 10.

Whenever you tie API calls to timers, be aware of the API call limit imposed by the owner of that API. Yahoo is typically quite large, but there are certain APIs that have lower restrictions and you must ensure that you don't accidentally exceed the limit simply because a user left the browser window open too long. Keep track of your usage, and consider updating every 5 seconds rather than every 1 second, for example.

Summary

In this chapter, you learned about the following:

- ❑ How to build a GeoRSS feed
- ❑ How to transform Amazon data using Amazon's own platform
- ❑ How to build a map and display map markers using the Yahoo interface
- ❑ How to compile and deploy an ASP.NET 2.0 Web site

Over the course of the last few chapters, you should have seen how versatile getdata.aspx is as a generic means of obtaining data. It can produce XML or XHTML, depending solely on the scenario's requirements and also serves as a common access point for abstracting API license keys and other sensitive pieces of information.

Chapter 12 shows you how to use the Yahoo API in conjunction with Amazon, but this time, using JSON notation instead of GeoRSS. The resulting application will load data directly from Amazon without the use of a proxy class in between.

Before continuing on, it's worth reviewing your knowledge with the following exercises.

Exercises

1. How would you modify this to include a YouTube Video inside the map marker?

2. How can you use Amazon's API to perform an XSL transformation?

3. In ASP.NET, how can you dynamically change the contentType of the content served by a page from, say, XML to HTML? What effect will that have on the browser?

4. How can you enhance the standard GeoRSS feed with Yahoo-specific tags?

5. What are some alternative mapping APIs that you could use in place of Yahoo?

A Customer Browser Using JSON

Ajax has received a lot of press in recent times as it pertains to enabling mashups and Web 2.0 applications. However, Ajax is not the only game in town. JavaScript Object Notation (JSON) is an effective alternative approach that supplies compelling functionality in its own right. What's more, the code for a JSON (pronounced "Jason") solution is, in many cases, less involved than the equivalent Ajax implementation.

In this chapter you learn about the following:

❑ The JSON notation and how it is structured

❑ How to add JavaScript to a page dynamically at run-time

❑ How to combine JSON with dynamic JavaScript to obtain customer data from Amazon

❑ How to create a mapping application using the Yahoo mapping API

The customer mapping mashup in this chapter is an interesting application, and one that should clearly display the potential of the JSON approach.

The Battle Plan: Yahoo Plus Amazon Using JSON and REST

In this chapter, you create a mapping application that plots the location of Amazon customers across the United States. Amazon provides access to data that its customers have chosen to make public, including general address information. Using Amazon APIs, this chapter's mashup will search the customer database, and then convert the data obtained into points on a Yahoo Map.

The goal of the tool is to provide a visualization on top of the Amazon data. The mashup in this chapter could be expanded to depict additional details such as which parts of the country are buying which products, or which customers are interested in which products.

Understanding the Architecture

Figure 12-1 shows the architecture of this specific Customer Browser architecture.

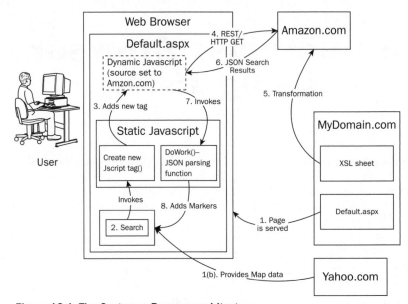

Figure 12-1: The Customer Browser architecture

How It Works

The Customer Browser application searches Amazon's customer information database and plots the customer's location on a Yahoo Map. The process flow is as follows:

1. When the application's main page is loaded, it includes a set of JavaScript, including a number of static functions. It also draws a map of the U.S. using Yahoo's API.

2. The user types in some search criteria, in this case a customer name, and clicks Search.

3. Clicking the Search button triggers a static JavaScript function on the page. Instead of submitting the page back to the server, this function modifies the page's structure to include a *new* <script> tag, thus creating a piece of dynamic JavaScript.

4. The source for this new JavaScript is specified as a URL pointing to Amazon.com. The browser resolves this and automatically issues an HTTP GET, in this case a REST request to obtain the <script> content.

5. Amazon receives the REST request and responds. Before it does, it uses an XSL sheet from the site's domain to perform a transformation on the results.

6. The result of the transformation is to convert the XML response into JSON in the form of text/JavaScript. The JSON is fed back into the page via the script tag added in Step 3. The script tag content now contains a function call like this:

```
DoWork( <some object> )
```

DoWork is a function that is already part of the page. The DoWork function expects a JavaScript object. Amazon supplies this object in the form of JSON.

7. Inside the DoWork function, the JSON object is examined and the data it contains is iterated through.

8. Map markers are created for each customer in the result set. Each marker is then added to the map.

Figure 12-2 shows the final application displaying a list of customers across the U.S.

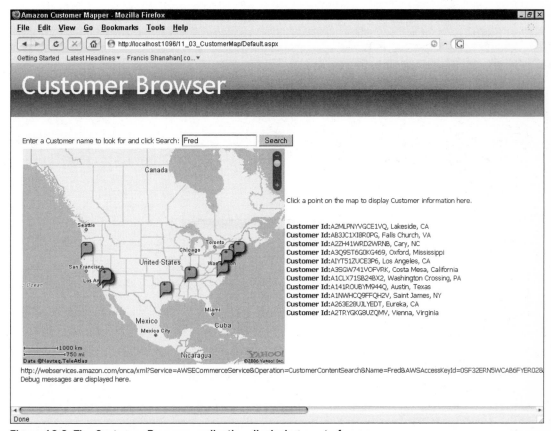

Figure 12-2: The Customer Browser application displaying a set of users

This is not necessarily a complex technique, but it does represent an approach that is slightly left of center. The elements of the solution are described in detail in subsequent sections.

Before diving into building the Customer Browser mashup, it's appropriate to understand JSON and the Dynamic Script technique that the application uses.

The Dynamic Script Method

When you view a page in a browser, the browser executes whatever JavaScript that the page includes. However, you can create a piece of JavaScript at run-time programmatically using JavaScript itself, and then include the created script in the page's Document Object Model (DOM). By altering the page's DOM in this manner, it makes it possible to create new pieces of JavaScript at the time the page is being viewed, which is then executed either immediately or upon user interaction. This is known informally as the Dynamic Script method.

Try It Out   A Simple Dynamic Script Example

The following example demonstrates how you can add a piece of JavaScript to a page at run-time (Figure 12-3). This is a key component of the ultimate JSON mashup.

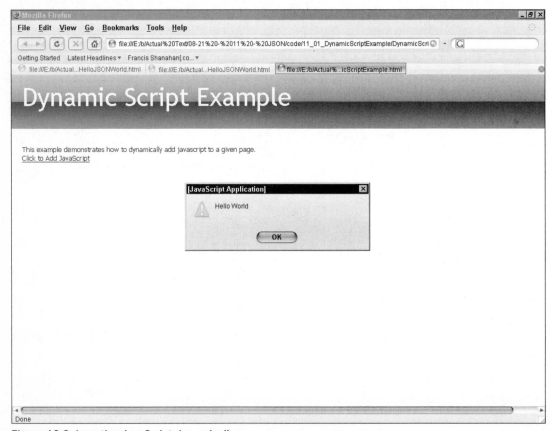

Figure 12-3: Inserting JavaScript dynamically

1. Create a new ASPX page in Visual Studio, named `default.aspx`. Note that for this example, you will not need to write any C# code.

2. Create a new file named `alert.js`. This will store the JavaScript code that gets inserted into the page. For now, this file should just contain a single instruction that launches a message box as follows:

```
alert("Helloworld");
```

3. Add a JavaScript `<script>` tag to the head of the `default.aspx` page and create a new JavaScript function named `CreateScriptTag`:

```
function CreateScriptTag (){
    var myScript = document.createElement("script");
    myScript.setAttribute("type", "text/javascript");
    myScript.setAttribute("src", "alert.js" );
    return myScript;
}
```

The `CreateScript` function creates a new JavaScript `<script>` tag. The source of this tag is specified as the `alert.js` file created in Step 2.

4. Assign an ID to the `<head>` element. This is to facilitate referencing it from within the JavaScript:

```
<head id="myHead">
```

5. Add another JavaScript function to the `default.aspx` page. This function should be named `AddScript` and looks like this:

```
function AddScript( ) {
    var myTag = CreateScriptTag();
    document.getElementById("myHead").appendChild(myTag);
}
```

The function calls `CreateScriptTag` to create the JavaScript page element, and then adds it to the page. The effect of the JavaScript element is that as soon as the tag is added, the script within the `alert.js` file is executed.

6. Finally, add a clickable link to the page to trigger the `AddScript` function:

```
<a href="javascript:void(0)" id="myTrigger" onclick="javascript:AddScript()">Click
to Add JavaScript</a>
```

How It Works

When you run the page and click the link, a new JavaScript tag is created. The source for this script is designated as `alert.js`. The static equivalent of this dynamic JavaScript is the following:

```
<script language="javascript" src="alert.js"/>
```

When this script tag is included in the page's header, the script within the tag is executed immediately. In this case, that means an alert pops up to greet you with "Hello World."

Dynamic scripting is a useful capability that can work in concert with JSON to facilitate mashup creation. In the case of a mashup, you can dynamically insert not only JavaScript *code* but also *data* in the form of a JavaScript object. This lets you get data from external sources and plug that data into the page at run-time. This is definitely useful if you want to build a mashup.

What Is JSON?

JSON is a way of writing down an object's members and their values in such a way that it can be converted from a string into an actual JavaScript object. Essentially, this means taking a string formatted according to the JSON structure and converting it into an object that can be parsed and processed similar to how you'd process an XML document. Said plainly, JSON lets you de-serialize data into an object.

You can learn more about the JSON specification at the following URL:

```
http://www.json.org
```

Try It Out   Hello World Using JSON

In this example, you create a single Web page that uses a single JSON object. This is just to familiarize you with the notation.

Create a single HTML page (you don't even need Visual Studio for this) and paste the following code into that page:

```html
<html>
<head>
<script language="javascript">

    // The JSON object
    var myJSON = {"MyJSON" : { "name" : "HelloWorld" } }

    function HelloJSONWorld( myObject) {
        document.getElementById('myResults').innerHTML = myObject.MyJSON.name;
    }
</script>
</head>
<body>
    <a href="javascript:void(0)" id="myTrigger"
onclick="javascript:HelloJSONWorld(myJSON)">Click me</a>
    <div id="myResults">Results Go Here</div>
</body>
</html>
```

Save the file and then open this newly created page in a browser. Click the link named "Click me" and you should see "Hello World" appear in the space where "Results Go Here" used to be. Figure 12-4 illustrates this, along with a slightly more complicated JSON object.

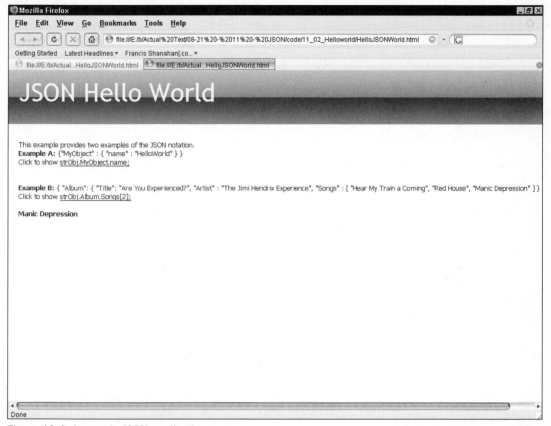

Figure 12-4: A sample JSON application

How It Works

Overall, this is an HTML page just like any other. The page is divided into typical head and body sections—nothing new there. The body contains a link whose sole purpose in life is to capture the click event of the user and fire off a JavaScript function. You'll learn more about this in a second. The page body also contains a div tag, which is where the results of the function will be placed.

The head contains the only JavaScript on the page. The first line declares a variable named myJSON. This variable's value is set to a weird-looking string-type thing. This is the JSON!

The only other thing in this section is a function called HelloJSONWorld. This function accepts a parameter named myObject. This parameter will contain the JSON object instance created by the JavaScript engine evaluating the JSON variable defined earlier.

The JSON Notation

As with many Web 2.0 technologies, JSON is surprisingly simple. The notation for an object is as follows:

```
{ Name : Value }
```

For example, the following notation describes an object with a single property named `myName` with a value of `Walter`:

```
{ "myName" : "Walter" }
```

The name is always a string, enclosed in quotation marks. The value could be another object, a literal (for example, `true`/`false`) or, in this case, a string (`"Walter"`).

This would evaluate to a single object containing a single property with a value of `"Walter"`.

A more complex example might be the following:

```
{"Album": { "Title": "Are You Experienced?", "Artist" : "The Jimi Hendrix
Experience" } }
```

This notation would evaluate to an object with a class definition that looked like this:

```
class Album {
    string Title;
    string Artist;
}
```

The member variables here are a simple type in that each has string values. To include a member variable whose value is an array, you can enclose the values using square brackets as follows:

```
var myAlbum = { "Album": { "Title": "Are You Experienced?", "Artist" : "The Jimi
Hendrix Experience", "Songs" : [ "Hear My Train a Coming", "Red House", "Manic
Depression" ] } } ;
```

This notation is the equivalent of the following class definition:

```
class Album {
    string Title;
    string Artist;
    string Songs[3];
}
```

Now, to access a value of the JSON object, you can use the same notation you'd use with any type of JavaScript object:

```
document.getElementById('myResults').innerHTML = strObj.Album.Songs[2];
```

This code accesses the "Manic Depression" song from the `Songs` array (assuming `strObj` is the JSON object).

Publicly Available JSON APIs

By now, you are probably wondering if there are sites out there that provide JSON as part of their service offering. Unfortunately, only a few have taken this step. Yahoo is one such company, and it has adopted JSON notation with open arms. To obtain JSON rather than the default XML from a Yahoo Web search, you need to specify the output parameter as follows:

```
http://api.search.yahoo.com/WebSearchService/V1/webSearch?appid=[YOUR ID
HERE]&query=Led Zeppelin&results=10&start=1&output=json&callback=MyFunction
```

Yahoo provides one other parameter, the *callback parameter*, which is only applicable when `output=json`. The callback parameter is used to wrap the JSON results in a function call. For example, if you have a function named `MyFunction` that expects an object, you can include that function name as the callback parameter. Yahoo responds with a string of JavaScript that looks like this:

```
MyFunction({ myJSONObject: ....<omitted> } ) ;
```

In this manner, the results from the Yahoo API call can be inserted into the HTML page, and then trigger a call to the `MyFunction` for further processing of the resulting data. Inside `MyFunction`, you can write code to inspect the JavaScript object returned by Yahoo and act accordingly.

Advantages of JSON

As you can see, there are some distinct advantages to the dynamic scripting method over an Ajax-based approach. The primary benefit is that data can be directly integrated from a third-party domain. There is no need for a proxy on the primary domain. In an Ajax implementation, you would generally need this proxy to avoid browser security restrictions.

Another advantage of JSON is that, on average, it is less verbose than XML. You can express the same information in a smaller payload with JSON than the equivalent XML.

Lastly, many developers are switching to JSON because it's simply easier to read than XML. I personally don't hold this view, but developers are all different.

The next section describes how to convert an Amazon XML response into JSON.

How to Get JSON from Amazon

Unfortunately, unlike Yahoo, Amazon doesn't (yet) provide JSON directly from its APIs. The good news is that it doesn't matter. Amazon provides capabilities to transform data using any publicly accessible XSL sheet that you specify. The API performs the transformation on Amazon servers and then responds with the results of the transformation. To get JSON from Amazon, all you need to do is write an XSL sheet that transforms an `ItemSearchResponse` document or a `CustomerSearchResponse` into the JSON notation.

The next section describes setting up the Customer Browser mashup application. Subsequent sections describe the mashup's components in detail.

Try It Out   Building the Customer Browser

To build this chapter's mashup application, start with the following steps:

1. Create a new project in Visual Studio and open up the `default.aspx` page. There will be no need for a code-beside file in this example.

2. Create a text input named `txtName` to store the search criteria.

3. Create a number of `<div>` tags as follows:

```
<div id="myMap"></div>
<div id="info">Click a point on the map to display Customer information here.
</div>
<div id="results"></div>
<div id="debug">Debug messages are displayed here. </div>
```

The `myMap div` will display the Yahoo Map. The `info div` will display customer information when the user clicks a map marker. The `results div` will show the output from processing JSON returned by Amazon. Lastly, the `debug div` is optional, but useful to capture and display any debug information during development. Feel free to arrange these as you see fit. Figure 12-5 shows the `default.aspx` page in Design view.

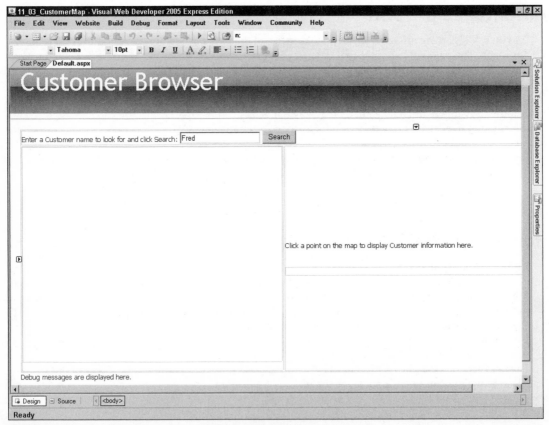

Figure 12-5: The Customer Browser main page in Design view

4. Create a link to the Yahoo `maps` JavaScript file in the `<head>` section of the page as follows:

```
<script type="text/javascript"
src="http://api.maps.yahoo.com/ajaxymap?v=3.0&appid=[YOUR APP ID HERE]">
   </script>
```

5. Create a new JavaScript file named `mashup.js` and place it in a new subfolder named `js`. Link this file into the page as follows:

```
<script type="text/javascript" src="js/mashup.js">
</script>
```

`mashup.js` will store all the JavaScript used in the application.

6. Create a new JavaScript function in `mashup.js` named `Init`:

```
function Init(){

     // Create a map object
     myMap = new YMap(document.getElementById('myMap'));
     // Display the map centered on given address
     myMap.drawZoomAndCenter("Nebraska", 15);
     // Add a zoom control
     myMap.addZoomLong();
}
```

This function takes care of initializing the map on the page.

7. Create one more JavaScript function named `myPrint`. This function just wraps access to the debug `div` and is purely a utility-type function:

```
function myPrint(strText){
        document.getElementById('debug').innerHTML = strText + "<br/>" +
   document.getElementById('debug').innerHTML;
}
```

That completes the main application setup. The next sections in this chapter describe the remaining functionality and how to implement it.

Searching Amazon for Customers

The Amazon REST API provides the `CustomerContentSearch` operation with which you can search customers by their name. This can be executed just like any other AWS operation using REST. The root of the URL looks like this:

```
http://webservices.amazon.com/onca/xml?Service=AWSECommerceService&AWSAccessKeyId=
[YOUR KEY HERE]&Operation=CustomerContentSearch
```

Currently, Customer search is only supported in the US locale. To search for a customer, you can specify either of the following parameters, but not both:

❑ `Name` — A free-form text entry of a customer name. No distinction is made between first or last name.

❑ `Email` — The customer email address.

A Customer search operation REST URI looks like this:

```
http://webservices.amazon.com/onca/xml?Service=AWSECommerceService&AWSAccessKeyId=[
YOUR KEY HERE]&Operation=CustomerContentSearch&Name=Jeff
```

A typical Customer search response is shown in Listing 12-1.

Listing 12-1: A `CustomerContentSearchResponse` **from Amazon**

```xml
<?xml version="1.0" encoding="UTF-8"?>
<CustomerContentSearchResponse
xmlns="http://webservices.amazon.com/AWSECommerceService/2005-10-05">
  <OperationRequest>
    ...
    <Arguments>
      <Argument Name="Name" Value="Jeff"></Argument>
      <Argument Name="Operation" Value="CustomerContentSearch"></Argument>
      <Argument Name="Service" Value="AWSECommerceService"></Argument>
      ...
    </Arguments>
    ...
  </OperationRequest>
  <Customers>
    <Request>
      ...
    </Request>
    <TotalResults>54799</TotalResults>
    <TotalPages>2740</TotalPages>
    <Customer>
      <CustomerId>AZN85XLJ651W9</CustomerId>
      <Location>
        <City>Webster</City>
        <State>MA</State>
        <Country>United States</Country>
      </Location>
    </Customer>
    <Customer>
      <CustomerId>A3HH6F1V7Z1AM5</CustomerId>
      <Nickname>jexx18288</Nickname>
    </Customer>
    <Customer>
      <CustomerId>A1Q23A9WY74A1E</CustomerId>
      <Location>
        <City>Hickory</City>
        <State>NC</State>
        <Country>United States</Country>
      </Location>
    </Customer>
    <Customer>
      <CustomerId>A3N6YYLZ9Y6LZY</CustomerId>
    </Customer>
    <Customer>
      <CustomerId>A17KNQ1H1CTXMK</CustomerId>
    </Customer>
```

```
    <Customer>
      <CustomerId>A12X406Y7R9W4X</CustomerId>
    </Customer>
    <Customer>
      <CustomerId>A1STAQK3JSR8YG</CustomerId>
      <Location>
        <City>Camas</City>
        <State>WA</State>
        <Country>United States</Country>
      </Location>
    </Customer>
    <Customer>
      <CustomerId>A1LVX1CRGVJ2TD</CustomerId>
      <Location>
        <City>Hayward</City>
        <State>CA</State>
        <Country>United States</Country>
      </Location>
    </Customer>
    <Customer>
      <CustomerId>AZ1A53FPFZM4Q</CustomerId>
      <Location>
        <City>Warren</City>
        <State>NJ</State>
        <Country>United States</Country>
      </Location>
    </Customer>
    ...
  </Customers>
</CustomerContentSearchResponse>
```

As you can see, it's fairly sparse in terms of details, but luckily the address and customer ID is all you need to plot a customer on the map.

The response consists primarily of customer nodes that always include a minimum of `CustomerId` nodes. Amazon customers may also specify nicknames and locations as public information. In those cases, those details are also included in the `CustomerContentSearch` response.

The JSON XSL File

The sample application uses an XSL file to convert the Amazon Customer Response into valid JSON notation. Whenever you write a transformation, it's important to visualize the desired output. In this case, I'd ultimately like a JavaScript object that looks like this:

```
Customer {
    CustomerId;
    City;
    State;
}

Customers {
    Customer[];
}
```

Essentially, I'd like a single object named `Customers` containing an array of `Customer` objects. This equates to a JSON structure that looks like this:

```
{"Customers" : [
  {
    "CustomerId" : "ABI2343247XFW5"
  } ,
  {
    "CustomerId" : "A2ML234VGCE1VQ",
    "City" : "Lakeside",
    "State" : "CA",
    "Country" : "United States"
  } ,
  {
    "CustomerId" : "AB123123I8R0PG",
    "City" : "Falls Church",
    "State" : "VA",
    "Country" : "USA"
  } ,

  {
    "CustomerId" : "123H41WRD2WRNB",
    "City" : "Cary",
    "State" : "NC",
    "Country" : "USA"
  } ]
} );
```

The JSON structure contains an array of customer nodes. Note the use of square brackets to denote an array. To produce this form of response, I need an XSL transformation that parses out each `<Customer>` node in turn. With this in mind, the XSL is fairly trivial to create. Listing 12-2 contains the XSL style sheet. Bear in mind that you could easily reuse this transformation with an `ItemSearchResponse` instead of a `CustomerContentSearchReponse` to produce JSON of a list of products instead of customers.

Listing 12-2: The `CustomerContentSearchResponse` **to JSON Transformation**

```
<xsl:stylesheet version="1.0"
    xmlns:xsl="http://www.w3.org/1999/XSL/Transform"
  xmlns:a="http://webservices.amazon.com/AWSECommerceService/2005-10-05"
  >

  <xsl:output method="html" omit-xml-declaration="yes"/>
  <xsl:template match="/">
    MyFunction( {"Customers" : [
    <xsl:apply-templates select="a:CustomerContentSearchResponse"/> ]
    } );

  </xsl:template>

  <xsl:template match="a:CustomerContentSearchResponse">
    <xsl:apply-templates select="a:Customers"/>
  </xsl:template>
```

```
<xsl:template match="a:Customers">
  <xsl:apply-templates select="a:Customer"/>
</xsl:template>

<xsl:template match="a:Customer">
  {
  "CustomerId" : "<xsl:value-of select="a:CustomerId"/>"
  <xsl:apply-templates select="a:Location" />
  } ,
</xsl:template>

<xsl:template match="a:Location">
  , "City" : "<xsl:value-of select="a:City"/>",
  "State" : "<xsl:value-of select="a:State"/>",
  "Country" : "<xsl:value-of select="a:Country"/>"
</xsl:template>

</xsl:stylesheet>
```

To continue development of the Customer Browser mashup, create a new XSL file named `AmazonJSON.xsl` and add it to the project. You should then place this XSL file at a publicly accessible location on the Internet (such as your personal Web site).

By placing the XSL sheet on a publicly accessible server, you can test the entire transformation using a single Amazon URL similar to the following:

```
http://webservices.amazon.com/onca/xml?Service=AWSECommerceService&Operation=Custom
erContentSearch&Name=Fred&AWSAccessKeyId=[YOUR KEY
HERE]&Style=http://mashups.FrancisShanahan.com/11_03_CustomerMap/AmazonJSON.xsl&con
tentType=text/javascript
```

Note the location of the specified XSL sheet is set using the following parameter:

```
Style=http://mashups.FrancisShanahan.com/11_03_CustomerMap/AmazonJSON.xsl
```

This is a publicly accessible server that you can leverage for your own testing.

You will not be able to alter or place files on this site. It is read-only and included here for your convenience.

Try It Out   Conducting the Search

To perform the Customer search you need to implement some code to power the Search button in the customer mashup. This code basically takes the users' search criteria and adds a new `<script>` tag (the dynamic script approach) to the page:

1. Open the `default.aspx` file and add a new input control of type `button`:

```
<input type="button" id="mySubmit" value="Search" onclick="FindCustomers()" />
```

2. Add a new function named `FindCustomers` to the `mashup.js`. The code for this function looks like this.

```
function FindCustomers() {
        // Build a customer search URL
        var strAWSAccessKey = "[YOUR KEY HERE]&";
        var strOperation = "Operation=CustomerContentSearch&";
        var strName="Name=" + document.getElementById("txtName").value + "&"

        var strRoot =
"http://webservices.amazon.com/onca/xml?Service=AWSECommerceService&";
        var strUrl = strRoot +  strOperation
            + strName + strAWSAccessKey +

"Style=http://mashups.FrancisShanahan.com/11_03_CustomerMap/AmazonJSON.xsl&contentT
ype=text/javascript";

        // Write out the URL for debugging purposes
        myPrint(strUrl);

        var myTag = CreateScriptTag(strUrl);
        document.getElementById("myHead").appendChild(myTag);
    }
```

How It Works

When the user clicks Search, the `FindCustomers` function is invoked. `FindCustomers` then constructs a new URL using the search criteria typed into the name input tag. This URL is similar to that shown in the last section. The URL is then used as the source for a new JavaScript `<script>` tag.

This URL resolves to a piece of JavaScript that includes a function call (to `MyFunction`) and passes in a new JavaScript object in the form of JSON.

The next section describes how to handle the response created when this new tag is added to the page.

Processing the JSON Object

When the application receives the response from Amazon, a JavaScript function named `MyFunction` is invoked and the JSON object is passed to that function. If you are wondering where the name of this function is specified, refer back to the XSL file used in the transformation.

`MyFunction` loops through the JSON object returned by Amazon and, if address information is present, uses it to add a marker for that customer to the Yahoo Map. `MyFunction` should be added to `Mashup.js` and the code looks like this:

```
// Parses out the JSON object Properties
    function MyFunction (myJSON){

        var strResults = "";

        if (myJSON.Customers) {
            var i;
            // Loop through all the customers.
            for (i = 0; i < myJSON.Customers.length ; i ++ ) {
```

```
                    var myCustomer = myJSON.Customers[i];

                    // Check the customer
                    if (myCustomer) {

                        // Check the address
                        if ((myCustomer.City) && (myCustomer.State)) {

                            // Write out the Customer details
                            strResults += "<b>Customer Id:</b>" + myCustomer.CustomerId
        + ", ";

                            strResults += myCustomer.City + ", " + myCustomer.State;
                            strResults += "<br/>";

                            // Create a new marker for the map
                            var myMarker = CreateMapMarker(myCustomer.CustomerId,
        myCustomer.City, myCustomer.State,
                            myCustomer.City + ", " + myCustomer.State);

                            // Add the marker to the map
                            myMap.addOverlay(myMarker);
                        }
                    }
                }
            }

            // Print out the customer list
            document.getElementById("results").innerHTML = strResults;
        }
```

You saw in Chapter 11 that points plotted on a Yahoo Map are known as YMarkers. The preceding code processes the Customers and calls "`CreateMapMarker`" for each one in turn.

In the old days, to plot a point on a map (either Yahoo or Google), you would need to convert the location's address into longitude and latitude coordinates. Vendors provide so-called *geo-coding* APIs to accomplish this. You pass the address to the geo-coding API and it responds with a longitude and latitude representing that location.

Luckily, this is no longer necessary. Yahoo now provides an API that accepts an actual address as a parameter and plots this address on the map without the need to obtain its longitude and latitude.

Open the `mashup.js` file and add the following dedicated function to create a map marker:

```
function CreateMapMarker(strCustomerId, strCity, strState) {
        // Create a new marker
        var myMarker = new YMarker(strCity + ", " + strState);

        // Add a label
        var label= "*";
        myMarker.addLabel(label);

        // Add some descriptive text
        var strText = "You Clicked: <b>Customer Id:</b>" + strCustomerId + " in " +
        strCity + ", " + strState;
```

```
            // Capture the click event
            YEvent.Capture(myMarker,EventsList.MouseClick,
                    function() { myMarker.openSmartWindow(strText) ;
                    document.getElementById('info').innerHTML = strText;});


            // Return the completed marker ready for the map
            return myMarker;
    }
```

This code accepts customer ID, city, and state as parameters, and uses these as input to create a new Yahoo map marker at that location.

Because you want each map marker to be clickable, you must assign an event handler to each map marker. This is shown highlighted in the preceding code using the YEvent.Capture method.

Testing the Finished Application

When you first run the application, you are presented with a blank map of the United States centered on Nebraska. Enter a name or partial name and click Search. The application goes out and retrieves data matching the search criteria and begins parsing it. As results are parsed, you will begin seeing markers appear on the map in various locations across the U.S. (Figure 12-6).

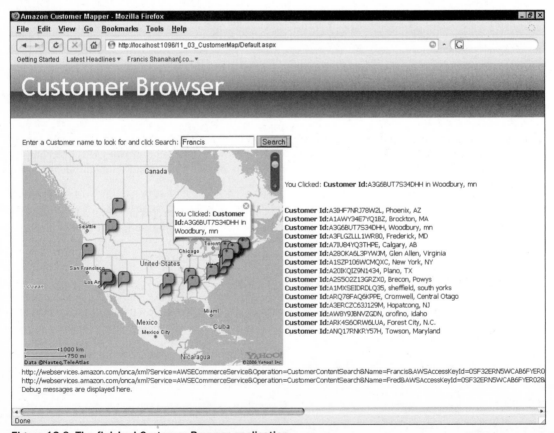

Figure 12-6: The finished Customer Browser application

Because you handled the click event in the map marker, if you click a customer, additional information for that customer is displayed on the map. The click event also writes out customer information to a `<div>` tag outside of the map.

Additional Suggestions

For the sake of clarity, I have kept the functionality in this chapter's application rather limited. The application provides a useful foundation for further experimentation.

Amazon provides access to various pieces of customer-related information—for example, Listmania lists, Product reviews, Restaurant reviews, and Wish Lists. The `CustomerContentSearch` operation returns the `CustomerId`, which can be used in subsequent `CustomerContentLookup` operations to obtain this additional information. Here's an example:

```
http://webservices.amazon.com/onca/xml?Service=AWSECommerceService&Operation=Custom
erContentLookup&CustomerId=ABBJC1XI8R0PG&AWSAccessKeyId=[YOUR KEY
HERE]&ResponseGroup=CustomerFull
```

Notice the operation is set to `CustomerContentLookup` and the `CustomerId` is specified in the querystring.

To obtain more than the default content response from the `CustomerContentLookup` operation, you need to specify a `ResponseGroup` of `CustomerFull`. By specifying the `CustomerFull` response group, Amazon supplies typical information such as `CustomerId`, `Name`, `Nickname`, and so on, as well as any lists the customer has set up and any reviews they have written.

Summary

JSON and the Dynamic Script method on the face of it can be confusing. This chapter has clearly laid out the various moving pieces so that you can take these and run with them on your own mashups.

You may have noticed this chapter did not involve any C# coding whatsoever. The solution is entirely based in JavaScript and extremely portable. This is one of the main advantages of the JSON approach to mashups.

The second advantage is that the solution entails the user's browser retrieving the data directly from the source; there is no need for a proxy on the Web site's server. The result is a more compact solution with better performance than the Ajax alternative.

Lastly, because the user's browser retrieves the data directly, it does not funnel in and out of your Web site. As a result, you don't incur the cost of the network bandwidth required to transmit the data.

Many developers prefer the use of JSON over XML because it can easily be parsed by the browser without the need to write browser-specific XML parsing code. JSON is also less verbose than XML, leading to smaller payloads and data transfers, which ultimately leads to a more performant solution.

Chapter 12

In this chapter you did the following:

- ❑ Implemented dynamic JavaScript on an ASPX page
- ❑ Created a JSON representation of Amazon data without using a proxy
- ❑ Built a working application using JSON and Amazon XSL transformation

This chapter should prove useful and informative as an alternative to the Ajax solutions presented earlier. That is not to say that Ajax and JSON are at odds with one another. On the contrary, JSON is being used more and more in place of XML in Ajax solutions.

Chapter 13 addresses the topic of performance and shows you how to leverage some of the advanced features in ASP.NET and Web services to optimize processing on your Web server.

Before reading on, I encourage you to review the following questions to ensure an accurate understanding of the material.

Exercises

1. Is JSON a technology, a platform, or a technique?
2. Is it possible to combine JSON with Ajax?
3. Are there any security issues with the JSON/Dynamic Scripting approach?
4. When JSON is delivered to the browser, what actually triggers the processing of that object?
5. What is the Dynamic Scripting method?

Improving Performance

Performance is a critical component of any application, and mashups are no exception. By "performance" I mean the efficient and responsive execution of application logic. Said differently, the application should make the most efficient use the resources available to perform whatever application logic is required. The goal is always to make your application, in this case a Web site, work as fast as possible.

In this chapter, you learn some advanced topics to speed up your application. Specifically, you learn how to do the following:

❑   Perform two (or more) actions in parallel using delegates and asynchronous Web services

❑   Use the Google Web Search API

❑   Create a search application that can be used with OpenSearch

The Battle Plan: Google Plus Amazon

Imagine you've just put the final semicolon on your killer new mashup. It's a killer app to beat all others. You fire it up and, sure enough, it works, mashing data from all over the Web. The only problem is it's incredibly slow. A slow application will frustrate a user just as much (if not more so) as an application with limited functionality. It's better to have a simple responsive application than a sophisticated slow one.

So far, I've talked about invoking Web services synchronously (in other words, one after another). The more data sources you have, the more Web service calls you must make. If a single service in the chain happens to be slow, then all subsequent calls will queue up waiting for the delinquent to finish. Worse still, the request could time-out.

Multithreading can help here. There are a number of ways of managing your application and executing simultaneous threads of processing. These waters can get murky fairly quickly. This chapter focuses on two main multithreading processing approaches. The first is Web service specific. The second is a generic mechanism that can be employed to execute any task, not just a Web service call, in parallel with the page's processing path.

Understanding the Architecture

The sample application accompanying this chapter is a search application that combines Google and Amazon results into a single result set. This mashup involves Amazon's search company, A9.com, along with Google and Amazon. Search results are federated using the OpenSearch specification and A9.com as a search aggregator.

You learn more about OpenSearch later in this chapter.

Figure 13-1 illustrates the architecture of this chapter's sample application.

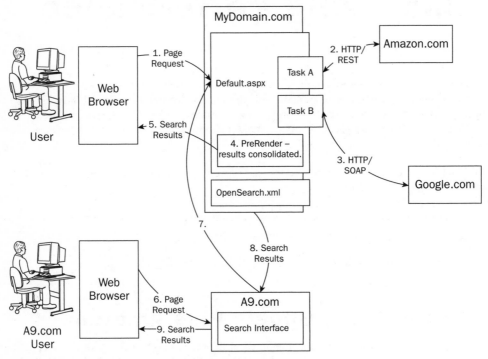

Figure 13-1: The Google/Amazon mashup architecture

How It Works

1. A user visits the site and views a search entry screen rendered by default.aspx. The user enters some keywords and clicks Submit.

2. The request comes to the server and is handled by the code-beside of default.aspx. This page initiates two tasks that execute in parallel. The first is search against Amazon using its REST-style API.

3. The second task is a search against Google using SOAP over HTTP.

4. These asynchronous tasks join back with the main page-rendering thread in the page `PreRenderComplete` event. Here, the results are consolidated into a single XML document.

5. The consolidated results are sent back to the browser.

6. An alternative flow exists where a visitor to `A9.com` searches against the mashup. This is possible because the mashup has already been registered with `A9` out-of-band.

7. The `A9` site generates a search interface using the `opensearch.xml` definition of the mashup. You learn how to create this file in this chapter. The search is submitted and the request forwarded on to the mashup site by `A9`.

8. The site executes as before and results are streamed back to `A9`.

9. `A9` presents the XML results back to the user as HTML.

Figure 13-2 shows the final application in action displaying Amazon and Google search results side-by-side with an `A9` search results set from Windows Live.

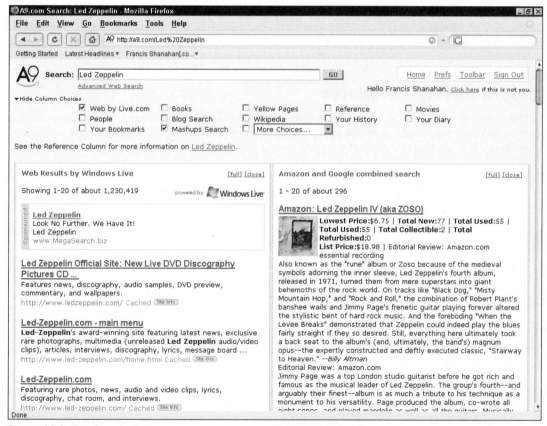

Figure 13-2: The Google/Amazon search results presented through `A9.com`

This chapter builds on some of the techniques in Chapter 7 where you remixed Amazon data as an RSS feed. Before diving into `PageAsyncTasks`, the next few sections set the stage with an overview of asynchronous programming in ASP.NET.

Asynchronous Techniques

In this chapter, you learn two separate techniques for asynchronous processing. The first is the .NET Web service–specific `MethodAsync/MethodCompleted` approach. You'll build a simple test application to demonstrate this technique.

The second one uses a non-Web service–specific approach utilizing a .NET Framework class called `PageAsyncTask`. You'll build a federated search application using this technique and deploy it into `A9.com`.

This chapter deals with .NET-specific technologies, although the concepts are generally transferable to other areas.

Each method makes use of delegates. Before going on, it's worth a quick review of delegates and what they are.

Understanding Delegates

The notion of a *delegate* is a programming concept that enables you to reference and pass around functions as you would data. Just as you can create a reference to an object of a specific type, a delegate is a reference to a function of a particular type.

So, you might ask, isn't a delegate just a function pointer? No, unlike function pointers, delegates are strongly typed. Strong typing enables compile-time verification that the code is correct, and, consequently leads to better quality than, say, a weak-typed function pointer.

Try It Out　　**Simple Named Delegate Example**

Start by creating a simple Web page that creates a delegate and invokes it:

1. To create a delegate, you first define a delegate type. This is the signature of the function:

    ```
    delegate string myDelegateType(string strMsg);
    ```

2. Create the function itself. This is the function that will be invoked through the delegate:

    ```
    static string DoSomething(string strMsg)
    {
        string strFuncName = System.Reflection.MethodBase.GetCurrentMethod().Name;
        return "My function name is this: " + strFuncName + " and you told me to do
    this: " + strMsg;
    }
    ```

3. Create an instance of the delegate:

    ```
    myDelegateType myDelegate = new myDelegateType(DoSomething);
    ```

4. Finally, you can invoke the delegate function by calling the `Invoke` method on the delegate:

```
this.lblResults.Text = myDelegate.Invoke("Say Hello!");
```

How It Works

This "Try It Out" is an example of a *named delegate* in the sense that the delegate function has a name, `DoSomething`. When you run the application, the delegate invokes its method and prints out the following statement:

```
My function name is this: DoSomething and you told me to do this: Say Hello!
```

The second type of delegate is an *anonymous delegate*, which has no name. The next section illustrates anonymous delegates.

Simple Anonymous Delegate

Anonymous delegates work just like their named counterparts, but are defined slightly differently. Here's an example:

```
// Declare an anonymous delegate
myDelegateType myDelegate = delegate(string strMsg) {
                return "You told me to say this: " + strMsg;
        };
```

The code inside the curly braces is actually the function code. There is no name assigned to the delegate, hence its anonymity.

Another Anonymous Delegate Example

When you declare an anonymous delegate, the delegate function is given a machine-generated name. You can prove this by using reflection to query the function name.

Reflection is a concept that allows you to query the run-time properties of a set of code, such as the currently executing method or the available public methods on a class.

To obtain the name the current function at run-time, do the following:

```
string strMyMessage = "Say Howdy!";

// Declare an anonymous delegate
myDelegateType myDelegate = delegate(string strMsg) {
    string strFuncName =
    System.Reflection.MethodBase.GetCurrentMethod().Name;
    return "My function name is this: " +
        strFuncName +
        " and you told me to do this: " + strMsg;
};

// Fire the delegate
lblResults.Text = myDelegate.Invoke(strMyMessage);
```

The highlighted code uses reflection to obtain the name of the function. Try it and see what you get!

The sample code associated with this chapter implements these delegate examples and should provide clear examples of how they work. The next section uses delegates with asynchronous Web services and `MethodAsync`.

Using MethodAsync

`MethodAsync` is the first of the two methods discussed in this chapter that enable parallel processing. It is Web service specific, meaning it only applies to SOAP Web services and cannot be used with, say, a REST-style approach.

In this section, you build a sample application that executes a Web service multiple times in the same time as it takes to execute once. This is a Web service–specific technique. Later on in this chapter you'll use the `PageAsyncTask` to achieve the same result, but without the need for a Web service.

When you generate a proxy class against a Web service WSDL, .NET 2.0 generates an `Async` method and corresponding `Completed` event for every method in the services. This pattern is known as `MethodAsync`.

For example, for a Web method named `HelloWorld`, .NET generates a method named `HelloWorld Async()` and an event named `HelloWorldCompleted`. The `Async` method invokes the service and takes care of forking off a thread.

To help figure out when the method is finished processing, .NET 2.0 generates a `Completed` event for every method. This is used in conjunction with the `Async` method. You call the Web method by invoking the `Async` method, and handle its results by registering an event handler against the `completion` event.

In the next "Try It Out," you use delegates and `Async` methods to build a proof-of-concept illustrating this technique.

Try It Out   Build the Test Web Service

It's far easier to test Asynchronous Web service calls with a Web service running locally than it is to use a third party's Web service. For this reason I created my own dummy Web service that returns a simple timestamp in string format. The point here is just to test the plumbing.

1. Create a new Web service in Visual Studio Web Developer Express Edition.

2. Set the Project property "Use Dynamic Ports" to false. Unlike Visual Studio 2003, which used Internet Information Server (IIS) as its Web server, VS Express uses its own lightweight Web server. To avoid conflicts with IIS if it's running on the same machine, the VS Express Web server uses a port other than port 80. This port is dynamically chosen each time the Web server is started. Changing the project properties will lock in that port for that project and allow you to bind consistently to the Web service from other projects.

3. Create a new Web method named `DoWork`. This method does nothing more than block on the current thread for a few seconds, and then return the current time in the form of a string. In this manner you can simulate the time it might take to invoke an external Web service such as Google's or MSN's search APIs. The code looks like this:

    ```
    [WebMethod]
    public string DoWork()
    {
    ```

```
//This is just a simple web service to demonstrate asynchronous calls.
// You could replace this logic with code that calls out to a third party.
string strStart = DateTime.Now.ToString() +
    ", " + DateTime.Now.Millisecond.ToString() +
    " milliseconds ";

// Sleep for a full second
System.Threading.Thread.Sleep(1000);
return "Web Service: DoWork started on thread " +
System.Threading.Thread.CurrentThread.ManagedThreadId + " at " + strStart + " and
ended at " + DateTime.Now.ToString() + ", " + DateTime.Now.Millisecond.ToString() +
" milliseconds ";
    }
```

This Web method does two things. First it sleeps for a full second, and then it prints out a message containing the ID of the thread it's executing on.

Run the application. You should be able to invoke the DoWork method from within the browser similar to Figure 13-3.

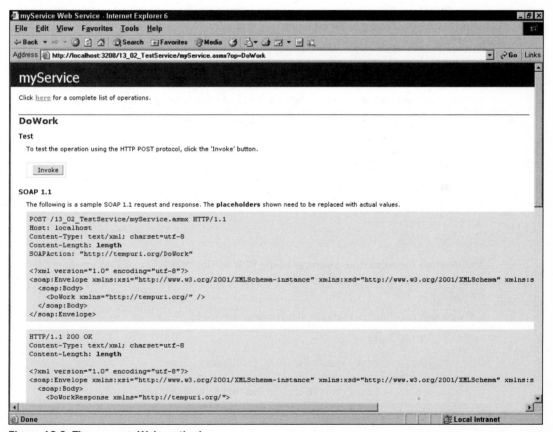

Figure 13-3: The DoWork **Web method**

The application will pause for 1 second and then print out the result. The output should look similar to the following:

```
<string>
    DoWork started on thread 12 at 5/16/2006 2:33:40 PM, 286 milliseconds and ended
at 5/16/2006 2:33:40 PM, 786 milliseconds
</string>
```

Try It Out   Building the Async Client

With the sample Web service complete, it's time to build the client. The client will invoke this test Web service in three different ways with three different outcomes.

1. Create a new Web project with a single page named `default.aspx`. Set the `Async` page directive in the ASPX page:

```
<%@ Page Language="C#" AutoEventWireup="true"
CodeFile="Default.aspx.cs" Inherits="_Default"
Async="true" %>
```

This tells ASP.NET that this page will execute asynchronous tasks. The page is not limited to using a single thread for both rendering and task execution.

2. In a separate instance of Visual Studio, open the Web service project and launch it. Add a reference to your sample Web service to the current client project.

3. Add three buttons and a label to the `default.aspx` page. The buttons are named `cmdOneService`, `cmdTwoSync`, and `cmdTwoAsync`. Assign the ID `lblResults` to the label.

4. In the code-beside for the page, add the following page-level variables:

```
// Two instances of the same service
localhost.myService serviceOne;
localhost.myService serviceTwo;

// Some vars to keep track of things
string strResults;
DateTime myStartTime;
DateTime myEndTime;
```

The first two variables store instances of the Web service proxy. The second group of variables simply stores the start and end times of the page execution, along with the results of the service methods.

5. Create a new function that sets the start time of the page:

```
void SetStartTime()
{
    // Get the current time
    myStartTime = DateTime.Now;
    strResults = "Page Started: " + myStartTime.ToString() + ", " +
    myStartTime.Millisecond.ToString() + " milliseconds<br/><br/>";
}
```

6. The first button, `cmdOneService`, executes the Web service a single time. Here's the code for that button:

```
protected void cmdOneService_Click(object sender, EventArgs e)
{
    SetStartTime();
    serviceOne = new localhost.myService();
    strResults += "One Service: " + serviceOne.DoWork() + "<br/><br/>";
}
```

7. The second button invokes the service twice in sequence, and the code looks like this:

```
protected void cmdTwoSync_Click(object sender, EventArgs e)
{
    SetStartTime();

    // Create two instances of the proxy
    serviceOne = new localhost.myService();
    serviceTwo = new localhost.myService();

    // Do some work
    strResults += serviceOne.DoWork() + "<br/><br/>";
    strResults += serviceTwo.DoWork() + "<br/><br/>";
}
```

In each case, the results of the method are written out to the label on the page.

8. The last button is the most interesting. It invokes the Web service twice, but the methods execute in parallel. Here's the code for the asynchronous button:

```
protected void cmdTwoAsync_Click(object sender, EventArgs e)
{
    SetStartTime();

    // Create two instances of the proxy
    serviceOne = new localhost.myService();
    serviceTwo = new localhost.myService();

    // Assign a new anonymous delegate to the
    // completed event of the first service
    serviceOne.DoWorkCompleted += delegate(object source,
DoWorkCompletedEventArgs args)
    {
        // Make sure no other thread is accessing the results.
        lock (strResults)
        {
            strResults += "Anonymous Delegate:" + args.Result + "<br/><br/>";
        }
    };

    // Register a named delegate to the completed event
    serviceTwo.DoWorkCompleted += new
            localhost.DoWorkCompletedEventHandler(MyFunction);
```

```
        // Do some work
        serviceOne.DoWorkAsync();
        serviceTwo.DoWorkAsync();
    }
```

Notice the use of both named and anonymous delegates in this event handler.

9.   In the page_load event, set the start time of the page. This is to help keep track of how long the work is taking:

```
        protected void Page_Load(object sender, EventArgs e)
    {
        if (!IsPostBack)
        {
            SetStartTime();
        }
    }
```

10.   Add a new function to handle the completed event of the DoWork service method. This function is hooked to the service in the cmdTwoAsync_Click code:

```
    void MyFunction(Object source, localhost.DoWorkCompletedEventArgs e)
    {
        // Make sure no other thread is accessing the results.
        lock (strResults)
        {
            strResults += "Named Delegate: " + e.Result + "<br/><br/>";
        }
    }
```

11.   In the Page_PreRenderComplete event, add some code to capture the end time, calculate the overall time taken, and then display the results:

```
    protected void Page_PreRenderComplete(object sender, EventArgs e)
    {
        // Finally print out some details so you know how long stuff took
        myEndTime = DateTime.Now;
        strResults += "Page Rendering Finished: " +
                myEndTime.ToString() + ", " +
                myEndTime.Millisecond.ToString() + " milliseconds<br/><br/>";
        strResults += "Page rendering took: " +
                (myEndTime -myStartTime).ToString();
        lblResults.Text = strResults;
    }
```

That completes the coding for this sample. You should be able to run the project at this time and click each button in turn.

Figure 13-4 shows the finished application at work.

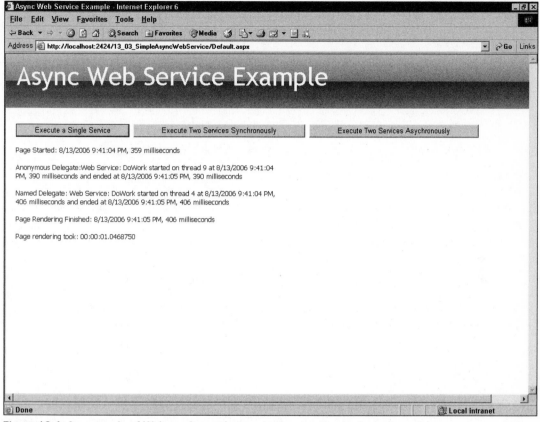

Figure 13-4: An example of Web services using `MethodAsync/MethodCompleted`

How It Works

The page executes the same method in three different ways:

1. When you click the first button, the service is executed a single time and the results are displayed. The invocation and should take about 1 second to execute, based on the delay built into the Web method. Here's the output:

```
Page Started: 7/21/2006 11:04:21 AM, 195 milliseconds

One Service: Web Service: DoWork started on thread 4 at 7/21/2006 11:04:21 AM, 195
milliseconds and ended at 7/21/2006 11:04:22 AM, 195 milliseconds

Page Rendering Finished: 7/21/2006 11:04:22 AM, 195 milliseconds

Page rendering took: 00:00:01.0000192
```

2. The second button invokes the same service twice, sequentially. Naturally, this takes twice as long as indicated by the following output:

```
Page Started: 7/21/2006 10:59:38 AM, 893 milliseconds

Web Service: DoWork started on thread 4 at 7/21/2006 10:59:38 AM, 893 milliseconds
and ended at 7/21/2006 10:59:39 AM, 893 milliseconds

Web Service: DoWork started on thread 4 at 7/21/2006 10:59:39 AM, 908 milliseconds
and ended at 7/21/2006 10:59:40 AM, 908 milliseconds

Page Rendering Finished: 7/21/2006 10:59:40 AM, 908 milliseconds
```

```
Page rendering took: 00:00:02.0156637
```

3. The third button is definitely the most interesting as seen by the output. The service is executed twice and results are consolidated:

```
Page Started: 7/21/2006 11:04:08 AM, 7 milliseconds

Anonymous Delegate:Web Service: DoWork started on thread 10 at 7/21/2006 11:04:08
AM, 54 milliseconds and ended at 7/21/2006 11:04:09 AM, 54 milliseconds

Named Delegate: Web Service: DoWork started on thread 4 at 7/21/2006 11:04:08 AM,
85 milliseconds and ended at 7/21/2006 11:04:09 AM, 85 milliseconds

Page Rendering Finished: 7/21/2006 11:04:09 AM, 85 milliseconds
```

```
Page rendering took: 00:00:01.0781457
```

Both method calls are initiated using the MethodAsync operation DoWorkAsync(). Completion is handled slightly differently. ServiceOne handles completion using an anonymous delegate. ServiceTwo uses the named delegate function, MyFunction().

The page blocks (waits) in the Page_PreRenderComplete event until all asynchronous methods have completed before continuing. This makes the PreRenderComplete event the ideal location to print out the output of the Web methods.

In each completion event handler, the shared variable strResults is accessed. To avoid a situation where the threads access this variable at the same time, a lock statement is used:

```
// Make sure no other thread is accessing the results.
lock (strResults)
{
    strResults += "Named Delegate: " + e.Result + "<br/><br/>";
}
```

lock provides a way to synchronize access to a resource, in this case the strResults string. Only the current thread can access the resource at any given time. Other threads will block until the lock is released.

As you can see, this is one way of executing multiple Web services without degrading performance. The service used in this example was a dummy service, but it is trivial to replace this with a third-party service such as Amazon's ECS.

Now, it's time to turn your attention to the Google API.

The Google API

Google exposes much of its search catalog and functionality through its Web service platform. To access it, of course, you need to register as a developer and obtain a key. There are the usual usage restrictions limiting the number of times you can call a service per day, but these are not prohibitive for the casual user.

Google's SOAP API Web service definition is located here:

```
http://api.google.com/GoogleSearch.wsdl
```

The Google search interface supports three main APIs, described in the following table.

Function Name	Description
DoGoogleSearch	Provides access to Google's search catalog.
DoGetCachedPage	Lets you access Google's copy of a particular page.
DoSpellingSuggestion on Google.com.	Provides alternative spelling, similar to what's available

A typical Google query consists of a set of search criteria or keywords and a set of directives indicating the type of results you are looking for.

The following table describes the search parameters in detail.

Parameter	Description
key	The Google API developer key, assigned to you during registration.
q	Search keywords. This can be refined using special directives such as `link:`, `related:`, `info:`, and so on.
start	Indicates which result to begin from. This is used to implement pagination. For example, the second page of results could be retrieved by specifying 10 as the start value.
maxResults	The number of results to retrieve, typically 10.
filter	Indicates whether Google should filter out similar results automatically.

Table continued on following page

Parameter	Description
restricts	You can restrict results by Country, Topic, or Language.
SafeSearch	SafeSearch indicates that Google should not return adult content in the result set.
lr	Language Restrict — Limits results to certain set of languages.
ie	Input encoding — no longer used.
oe	Output encoding — no longer used.

The next "Try It Out" uses the DoGoogleSearch method to implement a simple search application.

Try It Out   Simple Google Search Application

1. Create a new Web site project and add a Web reference to the Google API:

   ```
   http://api.google.com/GoogleSearch.wsdl
   ```

   A Web service proxy class is generated.

2. Create a simple client page (default.aspx) that contains a textbox to accept some keywords and a button to trigger the search. Add a label control to house the search results.

3. In the code-behind for the page, add a using statement for Google's Web service:

   ```
   using com.google.api;
   ```

4. In the event handler for the command button, insert the following code:

   ```
   // Create a Google Search object
   GoogleSearchService myService = new GoogleSearchService();

   // Invoke the search method
   GoogleSearchResult myResults ;

   myResults = myService.doGoogleSearch(
       "[YOUR API KEY HERE]",
       this.txtKeywords.Text,
       0, 10,
       true,
       "",
       true,
       "",
       "",
       "");

   // Prep the results area
   lblResults.Text = "<ol>";

   // Loop through each result and display it
   foreach (ResultElement myResult in myResults.resultElements)
   {
   ```

```
            lblResults.Text += "<li><a href=\"" +myResult.URL +  "\">" ;
            lblResults.Text += myResult.title ;
            lblResults.Text += "</a><br/>";
            lblResults.Text += myResult.snippet + "<br/><br/></li>";
        }
        lblResults.Text += "</ol>";
```

This code executes a search and then prints out the results in HTML.

5.   Run the application, enter some keywords, and click Go.

Congratulations! You just built your first Google application (Figure 13-5).

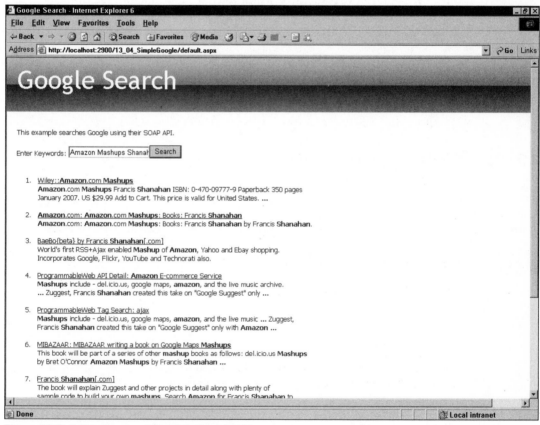

Figure 13-5: A Simple use of Google's Search API

You can tailor the results by adding directives to the search query. For example, to search for similar items, enter `related:www.mySite.com` where `mySite` is your Web site.

By now you have seen how delegates work, implemented asynchronous Web service calls, and built an interface into Google using SOAP. It's time to round out the chapter by building the sample application.

Building the Amazon Google Feed

The sample application for this chapter uses Amazon and Google to build a comprehensive search application leveraging the OpenSearch specification. It uses a new technique called `PageAsyncTasks` to execute the Amazon and Google API calls in parallel. As you will see, unlike `MethodAsync`, `PageAsyncTasks` do not require the use of Web services.

What Is OpenSearch?

OpenSearch is a mechanism by which search results can be syndicated and aggregated using simple XML-based formats. OpenSearch as a specification has been adopted by `A9.com`, which is an Amazon-owned company. `A9.com` provides a platform by which you can build your own search engine and then integrate it into their platform by virtue of it being OpenSearch-compliant. This is exactly what you'll do in this sample application. The results will be a combination of Amazon and Google search results, and will also support pagination.

You can learn more about OpenSearch at the following URL:

```
http://opensearch.a9.com/
```

Using PageAsyncTasks

`PageAsyncTasks` are a way to perform some type of processing in parallel with the execution of the ASP.NET. They are a complementary alternative to the `MethodAsync`/`MethodCompleted` mechanism shown earlier in the chapter. Unlike `MethodAsync`, `PageAsyncTasks` do not require a Web service proxy. As a result, they can be used to issue `HttpWebRequests`, as you will do in this next example.

Try It Out   Building the RSS Generator

1. Create a new Web application project in Visual Studio and add a reference to the Google SOAP API:

    ```
    http://api.google.com/GoogleSearch.wsdl
    ```

2. Design an input form (`default.aspx`) that contains two text inputs. The first accepts keywords, and the second accepts a numerical value that indicates which page of results to obtain. Set the `Async` page directive of `default.aspx` to `true`:

    ```
    <%@ Page Async="true" %>
    ```

3. In the code-beside for `default.aspx`, implement the following code, which sets up the `PageAsyncTasks`:

```
void GetResults()
  {
    strKeywords = Request["Keywords"]; // Keywords
    strSearchIndex = Request["SearchIndex"];
    iResultsPage = Convert.ToInt32(Request["ResultsPage"]);

    if ((strKeywords != "") & (strKeywords != null))
```

```
        {
            insufficientArguments = false;
            PageAsyncTask amazonTask = new PageAsyncTask(
                new BeginEventHandler(BeginAmazonSearch),
                new EndEventHandler(EndAmazonSearch),
                new EndEventHandler(TimeoutAmazonSearch),
                null);
            RegisterAsyncTask(amazonTask);

            PageAsyncTask googleTask = new PageAsyncTask(
                new BeginEventHandler(BeginGoogleSearch),
                new EndEventHandler(EndgoogleSearch),
                new EndEventHandler(TimeoutgoogleSearch),
                null);
            RegisterAsyncTask(googleTask);

        }
        else
        {
            insufficientArguments = true;
        }
    }
```

The code behind the button doesn't actually perform a search. Rather, it registers two PageAsyncTasks that are responsible for obtaining the results from both Amazon and Google.

Registering a PageAsyncTask

PageAsyncTasks must be registered with the page. It is a three-step process. The first step involves creating an instance of a PageAsyncTask by supplying three delegates to the PageAsyncTask constructor:

```
        PageAsyncTask amazonTask = new PageAsyncTask(
            new BeginEventHandler(BeginAmazonSearch),
            new EndEventHandler(EndAmazonSearch),
            new EndEventHandler(TimeoutAmazonSearch),
            null);
```

These delegates handle kicking off the task, ending the task, and handling any cleanup in the event of a timeout.

The default timeout value for a PageAsyncTask is 45 seconds, and can be overridden in the web.config file, or by adding the following page directive to your page:

```
    <%@ Page AsyncTimeout="30" %>
```

The second step is to register the newly created task:

```
    RegisterAsyncTask(amazonTask);
```

The third step is to actually implement the three functions referenced in the task's constructor. The next sections show you how to implement each function in detail.

SOAP Proxy Begin and End

Web services are typically invoked through a proxy class generated off of a Web service definition written in WSDL. The .NET Framework makes provision for asynchronous processing by generating `Begin` and `End` tasks for every Web method in the Web service. Any method in a Web service (`HelloWorld`, for example) will be created in the proxy; in addition, corresponding `BeginHelloWorld` and `EndHelloWorld` methods are also created. These can be used to invoke the Web service in an asynchronous manner, essentially forking the thread processing the page.

The Google Begin Task

Event handlers used in the `PageAsyncTasks` must return `IAsyncResults`. The `Begin` task method will invoke the `Begin` version of the `DoGoogleSearch` Web method. All `Begin` methods return `IAsyncResults`, so your function can simply return this object:

```
IAsyncResult BeginGoogleSearch(object sender, EventArgs e, AsyncCallback cb, object
state)
    {
        myGoogleService = new GoogleSearchService();
        string strKeywords = Request["keywords"];

        . . .

        // Get the Google Results
        // Invoke the search method
        return myGoogleService.BegindoGoogleSearch(
            "[YOUR KEY HERE]",
            strKeywords,
            iStartFrom, 10,
            true,
            "",
            true,
            "",
            "",
            "",
            cb, state
            );
    }
```

The Google End Task

Ending the Google Page task is slightly more complex. The code creates a `GoogleSearchResult` that is populated by invoking the `End` function on the Google Web service.

The remainder of the code is dedicated to converting the search results to an `XmlDocument` for easy processing:

```
void EndgoogleSearch(IAsyncResult ar)
    {
        GoogleSearchResult myGoogleResults;
        // Obtain the results
```

```
        myGoogleResults = myGoogleService.EnddoGoogleSearch(ar);

        myGoogleDoc = new XmlDocument();
        string googleNS = "urn:google:search";
        XmlNode myRoot = myGoogleDoc.CreateNode(XmlNodeType.Element,
                "MyGoogle", googleNS);

        foreach (ResultElement googleItem in myGoogleResults.resultElements)
        {
            XmlNode myItem = myGoogleDoc.CreateNode(XmlNodeType.Element,
                    "item", googleNS);

            // Create a new element node named "title"
            XmlNode myTitle = myGoogleDoc.CreateNode(XmlNodeType.Element,
                    "title", googleNS);
            myTitle.InnerText = googleItem.title;
            myItem.AppendChild(myTitle);

            // Another for the link
            XmlNode myLink = myGoogleDoc.CreateNode(XmlNodeType.Element,
                    "link", googleNS);
            myLink.InnerText = googleItem.URL;
            myItem.AppendChild(myLink);

            // One more for the description
            XmlNode myDescription = myGoogleDoc.CreateNode(XmlNodeType.Element,
                    "description", googleNS);
            myDescription.InnerText = googleItem.snippet;
            myItem.AppendChild(myDescription);

            // Append to the parent
            myRoot.AppendChild(myItem);
        }

        // Add the root to the google results.
        myGoogleDoc.AppendChild(myRoot);

    }
```

The Google Interim XML Document

The End task method converts the Google search results to an XML document that resembles the following format. This will be used later in the final transformation:

```
<MyGoogle>
    <item>
        <title>...</title>
        <link>...</link>
        <description>...</description>
    </item>
    <item>
        ...
    </item>
</MyGoogle>
```

The Google TimeOut Function

`PageAsyncTasks` also allow you to define a course of action should the operation time out. This is useful for cleaning up or aborting the transaction. In this case, the code simply writes out an error message to inform the user of an error:

```
void TimeoutAmazonSearch(IAsyncResult ar) {
        Response.Write("Amazon Data temporarily unavailable");
}
```

The Amazon Begin and End Tasks

Whereas Google uses SOAP to retrieve its results, Amazon uses a REST request issued via `HttpWebRequests`. The `Begin` task will look familiar:

```
IAsyncResult BeginAmazonSearch(object sender, EventArgs e, AsyncCallback cb, object
state)
    {
        myAmazonRequest =
(HttpWebRequest)WebRequest.Create("http://webservices.amazon.com..."
            + strSearchIndex +
            "&Keywords=" + strKeywords +
            "&ItemPage=" + iResultsPage);
        return myAmazonRequest.BeginGetResponse(cb, state);
    }
```

This constructs a new `HttpWebRequest` and issues its `Begin` method as shown. Once the task has completed, the `End` task gathers up the results in the form of an XML document:

```
void EndAmazonSearch(IAsyncResult ar)
    {
        myAmazonDoc = webUtility.GetUri(myAmazonRequest, ar);
    }
```

Because this is an asynchronous `HttpWebRequest`, the `webUtility.GetUri` function was overloaded to obtain the XML document. The overloaded method looks like this:

```
    public static XmlDocument GetUri(HttpWebRequest myRequest, IAsyncResult
myResult)
    {
        XmlDocument myDoc;
        HttpWebResponse myResponse =
    (HttpWebResponse)myRequest.EndGetResponse(myResult);
        StreamReader myReceiveStream = new
StreamReader(myResponse.GetResponseStream());

        // Create the doc and load it
        myDoc = new XmlDocument();
        myDoc.Load(myReceiveStream);

        // Return the doc
        if (myDoc != null) {
            return myDoc;
        } else {
```

```
                    return null;
            }
        }
```

As you can see, this code obtains the XML response using the `IAsyncResult` passed into it from the `End` task. The XML is converted into an `XmlDocument` and returned from the function. The next section deals with mashing the results into a single result set.

Combining the Results in the PreRenderComplete Event

Naturally, when you fork off a number of threads to perform some work, there is the issue of knowing when they will all have completed their processing. Thankfully, ASP.NET solves this issue with the `PageAsyncTask` implementation by waiting until all registered page tasks have executed and completed before entering the `PageRenderComplete` event. Once all the events have completed, the `PreRender Complete` event is fired making it a perfect place to consolidate the results from each worker task.

The `PreRenderComplete` event handler looks like this:

```
protected void Page_PreRenderComplete(object sender, EventArgs e)
    {
...
// Merge the results of all calls
XmlDocument resultsDoc = new XmlDocument();
XmlNode myRoot = resultsDoc.CreateElement("MyMashup");
resultsDoc.AppendChild(myRoot);

// first document to merge
XmlNode tmpNode;

if (myAmazonDoc != null)
{
    tmpNode = resultsDoc.ImportNode(myAmazonDoc.DocumentElement, true);
    resultsDoc.DocumentElement.AppendChild(tmpNode);
}

// second document to merge
if (myGoogleDoc != null)
{
    tmpNode = resultsDoc.ImportNode(myGoogleDoc.DocumentElement, true);
    resultsDoc.DocumentElement.AppendChild(tmpNode);
}

// print merged documents
if (resultsDoc != null)
{
    Response.Clear();
    Response.ContentType = "text/xml";
...
    Response.Write(webUtility.DoXSLTransformation(resultsDoc, "AmazonGoogle.xsl",
myArgs));
}
...
    }
```

How It Works

The `PreRenderComplete` event works like this:

1. First, a new XML document is created, with a single root node named `MyMashup`. This document will hold the consolidated XML responses from both searches.

2. Next, the Amazon XML document is checked and then appended to the new root node.

3. The Google results were delivered via SOAP and, if you recall, they were reconstituted in the `GoogleEndSearch` event handler into a temporary XML document. This document is now added to the consolidated results. The consolidated document has the following structure:

```
<MyMashup>
    <ItemSearchResult>
        <!-- Amazon results here -->
    </ItemSearchResult>
    <MyGoogle>
        <item>
            <title>...</title>
            <link>...</link>
            <description>...</description>
        </item>
        <item>
            ...
        </item>
    </MyGoogle>
</MyMashup>
```

4. The results are then transformed using `DoXSLTransformation` and a new XSL file. The result is an XML document based on the RSS specification.

OpenSearch uses RSS as its base format for transmitting results. The RSS document is extended using an OpenSearch namespace as follows:

```
<rss version="2.0" xmlns:openSearch="http://a9.com/-/spec/opensearch/1.1/" >
    <channel>
    ...
```

The XSL sheet adds three new nodes in the OpenSearch namespace to the RSS output. These are the current page (or `startIndex`), the number of items per page (20 in this case), and the `Total` results. I have assumed the total results equal to the Amazon result set, rather than the Google value:

```
<openSearch:startIndex>
    <xsl:value-of select="$resultPage"/>
</openSearch:startIndex>
<openSearch:itemsPerPage>20</openSearch:itemsPerPage>
<openSearch:totalResults>
    <xsl:value-of select="MyMashup/a:ItemSearchResponse/a:Items/a:TotalResults"/>
</openSearch:totalResults>
```

The highlighted code here tells OpenSearch users which page these results are from. Pagination is discussed in the next section.

Pagination of Results in Google and Amazon

It's not a requirement, but OpenSearch supports pagination of search results. To implement pagination, the application needs a parameter to be passed in named ResultsPage. This represents the page number of the results to retrieve. It gets parsed out in the GetResults function along with Keywords and SearchIndex:

```
void GetResults()
    {
        strKeywords = Request["Keywords"]; // Keywords
        strSearchIndex = Request["SearchIndex"];
        iResultsPage = Convert.ToInt32(Request["ResultsPage"]);
```

The page-level variable is then used within the Begin tasks of Google as follows:

```
// Google uses the result to start from
// not the page number to start from
int iStartFrom = iResultsPage * 10;

// Invoke the search method
return myGoogleService.BegindoGoogleSearch(
    "[YOUR KEY HERE]",
    strKeywords,
    iStartFrom, 10,
    true,
```

It's used again in the REST request to tell Amazon which page to return:

```
myAmazonRequest =
(HttpWebRequest)WebRequest.Create("http://webservices.amazon.com..."
            + strSearchIndex +
            "&Keywords=" + strKeywords +
        "&ItemPage=" + iResultsPage);
```

The iResultsPage variable is used one last time to format the results and indicate which page of results is being returned. This is done by passing iResultsPage into the XSL transformation.

Passing a Parameter to an XSL Sheet

The transformation using XSL should be fairly familiar by now. The only new thing to note in the transformation is the presence of an XSL parameter denoting the startIndex. This is a parameter defined in the head of the XSL sheet as follows:

```
<!-- Define a parameter -->
<xsl:param name="resultPage"></xsl:param>
```

The value is used later to denote the startIndex:

```
<openSearch:startIndex>
        <xsl:value-of select="$resultPage"/>
</openSearch:startIndex>
```

This value is actually passed into the transformation from C# code using an XSLArgumentList object. Here is the relevant code from the Page_PreRenderComplete event:

```
XsltArgumentList xslArg = new XsltArgumentList();

//Create a parameter
XsltArgumentList myArgs = new XsltArgumentList();
myArgs.AddParam("resultPage", "", iResultsPage);
Response.Write(webUtility.DoXSLTransformation(resultsDoc, "AmazonGoogle.xsl",
myArgs));
```

This enables the C# code to inform the transformation about which page the results are from.

Testing the Application

When you enter some search criteria and test the application, you should see an RSS output similar to Chapter 7 as follows:

```
<rss version="2.0" xmlns:openSearch="http://a9.com/-/spec/opensearch/1.1/">
  <channel>
    <title>AMZN + GOOGLE Search Results</title>
    <link>http://Mashups.FrancisShanahan.com</link>
    <description>Syndicated Amazon and Google Results</description>
    <language>en-us</language>
    <item>
      <title>
        Amazon: Led Zeppelin IV (aka ZOSO)
      </title>
      <description>
        ...
      </description>
      <link>http://www.amazon.com/...</link>
    </item>
    <item>
      <title>
        Google: Fred's Led Zeppelin Page
      </title>
      <description>...</description>
      <link>http://www..../</link>
    </item>
    <openSearch:startIndex>1</openSearch:startIndex>
    <openSearch:itemsPerPage>20</openSearch:itemsPerPage>
    <openSearch:totalResults>293</openSearch:totalResults>
  </channel>
</rss>
```

The output contains a block of results from Amazon followed by a block of results from Google. The last section contains the OpenSearch-specific items. The next step is to register this search application with an OpenSearch aggregator, namely A9.com.

Registering with A9.com

Point your browser at http://opensearch.a9.com/ and click "Submit your search to a9.com." You'll be shown a screen whereby you can "Enter OpenSearch Description URL." The OpenSearch specification uses a small XML file akin to a manifest that documents the various aspects of any given search. This metadata tells the search aggregator how to interact with the search application. The OpenSearch file for this application looks like this:

```
<?xml version="1.0" encoding="UTF-8"?>
<OpenSearchDescription xmlns="http://a9.com/-/spec/opensearch/1.1/">
  <ShortName>Mashups Search</ShortName>
  <LongName>Amazon and Google combined search</LongName>
  <Description>Search Amazon and Google in a single shot</Description>
  <Tags>amazon mashup google content rss</Tags>
  <Contact>email@address.com</Contact>
  <Url type="application/rss+xml"
       template="http://[YOUR SITE
HERE]/default.aspx?Keywords={searchTerms}&amp;SearchIndex=Music&amp;ResultsPage={st
artPage}"/>
</OpenSearchDescription>
```

This is called the OpenSearch Manifest file. You should create a new file, named opensearch.xml, and enter the preceding content. Upload this file to your server, along with the rest of the solution.

The most important element in this XML file is the URL element (highlighted). This describes the basic interface to the search application. What you have done is create a REST-style interface for your search results. The URL contains two statements, {startPage} and {searchTerms}. These are placeholders for the consumers of this API to place values. {startPage} will be replaced with the page number that the results should start from and {searchTerms} will be replaced with the search keywords.

You'll need to create an OpenSearch file of your own and upload it to your site. Supplying the location of the OpenSearch file to the A9 search registration page will bring up a preview page, as shown in Figure 13-6.

Looking at Figure 13-6, you'll notice the user interface generated for this application to the right-hand side of the screen. This is generated automatically by A9.

By registering your search application with A9 or any OpenSearch-compliant search aggregator, you can federate your results across a much wider audience than if you were to simply host them yourself.

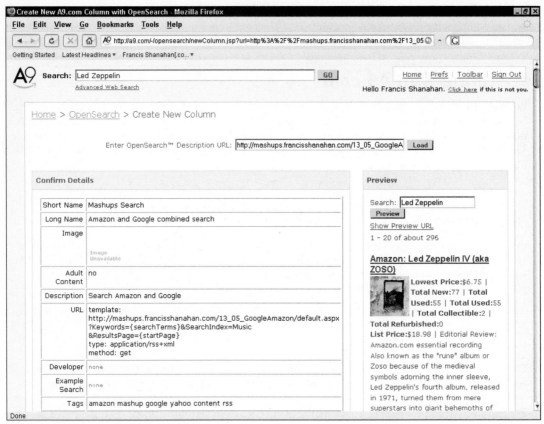

Figure 13-6: Submitting a new search to `A9`

Summary

This chapter covered a lot of ground. By completing the samples in this chapter, you have

- ❑ Utilized anonymous and named delegates
- ❑ Used `MethodAsync` and `MethodCompleted` features of .NET Web service proxies
- ❑ Learned how to do multithreaded processing in ASP.NET using `PageAsyncTask`
- ❑ Used RSS extensions to implement an OpenSearch-compliant search application
- ❑ Consolidated Google and Amazon search results into a single mashup

This chapter was a lot of fun and hopefully opened some doors for you in terms of the performance available within the .NET platform. ASP.NET has implemented some innovative threading patterns that greatly simplify multithreaded programming. By implementing the techniques outlined in this chapter, you will not only expand the possibilities of mashups beyond traditional Ajax and JSON, but also provide enhanced performance for your users.

Chapter 14 shows you how to build a mobile interface into Amazon that you can use from a BlackBerry or cell phone.

Before continuing on it's worth reviewing the following questions to ensure an accurate understanding of the material.

Exercises

1. How can you create a delegate in C#?

2. What advantages do delegates have over function pointers?

3. What capabilities are there in ASP.NET and SOAP for asynchronous execution?

4. What is OpenSearch?

5. What is the OpenSearch Manifest file?

6. How would you incorporate eBay or another set of results into the OpenSearch application?

Amazon Mobile

How many times have you been in a bookstore, just about to buy a book when the thought occurs to you that "maybe I could get this cheaper online"? You may not be as miserly (I prefer the term "frugal") as I am, but clearly a way to check the price online without leaving the store would be beneficial.

In this chapter, you build exactly that, an online interface into Amazon that's accessible from all manner of wireless devices with Internet access, including cell phones, BlackBerry devices, Palm devices, and Pocket PCs.

In this chapter, you do the following:

- ❑ Learn the essentials of the Wireless Markup Language (WML)
- ❑ Implement an interface into Amazon using XML and XSL exclusively
- ❑ Learn how to develop applications using mobile device emulators

The Battle Plan: Amazon in a BlackBerry Using REST

The plan in this chapter is to create an interface that's consumable by a mobile device. To limit the scope of the discussion, I chose a BlackBerry device as my target. BlackBerry devices are fairly widespread these days, and users of them have a strange (almost cult-like) affinity for their beloved devices.

The BlackBerry also has a rather strict WML browser and, hence, this makes it the perfect platform to target. If an application is accessible from a BlackBerry device, then there's a reasonable chance it'll be accessible from other, more forgiving devices such as the Pocket PC.

Understanding the Architecture

The architecture of the sample is fairly simple, as shown in Figure 14-1.

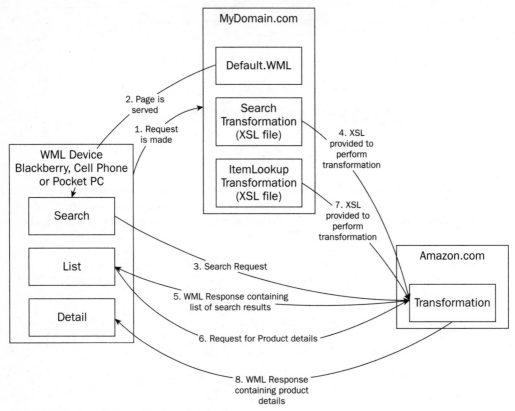

Figure 14-1: The WML application architecture

How It Works

The application works like this:

1. The user visits a specific URL using a wireless device.

2. The URL is served, but, in this case, instead of HTML, the Web server serves WML.

3. The user enters some search criteria and clicks Search.

4. Search actually directs to the Amazon servers and provides an XSL sheet to transform the results from XML into WML.

5. Amazon responds with a set of search results that are transformed into a listing screen in WML.

6. The user chooses a search result and requests more detail.

7. An Amazon `ItemLookup` is performed, and the results are transformed using another XSL sheet from the Web site's server (`myDomain.com`).

8. The converted results (now pure WML) are sent back to the browser.

That completes the overview. The next section describes some preliminary development environment setup that is necessary before getting your hands dirty with code.

Installing the Emulator

In this case, an *emulator* is a software application that looks and acts like an actual hardware device. It gets expensive to buy physical devices for each and every application you want to develop. In a commercial software company, the logistics of procurement can also be prohibitive. Of course, you are free to use a physical device for testing if you have access to one. A physical device is by far the highest assurance you can get that your application will work. In this case, I will use a software emulator.

Most device manufacturers provide free access to software emulators for developers. It's in the manufacturer's best interests to do this because the more software there is developed and available for a given device, the more likely people are to buy it.

You can download a BlackBerry emulator from the following URL:

```
http://www.BlackBerry.com/developers
```

Along with the BlackBerry emulator, you will need to download the BlackBerry Mobile Data Service (MDS). This is a separate download and specific to BlackBerry devices. You can find the MDS at the URL cited previously.

Try It Out   **Internet Access from the Emulator**

Once you've downloaded and installed the emulator, you can test its Internet connectivity from the desktop. The following instructions are specific to the BlackBerry emulator:

1. Click Start → Programs → Research In Motion and launch the emulator.

2. Click Start → Programs, Research In Motion and launch a program called MDS.

3. On the BlackBerry device, navigate to the Browser icon and launch the browser.

4. Type the following URL:

```
http://wap.yahoo.com
```

This will bring up Yahoo's wireless access page shown in Figure 14-2.

What Is WAP?

Wireless Access Protocol (WAP) is the protocol by which wireless devices communicate. It is the wireless equivalent of HTTP and it works to transmit WML in a similar fashion to HTML over HTTP and Transmission Control Protocol/Internet Protocol (TCPI/IP).

Figure 14-2: The BlackBerry emulator displaying Yahoo's site

The Mobile Data Service (MDS) application is what the BlackBerry uses to communicate with the Internet. The BlackBerry uses MDS as a gateway through which Internet traffic is routed.

An Overview of WML

Mobile devices have certain limitations not faced by a desktop. Here's a list of just some of the challenges faced when working on a mobile device:

❑ Less powerful CPU

❑ Less available memory

❑ Decreased amount of storage available

❑ Smaller screen

❑ Possibly fewer colors supported or a monochrome screen

❑ Slower network connection

❑ Limited user input mechanisms (for example, no "drag and drop")

❑ Not always connected to the Internet. Though certain BlackBerrys are generally always connected, other devices (such as the PocketPC) are not always connected to the network.

To best leverage the resources at hand, the HTML standard is just too bloated. WML is based on XML and IP, and it strips functionality down to the bare minimum.

Pages in WML

WML represents pages as cards in a deck. Unlike HTML (where a page can contain only one body), a WML document can contain multiple cards, each one representing an individual page:

```
<wml>
  <card id="main" title="WML HelloWorld">
    <p mode="wrap">
      <b>Hello World from Page 1</b>
      <a href="#card2" >Show Card2</a>
    </p>
  </card>
  <card id="card2" title="Page 2">
    <p>
      Hello world from Page 2
    </p>
  </card>
</wml>
```

By doing this, a WML application can download multiple cards at a time, saving a network hop when navigating between cards.

Forms in WML

WML uses input fields just as in HTML. The input fields are specified in a similar manner to HTML using an `<input>` tag:

```
<input name="Keywords" value="My Value"/>
```

The `name` attribute of the input field is used to refer to the field in the remaining sections of the page using a special WML syntax:

```
($Keywords)
```

WML does not use the `forms` element from HTML, but rather it uses a notion of do-and-go in its place. To build a form, you create a `<do>` tag. Inside the `<do>` tag, you add a `<go>` tag. The `<go>` tag is what actually specifies the action the form should take. Here's an example:

```
<do type="accept" label="My Form">
  <go href="http://www.MySite.com?Keywords=($Keywords)" method="get">
    <postfield name="myParameter" value="AWSECommerceService"/>
  </go>
</do>
```

In this code, the form's label is `"My Form"`. Notice the reference to the (`$Keywords`) variable defined earlier. When submitted, the form takes the value from this variable and inserts it into the form.

You can define additional parameters for inclusion in the form submission. These are similar to hidden fields in HTML, and are shown using the `<postfield>` tag.

Try It Out   Simple WML Page

1. Create a new empty project in Visual Studio.

2. Add a new file named `HelloWorld.wml` to the project. This will be your first WML page.

3. Add the following XML to the page:

```xml
<?xml version="1.0" ?>
<!DOCTYPE wml PUBLIC "-//PHONE.COM//DTD WML 1.1//EN"
"http://www.phone.com/dtd/wml11.dtd">
<wml>
  <card id="main" title="WML HelloWorld">
    <p mode="wrap">
      <b>Hello World from Page 1.</b>
    </p>
    <p>
      <a href="http://wap.yahoo.com">Here's a link to Yahoo</a>
      <br/>
      <br/>
      <a href="#card2" >Show Card2</a>
    </p>
  </card>
  <card id="card2" title="Page 2">
    <p mode="wrap">
      <b>Hello World from WML</b>
    </p>
    <p>
      Hello world from Page 2.
    </p>
  </card>
</wml>
```

4. Launch the project and note the address of the page.

5. Navigate to that location using the mobile device emulator.

Depending on the device emulator you are using, the local Web server may not be accessible. In those cases, you may need to host the page on a public URL to access it from the device.

Figure 14-3 shows the `HelloWorld` application at work. You can click the link named `Show Card 2` to display the second card in the deck.

Now that you've conquered `HelloWorld`, in the next section, you start building the Amazon interface.

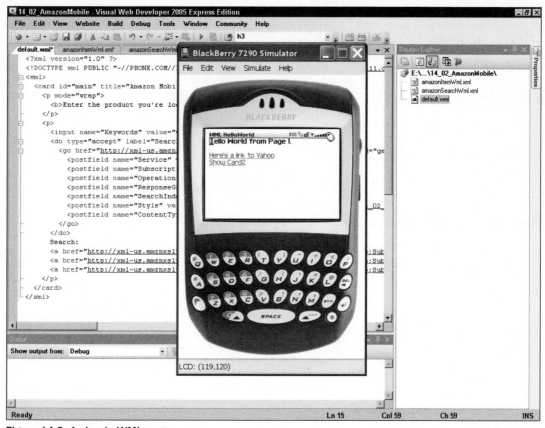

Figure 14-3: A simple WML page

Transforming Amazon Data into WML

To transform data into WML you'll again make use of Amazon's Web site to execute the transformation. Of course, you could implement the transformation in a proxy such as `getdata.aspx` developed earlier, depending on your requirements.

The cleanest solution is to provide the XSL sheet to Amazon via a publicly accessible URL. Amazon can then grab this sheet and execute the transformation.

WML has its own specific content type that you'll need to request from the Amazon server. To request a given content type in the Amazon results, you must specify the `contentType` parameter in the REST URL.

The content type for WML is `text/vnd.wap.wml`.

If you don't specify the content type, your device may not understand the response from Amazon. Even though the response is valid WML, the device may attempt to *download* the response, rather than *display* it as an actual WML page.

The Search List Detail Paradigm

The sample application implements the standard pattern of Search, List, and Detail. A user types in a search keyword on the first page, is presented a list of results, chooses an item from the results list, and is brought to the detail page for that product.

Each page requires a round-trip to the server and, consequently, is a new WML page.

Building the Search Page

The search page is a simple static WML page residing on the Web server. One important point to note is that the Web server serving this page has been configured with a specific MIME type for pages with an extension of WML.

To configure MIME types in Internet Information Services (IIS), perform the following steps:

1. Click Start → Administrative Tools and select Internet Information Server.

2. Right-click the local machine name under the root node in the console. Chose Properties from the menu.

3. Click the MIME Types button in the bottom of the Properties dialog (Figure 14-4). This launches the MIME Types window.

4. Ensure that there is an entry for file extensions of .wml. The correct content type for this extension is text/vnd.wap.wml.

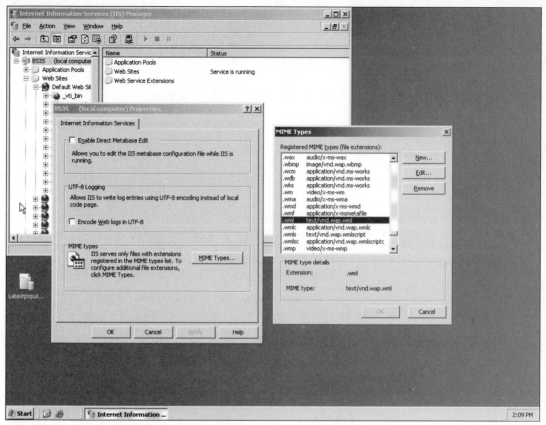

Figure 14-4: Setting the WML content type in IIS

Create a new page on your Web server and name it `default.wml`. The code for this page is shown in Listing 14-1.

Listing 14-1: The WML Home Page

```
<?xml version="1.0" ?>
<!DOCTYPE wml PUBLIC "-//PHONE.COM//DTD WML 1.1//EN"
"http://www.phone.com/dtd/wml11.dtd">
<wml>
  <card id="main" title="Amazon Mobile Search">
    <p mode="wrap">
      <b>Enter the product you're looking for and click "Search Amazon"</b>
    </p>
    <p>
      <input name="Keywords" value="Creative Zen"/><br/>
      <do type="accept" label="Search Amazon">
        <go href="http://xml-us.amznxslt.com/onca/xml?Keywords=($Keywords)"
method="get">
```

(continued)

Listing 14-1: *(continued)*

```
            <postfield name="Service" value="AWSECommerceService"/>
            <postfield name="SubscriptionId" value="[YOUR KEY HERE]"/>
            <postfield name="Operation" value="ItemSearch"/>
            <postfield name="ResponseGroup" value="Medium"/>
            <postfield name="SearchIndex" value="Blended"/>
            <postfield name="Style"
value="http://www.FrancisShanahan.com/mashups/14_02_AmazonMobile/AmazonSearchWml.xm
l" />
            <postfield name="ContentType" value="text/vnd.wap.wml" />
        </go>
    </do>
    Search:
    <a href="http://xml-
us.amznxslt.com/onca/xml?Service=AWSECommerceService&amp;SubscriptionId=[YOUR KEY
HERE]&amp;Operation=ItemSearch&amp;ResponseGroup=Medium&amp;SearchIndex=Books&amp;I
temPage=1&amp;Keywords=$(Keywords)&amp;Style=http://www.FrancisShanahan.com/mashups
/14_02_AmazonMobile/AmazonSearchWml.xml&amp;ContentType=text/vnd.wap.wml">[Books]</
a>
    <a href="http://xml-
us.amznxslt.com/onca/xml?Service=AWSECommerceService&amp;SubscriptionId=[YOUR KEY
HERE]&amp;Operation=ItemSearch&amp;ResponseGroup=Medium&amp;SearchIndex=DVD&amp;Ite
mPage=1&amp;Keywords=$(Keywords)&amp;Style=http://www.FrancisShanahan.com/mashups/1
4_02_AmazonMobile/AmazonSearchWml.xml&amp;ContentType=text/vnd.wap.wml">[DVDs]</a>
    <a href="http://xml-
us.amznxslt.com/onca/xml?Service=AWSECommerceService&amp;SubscriptionId=[YOUR KEY
HERE]&amp;Operation=ItemSearch&amp;ResponseGroup=Medium&amp;SearchIndex=Music&amp;I
temPage=1&amp;Keywords=$(Keywords)&amp;Style=http://www.FrancisShanahan.com/mashups
/14_02_AmazonMobile/AmazonSearchWml.xml&amp;ContentType=text/vnd.wap.wml">[Music]</
a>
    </p>
  </card>
</wml>
```

How It Works

The Search page accepts a single parameter, which is the keyword to search for. This is then plugged into a URL to the Amazon servers. The resulting URL looks like the following:

```
http://xml-us.amznxslt.com/onca/xml?Service=AWSECommerceService&SubscriptionId=[YOU
KEY
HERE]&Operation=ItemSearch&ResponseGroup=Medium&SearchIndex=Books&ItemPage=1&Keywor
ds=Mashups&Style=http://www.FrancisShanahan.com/mashups/14_02_AmazonMobile/AmazonSe
archWml.xml&ContentType=text/vnd.wap.wml
```

This URL is the key behind making Amazon serve WML, so the components of the URL have been described individually in the following table.

URL Component	Description
`http://xml-us.amznxslt.com/onca/xml?`	The Amazon service root URL. Everything after the question mark is part of the querystring.
`Service=AWSECommerceService`	The API in question, in this case the ECS service.
`SubscriptionId=[YOUR KEY HERE]`	Standard API parameters. Insert your own key into the `SubscriptionId`.
`Operation=ItemSearch`	It's performing a search.
`ResponseGroup=Medium`	Medium response size.
`SearchIndex=Books`	Searching books.
`ItemPage=1`	Provide the first page of results only.
`Keywords=Mashups`	The item to search for.
`Style=http://www.FrancisShanahan.com/mashups/ 14_02_AmazonMobile/ AmazonSearchWml.xml`	The XSL style sheet to use to transform the results. I have referenced my own server here, but you should set this value to the location of the file on your servers.
`ContentType=text/vnd.wap.wml`	The content type to set in the response header.

A handy tip you can use to test your application is to simply remove the `ContentType` parameter from the call. This will prompt Amazon to use the default content type in the response (which is XML). As a result, you can test the response from a standard browser.

Figure 14-5 shows the Search interface as seen from the device emulator. Notice in this screenshot that I'm using the BlackBerry 7520 emulator, as opposed to the 7290 used earlier. This is totally an arbitrary choice on my part. This XSL-driven architecture allows support for a large number of devices. If you need to customize something for a specific device, you just change the XSLT a little.

Figure 14-5: The WML home page

Building the List Page

The Search page makes a request against Amazon for search results. Amazon transforms its response into a WML listing page using the style sheet referenced in the request. In this case, it is `amazonSearchWml.xml`.

Create a new page on your Web server and name it `amazonSearchWml.xml`. Ensure that the path to this page is referenced in `default.wml` (Listing 14-2).

Listing 14-2: The WML XSLT Sheet

```
<?xml version="1.0" encoding="UTF-8"?>
<xsl:stylesheet version="1.0" xmlns:xsl="http://www.w3.org/1999/XSL/Transform"
xmlns:n="http://webservices.amazon.com/AWSECommerceService/2005-10-05" exclude-
result-prefixes="n">
  <xsl:output method="xml" omit-xml-declaration="yes"/>
  <xsl:template match="/" >
```

```
        <xsl:text disable-output-escaping="yes"><![CDATA[<!DOCTYPE wml PUBLIC "-
//WAPFORUM//DTD WML 1.1//EN"
"http://www.wapforum.org/DTD/wml_1.1.xml">]]></xsl:text>
    <wml>
      <card id="main1" title="Amazon Search Results">
        <p>
          Search Results from Amazon
        </p>
        <xsl:apply-templates select="n:ItemSearchResponse/n:Items/n:Item"/>
        <p>
          <a href="default.wml">[Go Back]</a>
        </p>
      </card>
    </wml>
  </xsl:template>


  <xsl:template match="n:ItemSearchResponse/n:Items/n:Item">
    <p>
      <a>
        <xsl:attribute name="href">
          http://xml-
us.amznxslt.com/onca/xml?Service=AWSECommerceService&amp;SubscriptionId=[YOUR KEY
HERE]&amp;Operation=ItemLookup&amp;ResponseGroup=Large&amp;ItemId=<xsl:value-of
select="n:ASIN"
/>&amp;Style=http://www.FrancisShanahan.com/mashups/14_02_AmazonMobile/AmazonItemWm
l.xml&amp;ContentType=text/vnd.wap.wml
        </xsl:attribute>
        <xsl:value-of select="n:ItemAttributes/n:Title" />
      </a><br/>
      ASIN: <xsl:value-of select="n:ASIN" />, Price $$<xsl:value-of
select="n:ItemAttributes/n:ListPrice/n:Amount div 100" />
    </p>
  </xsl:template>

</xsl:stylesheet>
```

How It Works

The listing page uses the same approach as before. It renders a list of search results. Each list item contains a URL to the detail page. This URL is again a pointer to Amazon's server. This time, the URL represents an `ItemLookup` operation and supplies a new sheet for use in transformation of the results.

When the user clicks a list item, Amazon renders a detail page for the given item. Remember to replace the path to the `AmazonItemWml.xml` file to point to your own servers.

Figure 14-6 shows the resulting listing page.

Figure 14-6: The WML listing page

The WML that is output from the transformation in Listing 14-2 begins with the typical XML tags. It also includes a new tag, which is the DOCTYPE:

```
<?xml version="1.0" encoding="UTF-8"?>
<!DOCTYPE wml PUBLIC "-//WAPFORUM//DTD WML 1.1//EN"
"http://www.wapforum.org/DTD/wml_1.1.xml">
<wml>
  <card id="main1" title="Amazon Search Results">
    <p>
      Search Results from Amazon
    </p>
    <p>
      <a href="http://xml-
us.amznxslt.com/onca/xml?Service=AWSECommerceService&amp;SubscriptionId=[YOUR KEY
HERE]&amp;Operation=ItemLookup&amp;ResponseGroup=Large&amp;ItemId=0470097779&amp;St
yle=http://www.FrancisShanahan.com/mashups/14_02_AmazonMobile/AmazonItemWml.xml&amp
;ContentType=text/vnd.wap.wml">Amazon Mashups (Wrox)</a><br/>
      ASIN: 0470097779, Price $$29.99
```

```
    </p>
    ...abridged...
    <p>
      <a href="http://xml-
us.amznxslt.com/onca/xml?Service=AWSECommerceService&amp;SubscriptionId=[YOUR KEY
HERE]&amp;Operation=ItemLookup& ItemId=B000H9I312&amp;... >Visionary Markets with
Mashup: An article from: Northwest Arkansas Business Journal</a><br/>
        ASIN: B000H9I312, Price $$3
    </p>
    <p>
      <a href="default.wml">[Go Back]</a>
    </p>
  </card>
</wml><?xml version="1.0" encoding="utf-8"?>
```

This is an abridged result, but you can clearly see the structure of the response. Each item is containined in its own <p> tag. Each item displays a link to the detail page for that item.

The detail page link itself is another call to Amazon. Notice that the detail link has been "escaped." The & signs are replaced by XML-compliant & elements. Failure to do this will result in an error during rendering.

One other item to note is the double dollar signs ($$). WML reserves the dollar symbol for use in its markup (to reference variables). To actually display a dollar sign, the sample code renders two dollar sign symbols back-to-back.

Building the Detail Page

Once a user chooses a search result from the listing page, Amazon is once again queried to provide the details for that item. This time, it uses an XSL transformation file named AmazonItemWml.xml.

Create a new page named AmazonItemWml.xml and place it on your Web server. The code for this transformation is shown in Listing 14-3.

Listing 14-3: The WML XSLT Sheet

```
<?xml version="1.0" encoding="UTF-8"?>
<xsl:stylesheet version="1.0" xmlns:xsl="http://www.w3.org/1999/XSL/Transform"
xmlns:n="http://webservices.amazon.com/AWSECommerceService/2005-10-05" exclude-
result-prefixes="n">
  <xsl:output method="xml" omit-xml-declaration="yes"/>

  <xsl:template match="/" >
    <xsl:text disable-output-escaping="yes"><![CDATA[<!DOCTYPE wml PUBLIC "-
//OPENWAVE.COM//DTD WML 1.3//EN" "http://www.openwave.com/dtd/wml13.dtd">
]]></xsl:text>
    <wml>
      <card id="main1" title="Amazon Item Details">
        <p>Amazon Item Details</p>
        <xsl:apply-templates select="n:ItemLookupResponse/n:Items/n:Item"/>
```

(continued)

Listing 14-3: *(continued)*

```
            <p>
              <a href="default.wml">[Home]</a>
            </p>
          </card>
        </wml>
      </xsl:template>

      <xsl:template match="n:Item">
        <p mode="wrap">
          <b>
            <xsl:value-of select="n:ItemAttributes/n:Title" />
          </b><br/>List Price $$<xsl:value-of
    select="n:ItemAttributes/n:ListPrice/n:Amount div 100" /><br/>
            ASIN: <xsl:value-of select="n:ASIN" /><br/>
            <xsl:apply-templates select="n:CustomerReviews/n:AverageRating"/><br/>
            <xsl:apply-templates select="n:ItemAttributes"/><br/>
        </p>
      </xsl:template>

      <xsl:template match="n:ItemAttributes">
        <xsl:apply-templates select="n:Feature"/>
        <xsl:apply-templates select="n:Director"/>
        <xsl:apply-templates select="n:Actor"/>
        <xsl:apply-templates select="n:Artist"/>
        <xsl:apply-templates select="n:Author"/>
        <xsl:apply-templates select="n:ISBN"/>
        <xsl:apply-templates select="n:PublicationDate"/>
        <xsl:apply-templates select="n:Publisher"/>
      </xsl:template>

      <xsl:template match="n:Author">
        Author: <xsl:value-of select="."/><br/>
      </xsl:template>
      <xsl:template match="n:ISBN">
        ISBN: <xsl:value-of select="."/><br/>
      </xsl:template>
      <xsl:template match="n:PublicationDate">
        Publication Date: <xsl:value-of select="."/><br/>
      </xsl:template>
      <xsl:template match="n:Publisher">
        Publisher: <xsl:value-of select="."/><br/>
      </xsl:template>
      <xsl:template match="n:Binding">
        Binding: <xsl:value-of select="."/><br/>
      </xsl:template>
      <xsl:template match="n:CustomerReviews/n:AverageRating">
        Average Rating: <xsl:value-of select="."/> out of 5<br/>
      </xsl:template>
      <xsl:template match="n:Feature">
        * <xsl:value-of select="." /><br/>
      </xsl:template>
      <xsl:template match="n:Director">
```

```
    <b>Director: </b>
    <xsl:value-of select="." />
    <br/>
  </xsl:template>
  <xsl:template match="n:Actor">
    <b>Actor: </b>
    <xsl:value-of select="." />
    <br/>
  </xsl:template>
  <xsl:template match="n:Artist">
    <b>Artist: </b>
    <xsl:value-of select="." />
    <br/>
  </xsl:template>
</xsl:stylesheet>
```

Listing 14-3 is similar to the ItemLookup transformations you have seen in the past. The primary difference is that the output is limited to XML that complies with the WML specification. The second difference is the inclusion of the WML-specific DOCTYPE element.

Figure 14-7 shows the detail page rendered into a BlackBerry emulator.

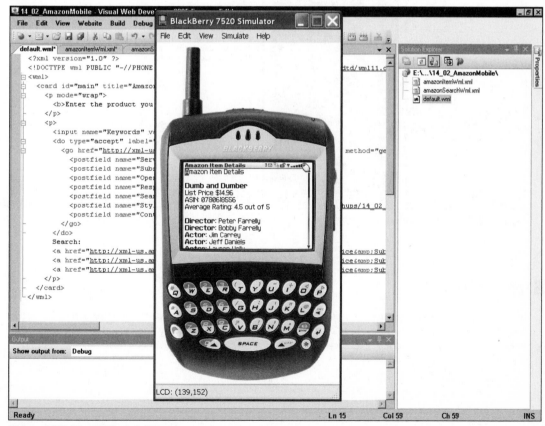

Figure 14-7: The WML detail page

Additional Ideas

As stated earlier, the WML interface is accessible from a variety of devices. By keeping the form design simple, the features set is reusable across physical devices with varying capabilities. For example, Figure 14-8 shows the sample application executing in a cell phone emulator.

Figure 14-8: The application executing in a cell phone emulator

Summary

In this chapter, you've seen an alternative access method for Amazon's data. Of course, the techniques implemented herein are applicable to other data sources, not necessarily Amazon. I am surprised that Amazon has not provided a WML-accessible site implementation as of this writing.

Specifically, this chapter showed the following:

- ❏ How to serve WML from a standard Web server
- ❏ How to create WML dynamically using Amazon's own servers
- ❏ How to develop solutions for hardware devices that you don't necessarily possess

Chapter 15 discusses one more sample based on Amazon's Simple Storage Service. Before continuing on, I recommend reviewing the following questions to test your knowledge of this chapters' content.

Exercises

1. What is WAP and what role does it play in WML access?
2. Why can't you just implement an HTML page and access it from a cell phone?
3. What approach could you take to provide WML access to a site that doesn't provide the transformation capabilities that Amazon offers?
4. What's the WML equivalent of an HTML page?
5. How can you support multiple devices using a single presentation approach?
6. The dollar sign is a reserved character in WML. How can you display dollar amounts?

A Generic Storage Solution Using Amazon S3

Imagine that you are an entrepreneur in the early days of 2000. You've just finished writing up your latest business model on the back of a napkin at a local restaurant. The plan calls for a photo-oriented Web site that allows users to upload their precious family photos to your servers for a small fee.

Of course, before you go live you'll need to create a capacity plan with the expected usage volumes, and then map that to your year-over-year projected growth. You'll then need to procure hardware and rack space from your favorite hardware vendor. With that complete, you'll commence setup of the environment and build out of the hardware cage. Don't forget to include provision for a disaster-recovery site, and the business contingency volumes that may never be used.

This is the approach many companies took in the Internet hey-day. I know, because I architected and facilitated many such ventures. Countless multimillion dollar environments were procured and set up, only to have the underlying business model prove shaky. The problem was that the barrier to entry was so high, only the luckiest companies actually got the venture capital required to procure the necessary infrastructure and begin building out their dreams.

Amazon has changed all of that with the launch of its pay-as-you go Simple Storage Service (S3). The Amazon S3 is a storage service that allows anyone to purchase industrial-quality storage space on an as-needed basis. You pay only for what you use.

This has major repercussions in terms of the business plans that it enables. A student working out of a dorm room can build a professional-quality photo storage site without requiring millions of dollars from venture capitalists up front. Budding media entrepreneurs can share content without a highly available redundant disaster-recovery site. The possibilities are endless.

In this chapter, you build a simple generic Web site that utilizes the Amazon S3 to securely store any type of file you see fit. The resultant application can be used as a basis on which to build your empire or at least store your business plan on something better than a napkin.

Specifically, this chapter shows the following:

❑ How the S3 service is organized

❑ How to authenticate securely against Amazon's S3 platform

❑ How to upload and store files and media to the S3 servers

❑ How to display what is stored in your S3 space and how to access that content

❑ How to delete items from S3

❑ How to access S3 billing information

The Battle Plan: Generic Online Storage Using S3 and SOAP

This chapter uses the Amazon S3 to store files on the Internet. You don't really know where or how these files are stored, only that they are stored securely and without fear of being lost.

Understanding the Architecture

The sample application uses SOAP over HTTP to communicate with the S3 service. The architecture of the sample application is depicted in Figure 15-1.

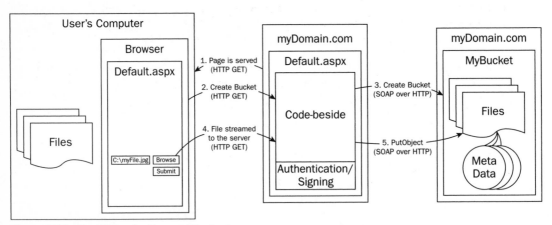

Figure 15-1: The S3 application architecture

How It Works

1. The default.aspx page is presented to the user. It contains a form with a number of pieces of functionality.

2. The user creates a bucket using the first set of controls on the sample page. This bucket can be used to store objects also known as files.

3. The user's request is forwarded onto the Amazon S3 server as a SOAP request. A bucket is created on Amazon.

4. The user locates a file on a local computer and clicks Submit. The file is converted into a stream and uploaded to the sample application's Web server.

5. The Web server then takes this stream and passes it on to the Amazon S3 server using SOAP over HTTP. The Amazon S3 server stores this stream as a file in its secure storage. The file is now associated with the bucket created in Step 1.

With this sample application the user can also delete a file or the bucket, list available buckets, or list the contents of a particular bucket.

Figure 15-2 displays the completed application. As you can see, this is a generic utility-type application. The code is written in such a way as to clearly articulate the steps involved. Feel free to take this code and build your own applications on top of it.

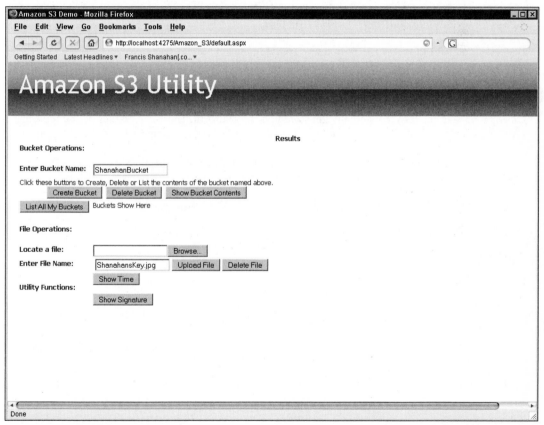

Figure 15-2: The finished application

The next section describes S3 in terms of registration requirements and key concepts.

Registering for S3 Access

Because S3 is a pay-per-use service, you will need to sign up for explicit access to the service to use it. If you are already an Amazon customer, you can use your billing and credit card information that Amazon already has. This makes signup literally a 1-minute procedure.

You will only be billed based on the storage space you use and the duration for which you use it. As someone who does this for a living, I can tell you that Amazon's rates are highly competitive, and will beat any dedicated hardware provider's estimates by a number of orders of magnitude.

Key Concepts

Amazon S3 uses a number of key concepts to organize data storage on its servers.

Buckets

Every object stored on S3 is placed in a bucket. A *bucket* is simply a way to group objects together and aggregate them for the purposes of usage tracking.

Bucket names have global scope. So, if a user creates a bucket named `"mybucket"`, no one else can create a bucket of the same name.

Objects

Objects represent the files that actually get stored on the platform. These can be files of any type, and are typically associated with a set of metadata. The object consists of the metadata and the file itself.

Objects can be created or deleted, and associated with a defined set of permissions. Only users or groups with the appropriate level of permissions can access a given object.

Every object in S3 is assigned a *key*, which is analogous to a filename, and is what uniquely identifies the object within your bucket.

Try It Out   **Setting Up the Project**

To build the generic S3 application, follow these steps:

1. Create a new project and add a class to the project named `S3Helper.cs`. This class should reside in the `App_Code` directory.

2. Add a function to this class named `GetTimeStamp`. This function will be implemented in the next section.

3. Add a Web reference to the S3 SOAP service. The WSDL endpoint for the service is located here:

    `http://s3.amazonaws.com/doc/2006-03-01/AmazonS3.wsdl`

4. Create a page named `default.aspx` and design it to look like Figure 15-3. The remainder of this chapter walks you through the specifics of each page element.

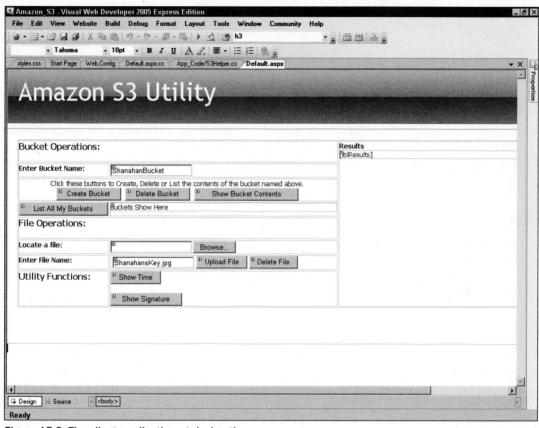

Figure 15-3: The client application at design time

Required Parameters

To make any call to the S3, you must supply a number of standard items:

1. The first is your `AWSAccessKeyId`. This is assigned when you register as a developer with the Amazon AWS service.

2. The second item is the current timestamp in Greenwich Mean Time (GMT). If the time you specify varies from the time on the Amazon servers by more than 15 minutes, the operation will be declined. This is for security reasons to ensure no one intercepts your request and attempts to replay it later.

3. The third item you need to specify is probably the most interesting. This is a string that acts as a signature. The *signature* is the cryptographic hash of a piece of data comprising the operation you are calling, a special *secret key,* and the timestamp sent as item 2.

These are standard items that are included in every call. The secret key is similar to the `AWSAccessKeyId` and is provided when you explicitly sign up for S3 access.

You must never disclose the secret key to anyone. Amazon will never ask for it, so if you are asked to disclose it, you know the requester is a fraud.

Authenticating with S3

The folks at Amazon have really done their homework when it comes to authentication. The Amazon S3 authenticates each and every method call. There is no notion of a session when working with S3. As a result, every call requires a set of parameters to be included, regardless of any other required information for the API.

The TimeStamp

There are two main instances when a timestamp is required:

❑ The first is for inclusion in a typical method call, in which case, the timestamp is included as a `DateTime` object.

❑ The second is in calculating the signature digest.

To create a valid `TimeStamp` value as a `DateTime` object, you must convert the current time to Universal Coordinated Time (UTC), also known as Greenwich Mean Time. The next section shows you how to do this.

Calculating the TimeStamp

To calculate a timestamp for use in an S3 call, the first step is to obtain the current time. This is then used in subsequent calls. It's important to store this value because time marches on, and you will not be able to recalculate a timestamp if you throw away the one you are working with.

I have provided a static helper class named `S3Helper` in the sample code that returns the correctly formatted timestamp. The code looks like this:

```
/// <summary>
/// Returns a new DateTime object set to the provided time
/// but with precision limited to milliseconds.
/// </summary>
/// <param name="myTime"></param>
/// <returns></returns>
public static DateTime GetTimeStamp(DateTime myTime)
{
    DateTime myUniversalTime = myTime.ToUniversalTime();
    DateTime myNewTime = new DateTime(myUniversalTime.Year,
            myUniversalTime.Month, myUniversalTime.Day,
            myUniversalTime.Hour, myUniversalTime.Minute,
            myUniversalTime.Second, myUniversalTime.Millisecond);

    return myNewTime;
}
```

This code accepts a `DateTime` as a parameter. This is the timestamp. That timestamp value is then converted into UTC, which is effectively mapped against GMT.

The precision of the `DateTime` is limited to milliseconds to conform to the expected format. Too much precision will break the Amazon API.

The second time helper function formats the same `TimeStamp` value as a string. This is used later in computing the message signature. The code looks like this:

```
/// <summary>
/// Formats the provided time as a string limited to millisecond precision
/// </summary>
/// <param name="myTime"></param>
/// <returns></returns>
public static string FormatTimeStamp(DateTime myTime)
{
    DateTime myUniversalTime = myTime.ToUniversalTime();
    return myUniversalTime.ToString("yyyy-MM-dd\\THH:mm:ss.fff\\Z",
System.Globalization.CultureInfo.InvariantCulture);
}
```

You should add both of these functions to the `S3Helper` class.

Calculating the Signature

The signature is the third component in the Amazon authentication scheme. The signature proves knowledge of the user's secret key (not the `AWSAccessKeyId`). This is a special key that is known only to the registered developer and should never be disclosed to anyone. By creating a digest with this key as input, Amazon can verify that the operation request came from a valid source, and has not been tampered with.

What Is a Digest?

A *digest* (or *message digest*) is a string value produced by applying a mathematical algorithm to a piece of content. The algorithm is such that if even a single character in the content is modified or changed, the resulting digest value will be affected, yielding a brand new digest value. A message digest is sometimes known as a *hash value*.

There are many algorithms available to calculate message digests. Amazon uses the HMACSHA1 algorithm, which is implemented in .NET using the `System.Security.Cryptography` namespace.

Add a `using` statement to your code in `S3Helper.cs` as follows:

```
using System.Security.Cryptography;
```

Amazon expects the digest to be created based on a concatenated string of the following data elements:

❑ The string `"AmazonS3"`

❑ The operation you are invoking (for example, "`PutObjectInline`")

❑ The string representation of the `TimeStamp` included in the call

HMACSHA1 constructs a *hash-based message authentication code* (HMAC) using a piece of data and a key input. The algorithm mixes the key with the data. It then applies a hash function to obtain a digest. The result is mixed with the key input again, and the result is hashed one more time. The result is a secure hash code that can be used to determine whether the data has been tampered with during transport.

Add the following code, which creates an HMACSHA1 hash or digest of the given data elements:

```
public static string GetSignature(string mySecretAccessKeyId, string strOperation,
DateTime myTime)
    {
        Encoding myEncoding = new UTF8Encoding();

        // Create the source string which is used to create the digest
        string mySource = "AmazonS3" + strOperation + FormatTimeStamp(myTime);

        // Create a new Cryptography class using the
        // Secret Access Key as the key
        HMACSHA1 myCrypto = new HMACSHA1(myEncoding.GetBytes(mySecretAccessKeyId));

        // Convert the source string to an array of bytes
        char[] mySourceArray = mySource.ToCharArray();

        // Convert the source to a UTF8 encoded array of bytes
        byte[] myUTF8Bytes = myEncoding.GetBytes(mySourceArray);

        // Calculate the digest
        byte[] strDigest = myCrypto.ComputeHash(myUTF8Bytes);

        return Convert.ToBase64String(strDigest);
    }
```

Now, you have generic `Signature` and `TimeStamp` functions that can be used with all the subsequent S3 operations.

Working with Buckets

As you would expect, buckets support a number of operations such as Create, Delete, and so on. This next section describes these operations and how to invoke them.

Creating a Bucket

The `CreateBucket` operation, as the name implies, creates a new bucket of a specific name.

The key takeaway when talking about buckets is that bucket names are not scoped per user. If I create a bucket named `MyBucket`, other users will not be able to create a bucket of the same name.

If a user named Fred has created a bucket named `MyBucket`, then any subsequent calls to `CreateBucket` by Fred using `MyBucket` as the bucket name will be successful. However, all other users will experience an error that says, "Bucket name already exists."

If successful, the `CreateBucket` operation returns null.

Adding a Bucket

To create a bucket using the Amazon S3 SOAP API, follow these steps:

1. Add a new textbox to `default.aspx` named `txtBucketName`.

2. Add a new button named `cmdCreateBucket`. Add the following code to its click event:

```
protected void cmdCreateBucket_Click(object sender, EventArgs e)
    {
        AmazonS3 myS3 = new AmazonS3();
        DateTime myTime = DateTime.Now;
        try
        {
            CreateBucketResult myCreateResult =
myS3.CreateBucket(txtBucketName.Text, null,
                myAWSAccessKeyId,
                S3Helper.GetTimeStamp(myTime),
                true,
                S3Helper.GetSignature(mySecretAccessKeyId, "CreateBucket",
myTime));

            MyPrint("Bucket successfully created.");
        }
        catch (Exception ex)
        {
            MyPrint("CreateBucket Error: " + ex.Message);
        }
    }
```

Creating a bucket is easy, but the returned information does little to indicate that anything has actually happened. You will want to quickly move on to the next section, which shows you how to display your list of buckets.

Listing Your Buckets

Once you have created some buckets, the next step will be to list them. Add the following code to the event handler for a new button named `cmdListBuckets`:

```
protected void cmdListBuckets_Click(object sender, EventArgs e)
    {
        AmazonS3 myS3 = new AmazonS3();
        DateTime myTime = DateTime.Now;

        /// Lists all buckets under this user
        ListAllMyBucketsResult myBuckets = myS3.ListAllMyBuckets(myAWSAccessKeyId,
            S3Helper.GetTimeStamp(myTime),
            true,
            S3Helper.GetSignature(mySecretAccessKeyId, "ListAllMyBuckets",
myTime));
```

```
lblBuckets.Text = "<b>My Buckets</b><br/>";
foreach (ListAllMyBucketsEntry b in myBuckets.Buckets)
{
    lblBuckets.Text += (b.Name + ", created " + b.CreationDate + "<br/>");
}
}
```

This code invokes `ListAllMyBuckets` and iterates through the results. Each result is returned as a `ListAllMyBucketsEntry`.

Now, you can create and list your buckets. The next step is to be able to delete the buckets associated with your account.

Deleting a Bucket

The `DeleteBucket` operation deletes a bucket. You can only delete your own buckets, and each bucket must be empty in order to delete it. That means you have to first delete all the files within a bucket before it can be removed.

`DeleteBucket` expects to be passed the name of the bucket to be deleted. Here's the code that goes in the Delete button's event handler:

```
protected void cmdDeleteBucket_Click(object sender, EventArgs e)
{
    AmazonS3 myS3 = new AmazonS3();
    DateTime myTime = DateTime.Now;
    try
    {
        Status myDeleteResult = myS3.DeleteBucket(txtBucketName.Text,
                myAWSAccessKeyId,
                S3Helper.GetTimeStamp(myTime),
                true,
                S3Helper.GetSignature(mySecretAccessKeyId,
                        "DeleteBucket", myTime),
                        null);

        MyPrint("Bucket successfully deleted.");
    }
    catch (Exception ex)
    {
        MyPrint("DeleteBucket Error: " + ex.Message);
    }
}
```

This code simply deletes whatever bucket is named in `txtBucketName`. You can modify this as you see fit (for example, to delete a given bucket returned by `ListAllMyBuckets`).

Deleting buckets is final, and, once they are gone, they are gone. There is no un-delete operation. Of course, you can re-create a bucket of the same name, if needed.

Uploading Objects

With the basic bucket housekeeping implemented, it's time to finally upload some files. The sample application uses an ASP.NET `FileUpload` control to obtain the file from the browser.

Add a `FileUpload` control to the page and name it `myFileUpload`:

```
<asp:FileUpload ID="myFileUpload" runat="server" />
```

Add a new button named `cmdSubmit`. This will handle the actual file upload to your Web server. Listing 15-1 shows the code for the event handler of the Submit button.

Listing 15-1: Uploading a File to the S3

```
protected void cmdSubmit_Click(object sender, EventArgs e)
    {
        if (myFileUpload.HasFile)
        {
            MyPrint("Server received " + myFileUpload.FileName);
            MyPrint("Attempting to save to S3");

            AmazonS3 myS3 = new AmazonS3();
            DateTime myTime = DateTime.Now;

            // Create a signature for this operation
            string strMySignature = S3Helper.GetSignature(
                mySecretAccessKeyId,
                "PutObjectInline",
                myTime);

            // Create a new Access grant for anonymous users.
            Grant myGrant = new Grant();
            Grant[] myGrants = new Grant[1];

            // Setup Access control, allow Read access to all
            Group myGroup = new Group();
            myGroup.URI = "http://acs.amazonaws.com/groups/global/AllUsers";
            myGrant.Grantee = myGroup;
            myGrant.Permission = Permission.READ;
            myGrants[0] = myGrant;

            // Setup some metadata to indicate the content type
            MetadataEntry myContentType = new MetadataEntry();
            myContentType.Name = "ContentType";
            myContentType.Value = myFileUpload.PostedFile.ContentType;

            MetadataEntry[] myMetaData = new MetadataEntry[1];
            myMetaData[0] = myContentType;

            // Finally upload the object
            PutObjectResult myResult = myS3.PutObjectInline(
                txtBucketName.Text,
                txtKey.Text,
```

(continued)

Listing 15-1: *(continued)*

```
                    myMetaData,
                    myFileUpload.FileBytes,
                    myFileUpload.FileBytes.Length,
                    myGrants,
                    StorageClass.STANDARD,
                    true,
                    myAWSAccessKeyId,
                    S3Helper.GetTimeStamp(myTime),
                    true,
                    strMySignature, null
                    );

            // Print out the results.
            if (myResult != null) MyPrint("ETag: " + myResult.ETag);
        }
    }
```

I am specifying the content type using a MetaData *entry. This allows me to store the file, which is essentially a stream of bytes, along with the actual MIME content type that those bytes represent.*

When you upload a file, you assign it a key name. This is analagous to a filename. If a file exists with a given key name, that file will be overwritten.

A successful file upload returns an eTag for the file. The eTag is a hash on the content of the file received by Amazon. The hashing algorithm used is Message Digest 5 (MD5).

For an added level of assurance, you can compute your own hash of the file content and compare it against the eTag. If the hash values match (as they should), you can be assured the file content was not tampered with or corrupted during transmission.

If the hash values don't match, it implies that something happened during transmission. You can conclude that the file was not accurately stored and should be re-transmitted.

Permissions

Every object or bucket stored on the S3 servers needs a set of grants or permissions. Only users with the required privileges can access a given bucket or object.

The sample code illustrates how to assign permissions on an object, but the process is similar for buckets. To create permissions on an object, you start by creating a new S3 Grant object:

```
// Create a new Access grant for anonymous users.
Grant myGrant = new Grant();
Grant[] myGrants = new Grant[1];
```

Next, specify the properties of the Grant object. A grant can apply to a group of users or an individual user. In this example, you want the grant to apply to all anonymous users, so you must create a new Group:

```
// Setup Access control, allow Read access to all
Group myGroup = new Group();
myGroup.URI = "http://acs.amazonaws.com/groups/global/AllUsers";
```

Then, assign this group to the `Grant`:

```
myGrant.Grantee = myGroup;
```

Next, specify the level of permission (in this case READ access):

```
myGrant.Permission = Permission.READ;
```

Finally, assign this `Grant` to the `Grants` array:

```
myGrants[0] = myGrant;
```

The `Grants` array is supplied to the `PutObjectInline` call and the `Grants` contained therein are assigned to the objects uploaded in the method call.

This example uses a group but you can also tie permissions to an individual user. By specifiying the user's Amazon email address, only that user will be granted the associated permissions.

Amazon S3 uses a set of predefined groups for grants. The following URL refers to the set of All Users, including anonymous users:

```
http://acs.amazonaws.com/groups/global/AllUsers
```

You must use only the predefined groups at this time and cannot currently define your own groups. The following table lists the predefined groups available.

Group URL	Description
http://acs/amazonaws.com/ groups/gobal/allUSers	All users, whether authenticated or otherwise.
http://acs/amazonaws.com/ groups/gobal/allUSers	Only users who have registered and authenticated with the S3 service will be part of this group.

By assigning the READ permission to non-authenticated users, any files uploaded will be available at the following URL:

```
https://s3.amazonaws.com/<Bucket Name>/<Key Name>
```

Listing a Bucket's Contents

With a file uploaded the next thing you'll want to do is list the contents of a bucket to ensure that files got uploaded OK:

```
protected void cmdShowContents_Click(object sender, EventArgs e)
{
    AmazonS3 myS3 = new AmazonS3();
    DateTime myTime = DateTime.Now;
    string strMySignature = S3Helper.GetSignature(
        mySecretAccessKeyId,
        "ListBucket",
        myTime);

    ListBucketResult myResults = myS3.ListBucket(
        this.txtBucketName.Text,
        "",
        "",
        0,
        false,
        "|",
        myAWSAccessKeyId,
        S3Helper.GetTimeStamp(myTime),
        true,
        strMySignature,
        null);

    // Iterate through the bucket contents
    if (myResults.Contents != null)
    {
        lblResults.Text = "<table>";
        foreach (ListEntry myEntry in myResults.Contents)
        {
            lblResults.Text += "<tr><td>";
            lblResults.Text += "<img src=https://s3.amazonaws.com/"+
txtBucketName.Text +"/" + myEntry.Key + " width=100px><br/>";
            lblResults.Text += "<a href=https://s3.amazonaws.com/"+
txtBucketName.Text +"/" + myEntry.Key + " target=_blank>" + myEntry.Key + "</a>";
            lblResults.Text += "</td></tr>";
        }
        lblResults.Text += "</table>";
    }
    else
    {
        MyPrint("Bucket is Empty");
    }
}
```

In this sample code, the results are iterated through, and a link to each item is provided. Because I assume the content is an image, I build an image tag referencing each bucket item. Figure 15-4 displays the output.

Deleting Objects

To delete a file, you need to specify the bucket in which that object resides, along with the name of the object to delete. This information is supplied along with the standard S3 required parameters.

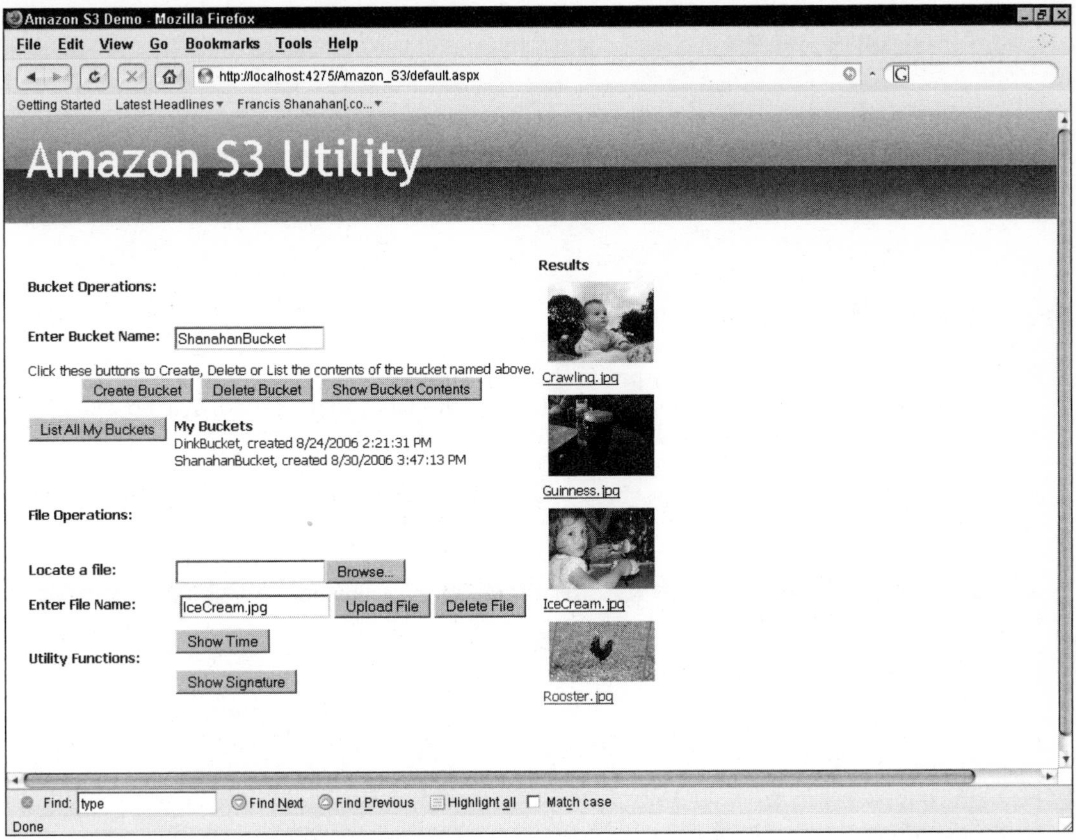

Figure 15-4: Listing the contents of a bucket

The following listing shows the code for the `DeleteFile` button:

```csharp
protected void cmdDeleteFile_Click(object sender, EventArgs e)
    {
        AmazonS3 myS3 = new AmazonS3();
        DateTime myTime = DateTime.Now;
        string strMySignature = S3Helper.GetSignature(
            mySecretAccessKeyId,
            "DeleteObject",
            myTime);

        Status myResults = myS3.DeleteObject(
            this.txtBucketName.Text,
            this.txtKey.Text,
            myAWSAccessKeyId,
            S3Helper.GetTimeStamp(myTime),
            true,
            strMySignature,
            null);
```

```
        MyPrint("Delete successful: " + myResults.Code + ", " +
myResults.Description);

    }
```

The Delete operation is unforgiving. Once a file is deleted, it cannot be un-deleted. The operation will not prompt you with an "Are You Sure?". I personally prefer this approach, but use with caution, because once an item is deleted from storage, it is not retrievable.

Tracking Usage

S3 is a pay-per-usage service. You only pay for what you use. To help figure out your bill, Amazon provides comprehensive usage reports that tell you how much space you have used, over how much time, and also how much network bandwidth you have consumed.

All of these items factor into the charges incurred. To view your usage reports, log in to the Amazon Web Service portal at aws.amazon.com and click "Usage Report" (Figure 15-5).

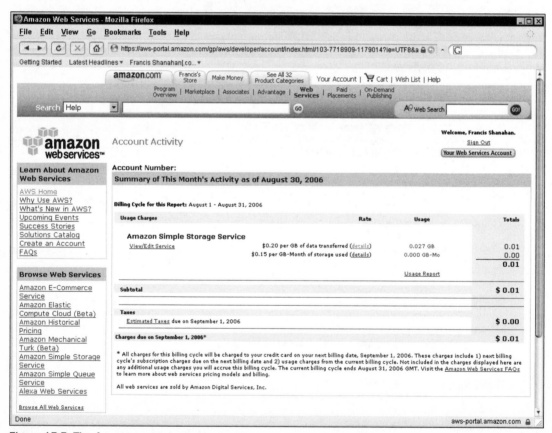

Figure 15-5: The Amazon usage reports

As of this writing, there is no way to obtain either billing or usage information via Web services. Developers have also asked for a way to cap the amount they are billed each month. Both of these features are under consideration for a future release.

Additional Ideas

S3 is just one of a suite of evolutionary services that Amazon is now offering. Among others are the Mechanical Turk and, most recently, the Elastic Computing Cloud environment.

The Mechanical Turk

The Mechanical Turk allows developers to submit tasks for completion using human intervention. These tasks might be trivial for a human to complete, but complex to automate. Amazon has taken the unique approach of providing a technology platform on top of a human work force. Jobs are submitted with an associated payment amount. Workers then complete these jobs and collect the payments.

Following are some examples:

- ❑ Determine whether a picture is of a girl or a boy.
- ❑ Type in the license plate number from this photo.
- ❑ Draw a picture of a cat.

As you can see, these tasks are trivial for humans, but require significant effort to automate.

The Mechanical Turk uses a similar authentication scheme to S3 to validate operations. The code supplied herein can easily be re-purposed for use with these platforms, should you so desire.

The Elastic Computing Cloud

The Elastic Computing Cloud (EC2) offers a pay-per-use computing platform through which you can submit an arbitrary application that will execute using Amazon CPU resources.

If your business plan calls for a scalable computing infrastructure, then you now have an option of starting small and growing the business over time, rather than investing in "big iron" on day one.

To use the EC2 requires that you create a machine image, including the operating system and any files or executables required by your application. EC2 uses S3 to store these machine images. The sample code could be used to manage such storage.

Summary

Amazon is branching out from the traditional Internet retailer business model. S3, along with Mechanical Turk and EC2, are evolutionary platforms that enable an entirely different approach to business development.

In this chapter you have done the following:

❑ Implemented HMACSHA1 message signing

❑ Built a generic S3 application

❑ Created a utility class that can be reused with other Amazon services (such as the Mechanical Turk or EC2)

The sample code with this chapter can easily be enhanced to support a wide range of storage scenarios, including file sharing, large email attachment storage, collaborative editing, and so on.

This chapter's application is the last sample application included with this book. I hope you have found the samples to be clearly written, easy to understand, and simple to implement.

Chapter 16 highlights some real-world applications built using the techniques already mentioned. Before going on, I recommend reviewing the following exercises.

Exercises

1. What is the S3 and what is its purpose?
2. What is SHA1?
3. What types of files can be stored on the S3 platform?
4. Is billing or usage information available via the S3 Web services themselves?
5. What are the pros and cons of a service like S3?

Further Ideas

This book has documented a lot of techniques and sample code to get you started along the path of mashup development. It would not be fitting to simply leave it at that, however. This chapter highlights some additional applications that have been developed using the techniques in this book. In this chapter, you learn further ideas that you might consider applying to your own specific development scenarios.

You're not going to build these applications in this chapter, because that would be redundant. Rather, I'll explain how the applications work, how they are structured, and how they were built. From there, you can take this information to build your own new creations.

TagLines

TagLines is an experiment in automatic tagging using news feeds in the form of RSS. Figure 16-1 shows TagLines in action. TagLines stores a repository of RSS feeds that it periodically analyzes for new content. The goal is to provide a visualization on the current news headlines, similar to a heatmap.

Hot topics are shown in larger font, and less-mentioned items appear smaller. By glancing at the TagLines visualization, you can get a feel for what people are talking about in their blogs and feeds. Larger items are being mentioned more (and perhaps are more important) than lesser-mentioned items.

Figure 16-1: TagLines displaying a group of tags

Understanding the Architecture

TagLines uses Ajax and a number of other tools to provide its functionality. The architecture of the application is displayed in Figure 16-2.

TagLines uses the Yahoo Content Term Extraction API to extract keywords from a piece of content. These keywords then become tags associated with that particular news item.

The Yahoo Term Extraction API

The Yahoo Term Extraction API accepts a blob of content as input and returns a set of tags or keywords in the form of XML. The tags returned are based on Yahoo's database and contextually related, and, hence, are very useful in terms of understanding the nature of a piece of content.

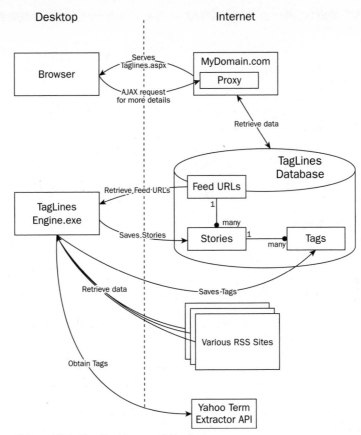

Figure 16-2: The TagLines architecture

Here's an example piece of content:

"Italian sculptors and painters of the renaissance favored the Virgin Mary for inspiration."

And here's the response obtained from the Yahoo API:

```
<?xml version="1.0" ?>
    <ResultSet xmlns:xsi="http://www.w3.org/2001/XMLSchema-instance"
xmlns="urn:yahoo:cate" xsi:schemaLocation="urn:yahoo:cate
http://api.search.yahoo.com/ContentAnalysisService/V1/TermExtractionResponse.xsd">
        <Result>italian sculptors</Result>
        <Result>virgin mary</Result>
        <Result>painters</Result>
        <Result>renaissance</Result>
        <Result>inspiration</Result>
    </ResultSet>
```

Relevant tags for this piece of content include italian sculptors, virgin mary, painters, renaissance, and inspiration.

How It Works

TagLines works like this:

1. A user can submit a feed for tagging. That feed URL gets stored in the TagLines database. TagLines uses a SQL Server database for storage.

2. Every so often the TagLines feed engine wakes up and begins polling for new content. The feed engine is written as a Windows forms application that I run on my desktop machine.

3. To poll for new content, the feed engine first retrieves a list of all the feed URLs in the TagLines database.

4. The feed engine then iterates through the list of feeds and issues an HTTP GET request for each one.

5. The result of each HTTP GET is a valid RSS document. Each RSS document contains news items.

6. Each news item includes a title, date, and description. This information is also stored in the TagLines database for convenience.

At this point, the content has been retrieved. The next step in the process is to tag this content. You could do this manually, but who has time to read every news story and tag it according to its content?

One of the goals in building TagLines was to understand whether content could be easily tagged in an automated fashion. For this, I chose to use the Yahoo Content Term Extraction API.

1. The Yahoo Term Extraction API is used to obtain a list of keywords based on the story description from the RSS feed.

2. This list of words or tags is then parsed out and each one in turn is stored in the TagLines database.

3. At this point, you have a database storing a set of feed URLs, the latest content at these URLs, and the associated keywords or tags for each story.

4. All of the processing thus far has taken place offline in the TagLines feed engine.

5. The final step is to build the content visualization on top of the data. With a sufficient number of stories indexed by the system, certain tags are likely to appear more than once. If there are a lot of news stories pertaining to the release of the latest iPod, for example, then the tag apple is likely to be present in the TagLines database many times.

6. The visualization retrieves the latest set of tags (usually around 1,000 or so) and counts the number of times each distinct tag appears in the database.

7. The presentation of each tag is based on how often the tag appears and in which categories. More-often-counted tags appear larger than others. Lesser counted ones appear smaller. The tags are displayed to the visitor, and each one can be clicked to retrieve further information. I've done this using XmlHttpRequest, SOAP, REST, and Yahoo Web Services.

Additional Enhancements

When TagLines was originally created, there were already a few Tag visualizations in existence. TagLines took the notion of Tag visualization a step further by Ajax-enabling each tag. By clicking a tag, the user can load related content (such as movies, photos, or RSS headlines) from sites such as Flickr and Yahoo (Figure 16-3).

Figure 16-3: TagLines displaying related content for a given tag

You can experiment with TagLines at the following URL:

```
http://www.FrancisShanahan.com/taglines
```

Zollage

I find recursion interesting and how it applies to real-life even more so. What would it feel like if you were somehow depicted by the images that make up your interests in life? If you could see yourself drawn out of images related to your favorite things in life, what would it look like?

Zollage is an application that takes that idea and combines it with the Amazon Web Services, XML/XSLT, SOAP, JavaScript, Ajax, c#.NET, Windows forms, SQL Server, and, lastly, GDI+. The result is an interactive collage made up of images of Amazon products. I call it Zollage!

Zollage is a series of smaller applications that, combined together, allow you to create pictures based on source images. Each picture is made up of tiny product images. The tiny pictures are clickable, so you can click each image and then be shown a view of the enlarged product. You can even read customer reviews of that product without a page refresh.

The Zollage shown in Figure 16-4 shows a picture of me. I'm drawn using images of thousands of Amazon products. The products are each related to my own personal interests, science and music.

Figure 16-4: Francis Shanahan as a Zollage

Understanding the Architecture

Just as with TagLines, there are a number of offline steps involved in the creation of a Zollage. The main components of the solution are shown in Figure 16-5.

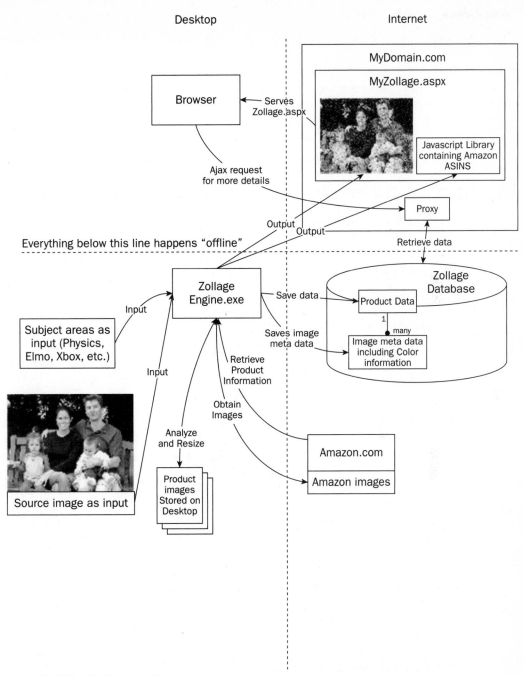

Figure 16-5: The Zollage architecture

How It Works

Creating a Zollage takes a few hours, but the entire process has been automated. Here's how it works:

1. Collect images.

   a. The process starts with the Zollage engine. This utility accepts a series of keywords and conducts a series of searches against Amazon's database for each keyword.

   b. Each search execution returns a set of results. These results are parsed and stored locally in a SQL Server database.

   c. The next step is to download the product images associated with each product. These are also stored locally on the file system.

2. Analyze the images.

   a. With a few hundred images available, the next step is to evaluate these images in terms of the overall average color content.

   b. Each image is examined in turn. The first step is to resize the images from their full size to a reduced size, suitable for using in the collage.

   c. Once the image is resized, it is examined for color content. Every pixel is examined for its red, green, and blue content. An entirely red pixel, for example, will have a red component of 100 percent and a green and blue of 0 percent.

   d. The overall image's red, green, and blue content is obtained by averaging out the aggregated values of every pixel. This information is then persisted to the Zollage database, along with a reference to the image it pertains to.

3. Create the Zollage image.

   a. The Zollage engine accepts a source image as input. This is typically a smaller image of 75×60 pixels or similar.

   b. Each pixel in the source image is examined and its red, green, blue (R, G, B) content is matched to a value in the Zollage database. The best-matching thumbnail image is selected and placed in the target image. In this manner, each thumbnail product becomes a tile in the target collage.

   c. Along with the Zollage image, a second file is simultaneously created. This file is a text file containing a JavaScript array. This is key in the creation of the interactive portion of the application.

   d. The JavaScript array is a collection of Amazon ASINs. Remember that the ASIN is Amazon's unique identifier for each of its products. The first entry in the array refers to the top-left tile (the first tile) in the Zollage image. The second ASIN in the array refers to the next tile over, and so on. The ASIN is all that is required to look up this tile's product on Amazon.

4. Publish the Zollage. With the Zollage image and JavaScript array created, the final step is to push it to the web server.

   a. Both the image and JavaScript file are posted to the Web server via FTP.

   b. These files are hosted within an HTML template. This template employs a generic Ajax library similar to the one provided in Chapter 10.

c. The mouseclick on the Zollage image is handled by the generic JavaScript library. When you click a pixel in the image, the JavaScript determines which pixel was clicked and resolves this to an entry in the ASIN array.

d. The ASIN is then used as an argument for an Ajax-powered ItemLookup request to Amazon.

e. Amazon responds with the product details, which are displayed in a <div> tag right where the user clicked (Figure 16-6). In this manner, each Zollage is more than just a static collage image. They are interactive art in a sense. It's not exactly Andy Warhol, but close enough.

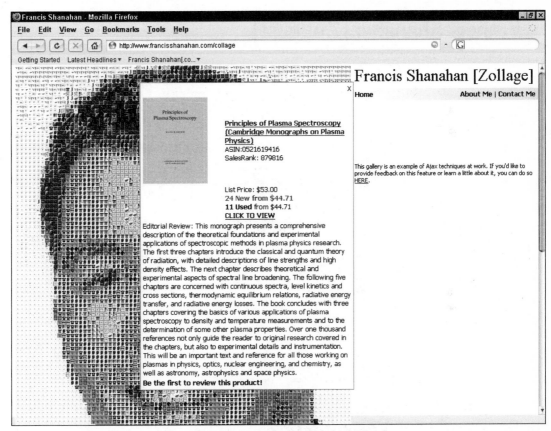

Figure 16-6: Zollage displaying Francis Shanahan drawn using physics books

The architectural implications of Zollage are the ability to represent a huge amount of data in the browser without the huge data payload or the heavy client-side applet traditionally associated with such functionality.

Amazon Zuggest

Amazon Zuggest is a search interface into Amazon. The application is essentially a remix using SOAP, but with a number of enhancements.

Figure 16-7 shows the user interface from Amazon Zuggest.

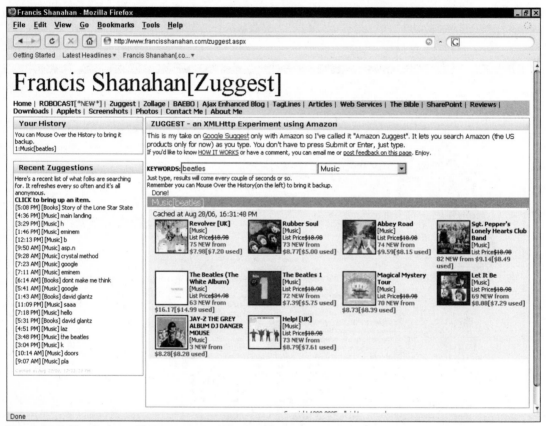

Figure 16-7: The Amazon Zuggest user interface

Understanding the Architecture

The architecture of the Zuggest similar to what you have already seen. It does contain a few performance and caching enhancements that are worthy of review. The architecture is shown in Figure 16-8.

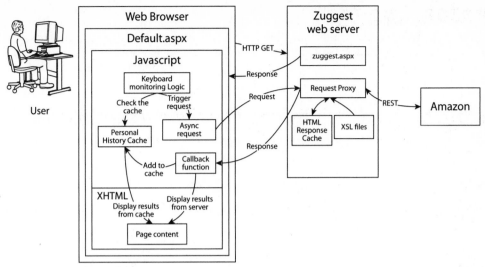

Figure 16-8: Amazon Zuggest technical architecture

How It Works

The user is presented with a typical search interface minus the actual Search button. The user can choose an Amazon search index to query and type in a search item.

As the user types the browser page begins retrieving results from Amazon. Each search result includes a thumbnail of the Amazon product.

The user can stop typing at any moment and click a product to be brought to that product page on Amazon.

Zuggest Features

One of the factors contributing to the success of Zuggest is its overall speed. I have received many requests from curious users inquiring about how the application can provide results as fast as it does. To enable this level of performance, Zuggest uses a number of strategies under the covers.

The first is a pre-emptive strategy on the client side. Rather than conducting a search for each and every keyboard click, the application uses a timer in JavaScript to detect when the user has stopped typing.

There is an assumption here that most users will type a series of keys in rapid succession. In practice, this has proven to be true. Most users will type about three characters within 1 or 2 seconds.

The Zuggest interface waits until there is a pause of about 700 milliseconds in the keystrokes. When this happens, it is assumed that the user has stopped typing.

Chapter 16

The second optimization has been made to the data proxy on the server. The proxy class on the Web server maintains a rolling cache of search criteria in the application cache. Before issuing a Web service call, the application will check if the same call has recently been made and, if so, it simply takes the search results and passes them back to the browser. This not only increases performance, but also reduces the load on the Amazon ECS servers and helps keep the application within the daily allowed request limits.

The final optimization is yet another JavaScript strategy. All results obtained by the page from the server are stored in a local JavaScript array. In this manner, if users want to bring back up a set of search results previously viewed, they can simply click their history, and the results are displayed instantly with no additional server traffic.

You can view Zuggest at the following URL:

```
http://www.FrancisShanahan.com/zuggest.aspx
```

Robocast

Robocast is an example of how mashups can take a service and re-package it to increase data accessibility. Robocast is the world's first (and only) *robotic feed podcast generator*.

What's a Podcast?

A *podcast* is an audio blog. What's that you say? If you write a blog, each RSS entry contains text. Some people choose to record their blog as an audio file (typically an MP3 file) that is enclosed in the RSS feed items. Subscribers can listen to these blogs instead of reading them. The associated audio MP3 files are typically downloaded to an MP3 player and updated, just as traditional RSS content is updated.

How It Works

Robocast works by literally reading an RSS feed and recording the result. By using the Microsoft's Speech API (SAPI 5.1), I was able to easily convert the text from the RSS feeds into MP3 files.

The resulting MP3s are published via FTP to my personal Web site, along with a new RSS feed that includes an <enclosure> tag.

With Robocast, you can convert *any* RSS 2.0 feed into a podcast. This is great if you want to monitor a blog, but aren't going to be at a computer to read it. It's also very useful if you're partially sighted and just can't be bothered straining your eyes. For the blind, it opens up a new avenue to explore the world of blogging and RSS.

You can try out Robocast here:

```
http://www.FrancisShanahan.com/robocast
```

BaeBo

BaeBo is an online store that combines almost every technique in this book. BaeBo integrates a wide range of APIs together, and attempts to cross-pollinate content in the context of the shopping experience (Figure 16-9).

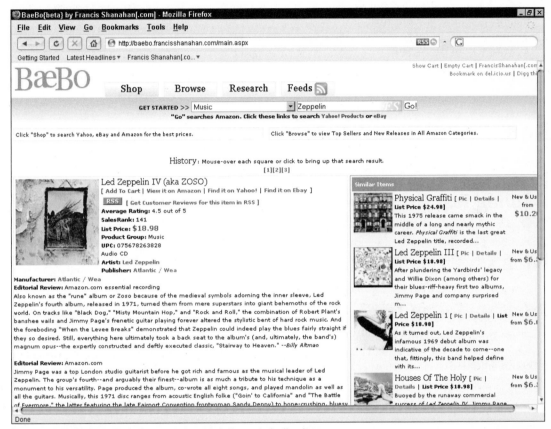

Figure 16-9: BaeBo displaying product details and similar items

Through BaeBo, you can browse, search, and purchase products from Amazon's entire product catalog. When you search Amazon, BaeBo will load eBay results in the background. When you view details of an Amazon product, BaeBo will load similar products in the background! You can create Product feeds through RSS for Amazon Product data. This allows you to stay up-to-date on any set of products and their prices, so you never miss a deal.

BaeBo has a WML interface similar to that implemented in Chapter 14. When you're on the move, you can search Amazon's product database using your BlackBerry! You can comparison-shop with eBay and Yahoo Products to find the absolute best price.

As you're shopping, you can search Google for Web sites referencing the products you're interested in, or *any* Web result for that matter. You can query Flickr for photos of a specific product, or Technorati for people blogging about a product in real time! BaeBo will also let you find Top Selling products and New Releases in a given category.

BaeBo supports Amazon's remote shopping cart so you can add and purchase items on BaeBo through Amazon without affecting your existing shopping cart at Amazon. The site maintains no personal information; it's entirely confidential.

You can try out BaeBo here:

```
http://baebo.FrancisShanahan.com
```

Some Additional Ideas

The following are ideas that I have not implemented, but that you may find useful to explore.

A Turing Test Using Amazon Images

Here's a thought that illustrates the power of Web services when combined with a little lateral thinking. Spam is a big problem for sites today. One form of spam is that of automated robots creating fake registrations for online services. Registration pages today typically employ some means of determining if the registrant is a human as opposed to an automated Web robot. This is a Turing test of sorts.

What's a Turing Test?

Alan Turing was a British mathematician who invented the notion of a test to tell a computer apart from a human being. The human and machine are kept hidden, and only interacted with through a common communication channel, typically a keyboard.

Questions are asked and responses are given. The goal is to figure out, based on the responses, which is the computer and which is the human.

This mechanism deters fake registrations. Typically, this is implemented by generating an image (which a robot can't read) of a word. That image is obscured somehow, perhaps by skewing the lettering in the word. This essentially defeats optical character-recognition software.

An alternative idea is to perform two `ItemSearches` against the Amazon database, one for a known element, the other for something unknown. For example, try searching for Eggs and Meat. This will yield two sets of products.

Next, present the images from the results in a grid, let's say 9×9 — six of the images from the meat and three from the egg result.

The user would then be prompted to click the egg-related images. Three correct results would affirm with some reasonable level of assurance that the candidate was indeed a human. Because the results are different every time, it would be impossible to create an automated Web 'bot to crack the code.

Leveraging Microsoft Atlas

In this book, you've learned how to implement Ajax from the ground up. There are commercial libraries available, however, that insulate you from the trials and tribulations of XmlHttpRequest. Atlas is Microsoft's Ajax library and, as of this writing, it is still in beta.

You can learn more about Atlas at the following URL:

```
http://atlas.asp.net/Default.aspx
```

What Is Atlas?

Atlas is a set of .NET assemblies and ASP.NET server-side controls that provide asynchronous processing to existing ASP.NET Web sites.

Atlas uses a declarative programming model. By adding tags to a page, you can easily enable asynchronous communication and rich client-side behavior in an application.

For example, Atlas provides a new control called the UpdatePanel. This control allows you to identify a region of a page that should update independently of the remainder of the page. Traditional ASP.NET server-side controls can be placed on an UpdatePanel, and the UpdatePanel will take care of generating the appropriate JavaScript to update those controls asynchronously.

If you have existing ASP.NET applications, consider Atlas as the path of least resistance toward rich browser functionality.

Integration with the Microsoft Portals

Microsoft has two popular portal offerings on the Internet today: the Live.com portal and the Start.com portal. If you take a look at these sites, you will immediately notice that they follow a very similar visual metaphor. Wow, a "visual metaphor" sounds complicated. This just means they approach things such as navigation, layout, and so on, in a similar way.

Each screen is composed of various portlets displaying various news headlines and assorted data. These screen portlets are known as *gadgets*, and they follow a specific development paradigm.

You can take the development techniques and code from earlier chapters in this book and use them to build a gadget that can be deployed and installed into Microsoft Live.

The Microsoft Gadget

A gadget consists of the source code of the gadget itself, and a specific file that describes the gadget and its resources. This is the *gadget manifest* and every gadget must have one. The manifest file is an XML document and follows the RSS format. The manifest defines various properties of the gadget (such as the title, a link to the publisher's site, a description, and so on). It also defines where to obtain the source code for the gadget.

The following is an example gadget manifest. As you can see, gadgets are not in any way complicated:

```xml
<?xml version="1.0" ?>
    <rss version="2.0" xmlns:binding="http://www.start.com">
        <channel>
            <title>Baebo Search</title>
            <link>http://baebo.francisshanahan.com</link>
            <description>Search Amazon products through Baebo from within Live.com or
Start.com and get RSS feeds of the search results. </description>
            <language>en-us</language>
            <pubDate>Tue, 15 Mar 2006 16:30:00 GMT</pubDate>
            <binding:type>Gadget.BaeboSearch</binding:type>
            <item>
                <link>http://www.francisshanahan.com/baebogadget/BaeboSearch.js</link>
            </item>
            <item>
            <link
binding:type="css">http://www.francisshanahan.com/baebogadget/BaeboSearch.css</link
>
            </item>
        </channel>
</rss>
```

By implementing a gadget and deploying it to a site like Live.com, you can potentially reach a far broader audience with your application than writing a mashup and deploying it on your own site.

Gadget Design Guidelines

Gadgets are tiny little areas on a page, so there are some general design guidelines you should consider when creating the user interface:

❑ *Keep the user interface clean* — Don't try to clutter up the area with complicated backgrounds and so on. Neutral text on a white background is a classic look that won't confuse the user.

❑ *Keep the gadget's purpose clear* — Typically, a gadget should provide just one service or feature. Don't try building the be-all and end-all Swiss army knife of gadgets.

An Email Attachment Manager Using S3

How many times have you tried to attach a large file to an email, only to have it get bounced back by the recipient's mailbox? Amazon's Simple Storage Service could be used to solve this problem.

A sample implementation might look like this:

1. Create a plug-in into your mail client (for example, Microsoft Outlook).

2. When attaching large files to your email, the files are uploaded to the Amazon S3 servers.

3. A link to the Amazon S3 object is inserted into the email.

4. The recipient can the use this link to access the attachment.

Your email account benefits by not having to store the attachment in your Sent Items, the email server benefits by not having to send this file, and the recipient's Inbox benefits by not having to accept such a large attachment.

You could further enhance this notion to allow collaborative development of files by implementing a check-in, check-out paradigm, for example.

Amazon Access via Windows Media Center

Windows Media Center is Microsoft's implementation of a personal video recorder. It's essentially a PC-powered television. With Windows Media Center, you can view and record television, pause live television, view an enhanced programming guide, and easily set up recurring recording schedules that update even if the time and date of the broadcast changes.

It would be nice to be able to browse Amazon's database from within the Media Center experience. Initial investigation reveals that the Windows Media Center environment uses an HTML-based interface. Using the techniques in this book and some experimentation, it would be a relatively simple task to build an interface into Amazon that was accessible for users of Media Center.

This channel is still emerging, and the user base is in its infancy. A smart Amazon affiliate could quickly capture the Media Center market with little competition.

Summary

In this chapter, I've described a number of applications that are built on the techniques described throughout this book. That list includes the following applications:

- ❑ *TagLines* — An up-to-the-minute news-tag visualization
- ❑ *Zollage* — An unorthodox combination of art and entropy
- ❑ *Zuggest* — A search interface that provides Amazon results in near real time
- ❑ *Robocast* — An automated tool that converts RSS feeds into MP3 audio podcast feeds
- ❑ *BaeBo* — An online shopping experience combining more than ten different Web APIs

As you can see, the earlier chapters are essentially building blocks that you can use as you see fit to create your own remarkable creations.

I've also provided a few ideas that have yet to be implemented. Again, these are just intended to stimulate the imagination and provoke some lateral thinking.

I hope you have enjoyed this book. I have certainly enjoyed writing it. I encourage you to take the lessons learned in this book and combine them with a nice bottle of red wine over dinner, and get out there and invent your own Web 2.0.

The E-Commerce Service FAQ

This appendix provides valuable information about the ECS in the form of commonly asked questions and answers.

Q: What's an FAQ?

A: An FAQ is a list of Frequently Asked Questions.

Accessing the ECS

Q: If I sign up and obtain an `AWSAccessKeyId`, *do I have to use it?*

A: No, once you register you are under no obligation to actually use the service.

Q: Does is cost anything to register?

A: No. Registration with the Amazon Web Services Platform is free.

Q: Where is the Amazon ECS WSDL located?

A: The ECS WSDL is located here:

```
http://webservices.amazon.com/AWSECommerceService/AWSECommerceService.wsdl
```

General ECS Questions

Q: Where can I find sample code?

A: Amazon has sample code available in a number of languages. Find it at the following URL:

```
http://aws.amazon.com
```

Q: Can I submit content to Amazon through the ECS?

A: The Amazon ECS is a read-only service. You can only extract information from Amazon. You can, however, create and manage shopping carts that are temporary storage for the purpose of online shopping.

Q: Can users set up an Amazon customer account through my site?

A: Unfortunately, no. Accounts can only be set up directly through the `Amazon.com` Web site.

Q: Do I have to fulfill orders sold on my site?

A: No. Product delivery is taken care of by Amazon.

Q. *How can I be notified when the Amazon API changes?*

A: Amazon provides email notifications through the developer connection for a specific topic. Log in to your developer account at `http://developer.amazonwebservices.com`. Navigate to the Release Notes listing page. To the right of the screen is a "Watch Category." Click this link to be notified whenever new release notes are posted.

Q. *Will my code break if Amazon changes its API?*

A. Amazon tends to maintain backward-compatibility when it updates the API. In most cases, your code will not break. It's important to review what has changed, however, to mitigate any potential risks of downtime. Use the email and RSS feeds mentioned earlier to stay up-to-date with the latest changes.

Q: Can my users be assured their information is confidential?

A: Yes. The Amazon Shopping Cart is stored on Amazon's Web servers. The checkout process involves directing the user to Amazon's site, and completing the order from within `Amazon.com`. The user's credit card is never exposed to the third-party site.

ECS Detailed Usage

Q: How can I find the Top Sellers for a particular category?

A: The `Amazon.com` Web site often has links to display the top-selling items within a specific category. To obtain the same results from the ECS, you need to perform a `BrowseNodeLookup` operation, specify the `BrowseNodeId` of the category you are interested in, and, finally, specify the `TopSellers` `ResponseGroup` to be included in the response.

The following example shows how to obtain the top-selling items in Books:

```
http://ecs.amazonaws.com/onca/xml?Service=AWSECommerceService&AWSAccessKeyId=[YOUR
ID HERE]&Operation=BrowseNodeLookup&BrowseNodeId=283155&ResponseGroup=TopSellers
```

Q: How can I find the New Releases for a particular category?

A: To obtain new releases for a given category, use the `BrowseNodeLookup` operation, specify the `BrowseNodeId` of the category you're interested in, and request the `NewReleases ResponseGroup` to be returned.

You can combine multiple `ResponseGroups` in a single request by separating them with a comma. The following URL will retrieve top-selling items, as well as new releases, in a single request/response:

```
http://ecs.amazonaws.com/onca/xml?Service=AWSECommerceService&AWSAccessKeyId=[YOUR ID
HERE]&Operation=BrowseNodeLookup&BrowseNodeId=283155&ResponseGroup=TopSellers,
NewReleases
```

Q: Can I get more than ten results returned for either a Top Sellers or New Releases query?

A: Not at this time. Only ten Top Sellers or New Releases are available in a single request. You can also combine Top Sellers and New Releases to get 20 total results in a single request.

Q: Can customers create Wish Lists through my site?

A: Not at this time. Currently, Wish Lists can only be created through Amazon's Web site. There are no APIs available for creating a wish list.

Q: Do I have to manage returned items?

A: No. Items sold through the ECS that end up being returned are managed through the normal process defined at `Amazon.com`.

Q: Do all products have images?

A: No. Some products do not have any images at all; others contain only a `SmallImage` and no `Medium` or `Large`. Be sure to always test for the existence of a value before using these properties.

Q: How many requests can I make to the ECS per day?

A: You can make as many requests as needed, as long as you do not exceed more than one request per second from a single IP address.

Q: How can I determine if an item is available for sale?

A: The ECS can return items in search results that are not always available for sale. This might be for a number of reasons (for example, the item is out of stock or has not yet been released). To check availability, you can refer to the `Availability` node within the `ItemLookupResponse`. This node is contained within the `ItemLookupResponse/Items/Item/Offers/Offer/OfferListing/Availability` node.

Alternatively, if you know the `MerchantId` of a given merchant, you can perform an `ItemSearch` against that merchant and specify the `Availability` parameter. Setting `Availability` to `"Available"` and specifying the condition of the item in an `ItemSearch` will return only items that are currently available for purchase.

Q: Is the Amazon REST API case-sensitive?

A: Yes, case is important. `ItemSearch`, for example, is a valid operation, whereas `itemsearch` is not valid.

Q: How can I ensure prices displayed are in the right currency?

A: You can get location-specific currencies by using the right locale with your queries. To specify the locale in REST, simply send the request to the right base URL.

Q: What are the available locales?

A: There are six available locales. To search against a given locale, you must change the base URL of the request. The following tables list the URL for each locale.

Locale	Code	URL
United States	US	`http://webservices.amazon.com/onca/xml`
France	FR	`http://webservices.amazon.fr/onca/xml`
United Kingdom	UK	`http://webservices.amazon.co.uk/onca/xml`
Canada	CA	`http://webservices.amazon.ca/onca/xml`
Japan	JP	`http://webservices.amazon.co.jp/onca/xml`
Germany	DE	`http://webservices.amazon.de/onca/xml`

Access Keys and Identifiers

Q: What is a `SubscriptionId`?

A: The `SubscriptionId` is a legacy identifier that was used to identify developers in the ECS. This identifier has been replaced by the `AWSAccessKeyId` and is no longer used, although you may see it referenced in documentation from time to time. You should use `AWSAccessKeyId` moving forward.

Q: Do I need a Secret Access Key Id to use the ECS?

A: No. The Secret Access Key Id is not needed for the ECS. It is used with other Amazon services such as the S3.

Q: What's the difference between an `AssociateID` *and an* `AWSAccessKeyID`*?*

A: The `AWSAccessKeyId` is a developer access code. An `AssociateId` enables tracking of usage and referrals from third-party sites. You can have an `AWSAccessKeyId` without having an `AssociateId`, and vice versa. You need to include the `AWSAccessKeyId` in every request into the Amazon ECS. The `AssociateId` is optional, and only required to earn commission on sales.

Q: How can I ensure that I'm using a specific version of the ECS?

A: Specify the `Version` parameter in your REST requests to limit execution to that version of the API. The following requests data from the `2005-03-23` version of the ECS:

```
http://ecs.amazonaws.com/onca/xml?Service=AWSECommerceService&AWSAccessKeyId=[YOUR
ID HERE]&Operation=ItemLookup&ItemId=0470097779&Version=2005-03-23
```

Note that this executes against the `March` version of the ECS, not the `March` version of the Amazon database.

To use the most recent version of the API, simply leave off the `Version` parameter.

Amazon Associates

Q: How do I know if I'm earning money?

A: You can obtain a report or any earnings from the Amazon Associates' Web site located at `http://associates.amazon.com`.

Q: How much does the Amazon Associate Program pay?

A: Amazon uses a tiered referral rate structure to calculate earnings. The tier structure is shown in the following table.

Total Items Shipped	Referral Fee (Consumer Electronics)	Referral Fee All other Categories
1-20	4.00%	4.00%
21-90	4.00%	6.00%
91-330	4.00%	6.50%
331-940	4.00%	7.00%
941-1880	4.00%	8.00%
1881-4700	4.00%	8.00%
4701-9400	4.00%	8.25%
9401+	4.00%	8.50%

Q: Are referral fees calculated on the sales price or the retail price of the item?

A: Referral fees are calculated on the Sales price of the item shipped.

Q: When will I be paid?

A: Associates are paid quarterly, shortly after the calendar quarter has ended.

Q: Do I have to register as a credit card merchant?

A: No. You don't need a merchant ID, nor do you have to handle credit card transactions. The checkout process is entirely managed by Amazon.

Q: I'm not a developer; can I still become an Amazon Associate?

A: Yes, absolutely. In fact, there is little to no programming required to get an Amazon Associates store up and running.

Q: What types of resources are available for non-programmers?

A: The Amazon Associates site provides tools to facilitate building HTML snippets and links to products that contain your Associate ID. The HTML for these elements can then be copied and pasted directly into your own Web site.

Q: I'd like to defer payment owed through the Associates program for tax purposes. Is there a way to do this?

A: You will need to discuss this with Amazon directly. Contact the Amazon Associates group at the following URL:

```
http://associates.amazon.com
```

Q: Can I include links to Amazon products on pages other than my own site? Will I earn commissions if this item is purchased?

A: Yes. As long as the link is built correctly and contains your Associate ID, click-throughs will be tracked and commission earned in the event of a sale.

Q: Can I become an associate and then purchase items from myself to earn commission?

A: No. Amazon discourages this practice, and filters out items bought in this manner from commissions earned.

Remote Cart

Q: How can I add multiple items to the Amazon shopping cart?

A: You can add multiple items in a single CartAdd operation by specifying additional Item parameters in the REST URL, as shown here:

```
http://ecs.amazonaws.com/onca/xml?Service=AWSECommerceService&AWSAccessKeyId=[YOUR
ID HERE]&Operation=CartAdd&Item.1.ASIN=[FIRST ITEM ASIN HERE]&Item.2.ASIN=[SECOND
ITEM ASIN HERE]
```

Searching and Browsing

Q: How can I test if a node is present in the Amazon response?

A: To check if a node exists in an XML response, use the XSL `exists` method as follows:

```
<xsl:if test="exists(/MyNode) ">
 <!-- Do Something here -->
</xsl:if>
```

Q: Can I do an `ItemLookup` *for more than one product at a time?*

A: Yes. Perform an `ItemLookup` and specify the `ItemIds` as a comma-separated list to request details for more than one product in a single request.

Q: I need to sort results. What can I sort by?

A: Valid sort values vary by `SearchIndex`. For example, you can generally sort all products by price or sales rank, but only books can be sorted by publication date. For a full list of the valid sort values by `SearchIndex`, refer to the ECS documentation.

Q: How do I include ampersands in the search keywords?

A: You need to encode ampersands using standard URL encoding. For example, `%26` is the equivalent of & in a URL.

To search for the Coldplay album "X&Y," the REST URL would look like this:

```
http://ecs.amazonaws.com/onca/xml?Service=AWSECommerceService&AWSAccessKeyId=[YOUR
KEY HERE]&Operation=ItemSearch&SearchIndex=Music&Keywords=X%26Y
```

Q: I have an ISBN for a book but no ASIN. How can I look it up?

A: You can specify the ISBN number as the `ItemId` in place of the ASIN. The following example locates this book on Amazon. In most cases, a book's ISBN is also its ASIN.

```
http://ecs.amazonaws.com/onca/xml?Service=AWSECommerceService&AWSAccessKeyId=[YOUR
KEY HERE]&Operation=ItemLookup&ItemId=0470097779
```

Q: Do `BrowseNodeId` *values ever change?*

A: Yes. `BrowseNodeIds` sometimes change. Changes are infrequent but `BrowseNodeIds` are not guaranteed static.

Q: What is the list of all available `SearchIndexes`?

A: As of this writing, the `SearchIndex` parameter possible values were as follows: `Blended`, `Apparel`, `Baby`, `Beauty`, `Books`, `Classical`, `DigitalMusic`, `DVD`, `Electronics`, `GourmetFood`, `HealthPersonalCare`, `Jewelry`, `Kitchen`, `Magazines`, `Merchants`, `Miscellaneous`, `Music`, `MusicalInstruments`, `MusicTracks`, `OfficeProducts`, `OutdoorLiving`, `PCHardware`, `PetSupplies`, `Photo`, `Restaurants`, `Software`, `SportingGoods`, `Tools`, `Toys`, `VHS`, `Video`, `VideoGames`, `Wireless`, `WirelessAccessories`.

Always refer to the documentation for the most up-to-date list of values.

Q: What is the `SearchBins ResponseGroup` *and what can I use it for?*

A: Specifying the `SearchBins ResponseGroup` will categorize items returned by an `ItemSearch` into groups or bins. Bins are predefined, and can be specified with an additional parameter named `NarrowBy`. Valid `NarrowBy` values vary by `SearchIndex`, but the main values are `PriceRange`, `SpecialSize`, `Merchant`, `Subject`, or `BrandName`.

Q: What are the `BrowseNodeIds` *for the major product categories?*

A: The major product categories and their associated `BrowseNodeIds` are listed in the following table.

SearchIndex	BrowseNodeId
Books	283155
Music	5174
DVD	130
Unbox Video Downloads	16261631
VHS	404272
Magazines & Newspapers	599858
Computer & Video Games	468642
Software	229534
Amazon Shorts	13993911
Electronics	172282
Audio & Video	1065836
Camera & Photo	502394
Cell Phones & Service	301185
Computers & PC Hardware	541966
Office Products	1064954
Musical Instruments	11091801

SearchIndex	BrowseNodeId
Home & Garden	1055398
Bed & Bath	1057792
Furniture & Décor	1057794
Gourmet Food	3370831
Kitchen & Housewares	284507
Outdoor Living	286168
Pet Supplies	12923371
Automotive	15684181
Tools & Hardware	228013
Industrial & Scientific	16310091
Apparel & Accessories	1036592
Shoes	1040068
Jewelry & Watches	3367581
Grocery	16310101
Beauty	3760911
Health & Personal Care	3760901
Sports & Outdoors	3375251
Toys & Games	165793011
Baby	165796011

Q: Are all SearchIndex *values valid in all locales?*

A: No. Certain SearchIndex values are not valid in certain locales. For example, searching GourmetFood against the UK local will not work. The ECS documentation contains a matrix of valid locale versus SearchIndex values.

Resources

Q: Where are the developer forums located?

A: Amazon developer forums are available from the AWS developer connection site, located at the following address:

```
http://developer.amazonwebservices.com/connect/forumindex.jspa
```

Q: I just created a great new application. How can I tell the world about it?

A: You can submit your application to the Amazon Web Services Blog at the following URL:

```
http://aws.typepad.com
```

They will be happy to announce it for you.

Q: Where can I find more information about the author?

A: You can read my blog, access source code, and play with various experiments of mine at the following URL:

```
http://www.FrancisShanahan.com
```

Q: Where can I find a good list of all the Web 2.0 APIs available?

A: One of the best resources for mashup and API information is the following:

```
http://www.ProgrammableWeb.com
```

Exercise Answers

Chapter 4 Answers

1. There are three ways to add a style sheet to a page in ASP.NET:

   a. Drag and drop the style sheet from the Solution Explorer onto a page's design surface.

   b. Manually add the `<link href="myStyles.css" type="text/css" rel="stylesheet"/>` tag in the page's `<head>` section.

   c. Add the style sheet using a Theme.

2. ASP.NET supports dynamically re-styling a site through Themes and Skins.

3. ASP.NET supports Microsoft Access, any ADO.NET-compliant datasource (such as SQL Server 2005 or SQL Server Express), any .NET class (such as a business class), an ASP.NET sitemap, or a plain old XML file as valid datasources.

4. To bind a `GridView` to an XML file, simply create a datasource using the Data Configuration Wizard and specify which set of nodes to present in the `GridView` using either an XSLT file or an XPath expression.

5. ASP.NET supports storing a sitemap in XML. ASP.NET comes with a set of navigation controls whose content can be driven off of this sitemap file. The main Navigation controls are a `SiteMapPath`, `Menu`, and `TreeView`.

6. A *theme* in ASP.NET is a collection of resources applied to a site. The theme forms the overall visual appearance of the site. *Skins* are specific styles tied to a given control type (for example, a calendar control or grid control). Skins can be specific to a particular instance of a control, or applied to all controls of a given type. Themes *include* skins, as well as CSS sheets, images, and other resources.

Here's an example of a skin for a `GridView` control:

```
<asp:GridView runat="server" CellPadding="4" ForeColor="#333333"
        GridLines="None">
        <FooterStyle BackColor="#507CD1" Font-Bold="True" ForeColor="White" />
        <RowStyle BackColor="#EFF3FB" />
        <EditRowStyle BackColor="#2461BF" />
        <SelectedRowStyle BackColor="#D1DDF1" Font-Bold="True" ForeColor="#333333"
/>
        <PagerStyle BackColor="#2461BF" ForeColor="White" HorizontalAlign="Center"
/>
        <HeaderStyle BackColor="#507CD1" Font-Bold="True" ForeColor="White" />
        <AlternatingRowStyle BackColor="White" />
    </asp:GridView>
```

7. Master Pages are a feature of ASP.NET that allows developers to create a generic page template, including layout and content regions. That template can then be reused in a declarative way by other pages within the site.

8. No. You can use whatever tools you're comfortable with. This book uses the Microsoft Visual Studio tool set because it is arguably one of the most productive development environments available — and it's free.

Chapter 5 Answers

1. HTML is not necessarily well-formed XML, whereas XHTML is. XHTML adheres to an XML DTD.

2. RSS and Atom are both XML-based structures used to syndicate content.

3. Any service that relies on the caller to provide all necessary state information can be called a REST-style API. REST APIs are stateless, and assume no state management on the part of the service provider.

4. XML-RPC and SOAP are both approaches to invoking Web methods using XML and HTTP.

5. hCard is a microformat aimed at describing personal contact information on a Web site.

6. No. REST can use any mechanism that transfers state into the method.

7. No. REST is, strictly speaking, an architectural style. It's a way of programming, not a specification or rigid mechanism.

8. Microformats are situational solutions to specific problems. Again, they are not rigid specifications aimed at being extensible and infinitely scalable. They are simple formats or approaches combining presentation and structure to display information. Why not invent your own?

9. This is a trick question. The truth is they each have their place. Each has its own set of pros and cons. SOAP is a rigid specification and, as such, can be heavyweight in terms of the amount of data traveling across the network. REST tends to be more free-form, which lends itself to getting an application up and running quickly. On the other hand, it is poorly structured and doesn't perhaps have the same support for long-running transactions, secure conversations, and addressability as SOAP. So, you see there is no real answer to this. It's best to be aware of each style, and then choose what's right for a given situation.

Chapter 6 Answers

1. The three main approaches to mashing data include the following:

- ❑ Mashing on the server
- ❑ Ajax
- ❑ JSON/Dynamic Scripting

2. "Ajax" is an acronym for "Asynchronous JavaScript and XML." Ajax is the name of the approach whereby data is requested from a Web server using JavaScript, and the Web server responds with XML.

3. Following are the pros of Ajax:

- ❑ Better perceived performance
- ❑ Good separation of presentation and business logic
- ❑ Good scalability (offloads processing to the browser)

Following are the cons of Ajax:

- ❑ Many moving parts that can be difficult to develop and debug
- ❑ The browser's Back button and history functionality are essentially disabled by using an Ajax model

4. Following are the pros of JSON:

- ❑ Simple and direct communication with the partner site
- ❑ Can be easier to read than XML

Following are the cons of a JSON/Dynamic Scripting approach:

- ❑ No opportunity to mash data on the server using the Dynamic Script method
- ❑ Not as many parsers for JSON as say XML

Chapter 7 Answers

1. You can easily switch locales by pointing the SOAP client to a new Amazon SOAP endpoint. This setting is stored in the `web.config` file.

```
<appSettings>
    <add key="com.amazon.webservices.AWSECommerceService"
value="http://soap.amazon.co.uk/onca/soap?Service=AWSECommerceService"/>
    </appSettings>
```

Change it to one of the values in the following table, depending on the desired locale.

Locale	WSDL Endpoint URI
US	http://soap.amazon.com/onca/soap?Service=AWSECommerceService
UK	http://soap.amazon.co.uk/onca/soap?Service=AWSECommerceService
DE	http://soap.amazon.de/onca/soap?Service=AWSECommerceService
JP	http://soap.amazon.co.jp/onca/soap?Service=AWSECommerceService
FR	http://soap.amazon.fr/onca/soap?Service=AWSECommerceService
CA	http://soap.amazon.ca/onca/soap?Service=AWSECommerceService

2. To create an `XmlDocument` from scratch, utilize the `XmlDocument`, `XmlNode`, and `XmlAttribute` classes within the `System.Xml` namespace. Here's some example code that builds the following output:

```
<album title="BBC Sessions">
    <song>Out on the Tiles</song>
    <song />
    <song>Achilles Last Stand</song>
</album>

// Create a new document
XmlDocument myXml = new XmlDocument();

// Create a new element node named "album"
XmlNode myAlbum = myXml.CreateNode(XmlNodeType.Element, "album", "");

// Create an attribute for this node, called "title" with a value of "BBC Sessions"
XmlAttribute albumName = myXml.CreateAttribute("title");
albumName.Value = "BBC Sessions";

// Add the attribute to the node
myAlbum.Attributes.Append(albumName);

// Add the album node to the document
myXml.AppendChild(myAlbum);

// Create some "song" nodes
XmlNode mySongA = myXml.CreateNode(XmlNodeType.Element, "song", "");
XmlNode mySongB = myXml.CreateNode(XmlNodeType.Element, "song", "");
XmlNode mySongC = myXml.CreateNode(XmlNodeType.Element, "song", "");
mySongA.InnerText = "Out on the Tiles";
mySongC.InnerText = "Achilles Last Stand";

// Add the child nodes this node
myAlbum.AppendChild(mySongA);
myAlbum.AppendChild(mySongB);
myAlbum.AppendChild(mySongC);
```

3. To search Amazon using the SOAP interface, you must construct an `ItemSearch` query as follows:

```
// Create a new instance of the proxy class
AWSECommerceService myProxy = new AWSECommerceService();

// Create a new instance of the ItemSearch class
ItemSearch mySearch = new ItemSearch();

// ItemSearchRequest stores the actual request parameters
ItemSearchRequest mySearchRequest = new ItemSearchRequest();

// Set some parameters, Keyword and Search Index
mySearchRequest.Keywords = strKeywords;
mySearchRequest.SearchIndex = strSearchIndex;

// Just need Small results, not the full enchilada
mySearchRequest.ResponseGroup = new string[] { "Medium", "Request" };

// Set the subscription and associate tags here
mySearch.AWSAccessKeyId = ConfigurationManager.AppSettings["AWSAccessKeyId"];
mySearch.AssociateTag = ConfigurationManager.AppSettings["AssociateTag"];

// Setup request
mySearch.Request = new ItemSearchRequest[] { mySearchRequest };

// Execute the request and get the response
ItemSearchResponse myResponse = myProxy.ItemSearch(mySearch);
```

4. The `appSettings` section of the `web.config` file is a great place to store configuration information in an ASP.NET Web site. You can access values using the following code:

```
string myVar = ConfigurationManager.AppSettings["AWSAccessKeyId"];
```

Chapter 8 Answers

1. Assuming you have a valid XML document, it can be used to populate a `DataSet` using an `XmlNodeReader`.

```
XmlNodeReader myReader = new XmlNodeReader(myDoc);
DataSet ds = new DataSet();
ds.ReadXml(myReader);
```

2. XSL can be used to transform XML documents using the following code snippet:

```
/// <summary>
/// Transforms an xml document using an XSL style sheet
/// </summary>
/// <param name="myDoc">the XML to tranform</param>
/// <param name="strXsl">The filename of the XSL file to use</param>
/// <returns>The transformed document as a string</returns>
public static string DoXSLTransformation(XmlDocument myDoc, string strXsl)
{
```

```
// Create an XSL transformation
XslCompiledTransform myProcessor = new XslCompiledTransform();

// Load the XSL document
myProcessor.Load(
  System.Web.HttpContext.Current.Server.MapPath(strXsl));

// Create a text writer for use in the transformation
StringWriter myWriter = new StringWriter();

// Transform the source XML document
myProcessor.Transform(myDoc, (XsltArgumentList)null, myWriter);

// Return the result as a string
return myWriter.ToString();
}
```

3.   HTTP GET requests can be issued using the following function:

```
/// <summary>
/// Retrieves a Uri using HTTP GET and returns the results as XML
/// </summary>
/// <param name="strURL">Uri to retrive</param>
/// <returns>Xml document results</returns>
public static XmlDocument GetUri(string strURI){

    // Create a request object
    HttpWebRequest myRequest = (HttpWebRequest)WebRequest.Create(strURI);

    // Obtain the response from the server
    HttpWebResponse myResponse = (HttpWebResponse)myRequest.GetResponse();
    Stream myResponseStream = myResponse.GetResponseStream();

    // Load the result into an XML document
    XmlDocument myDoc = new XmlDocument();
    myDoc.Load(myResponseStream);

    // return the XML document
    return myDoc;
}
```

Chapter 9 Answers

1.   XSL can parse hierarchical tree structures using named templates and recursion. The following template will parse a BrowseNode structure recursively, printing ancestor nodes before child nodes:

```
<xsl:template match="a:BrowseNode" name="myBranch">
  <xsl:choose>
    <xsl:when test="a:Ancestors/a:BrowseNode">
      <xsl:for-each select="a:Ancestors/a:BrowseNode">
        <xsl:call-template name="myBranch" />
```

```
        </xsl:for-each>
      </xsl:when>
      <xsl:otherwise>
        <br/>
      </xsl:otherwise>
    </xsl:choose>
    &gt;&gt; <xsl:value-of select="a:Name" />
  </xsl:template>
```

2. `XmlHttpRequest` can be used within JavaScript to call back to the server from which the page was served. The following JavaScript code implements a callback in this manner:

```
...
myRequest = new ActiveXObject("Microsoft.XMLHTTP");
if (myRequest) {
            myRequest.onreadystatechange = HandleResponse;
            myRequest.open("GET", myUrl, true);
            myRequest.send();
 }
...


function HandleResponse() {
...
    // Readystate 4 means we're done
    if (myRequest.readyState == 4) {

        // If the server returned OK
        if (myRequest.status == 200) {

            ... Access results using myRequest.responseText...
            myDiv.innerHTML = myRequest.responseText;
    }
 }
```

3. Amazon provides comprehensive error information in the form of a specific set of elements contained in the XML response. These elements are located in the `Items/Request/Errors/Error` branch of the XML response.

4. This is a trick question. The ports are dynamic by default in Visual Studio 2005 and Express editions. Studio no longer requires Internet Explorer as its Web server, so, to avoid conflicts on port 80, a dynamic port is assigned to the IDE's Web server.

5. You never know what a malicious user will do to your site. It's conceivable that a malicious visitor could hack your code and attempt to send malicious content to Amazon on your behalf. Worse still, a malicious user may use your site as a phishing vehicle to fool other users. Validating URLs sent from the browser before forwarding them on is a good practice that you should perform whenever possible.

6. Using `Response.Clear` before you write to the `Response` stream and `Response.End` when you are finished allows you to be sure of what's written to the `Response` stream. Leaving these out may result in ASP.NET tacking on content from the ASPX presentation file.

Chapter 10 Answers

1.   To support YouTube or other data sources, you simply need to augment the code within `getdata.aspx` to support calling out to these services.

2.   To support other forms of Amazon query (such as Baby Registries List lookups or Wedding Registry List inquiries), you would simply need to modify the query sent into `getdata.aspx`. Just as you'd add support for YouTube, you need to modify the `getdata` logic to perform additional query types against Amazon. The `BuildAmazonURL` function would need to be modified to support additional Amazon parameters. This is a relatively straightforward procedure.

3.   Live Search is a paradigm whereby users are searching and results are presented to them as they type in their search criteria. The user doesn't have to click a search button to trigger the query. To implement Live Search using Ajax, there are a couple of options.

    The first is to simply capture the `keypress` event of an HTML text input field. Whenever a key is pressed, that means the text in that input field has changed. Write a JavaScript function to obtain the current value of the text entry and use that to construct a query to your Web server.

    An alternative approach is to use a combination of a JavaScript `timer` object and a `keypress` event handler.

    To start a JavaScript timer use the following code:

```
setTimeout("TimeUp()", 5000);
```

    This will trigger the `TimeUp` function in 5 seconds (5000 milliseconds). Whenever a `keypress` is detected, instead of making an Ajax call, you set a global variable (indicating that the user is still typing) and a timer. That timer expires in, let's say, 2 seconds. When 2 seconds are up, you may choose to make an Ajax call or not, depending on whether the user is still typing.

    In this manner, you can give users a chance to complete entering their search criteria before invoking the actual search. This is a very subtle nuance, but makes a huge difference to the effectiveness of the Live Search.

4.   You can create a JavaScript array with a simple statement:

```
var gXsl = new Array;
```

    There is no need to dimension the array. Simply create a new item and assign an object or variable to that position in the array. In this manner, you can cache a set of XSL documents in an array to improve performance.

5.   If you have a variety of XSL sheets, it's worthwhile considering using JavaScript arrays to cache these once loaded in the browser. You can easily load the XSL sheets once the application loads in the browser and maintain this cache for the duration of the session.

6.   Depending on the browser you're using, the browser may intercept your HTTP calls and match them to its built-in cache. The browser does this to cut down on unnecessary network traffic and improve performance. Being aware of this during your testing can save you hours of detective work.

Chapter 11 Answers

1. You could modify the `iFrame` XSL sheet to produce a thumbnail preview of the You Tube movie. The XSL code from the Movie Mogul example in Chapter 9 could be reused and tweaked to produce the desired layout.

2. You can have Amazon perform a transformation using a publicly available XSL sheet by specifying the `Style` parameter in the URL and providing the fully qualified URL to that file.

3. In ASP.NET, you can specify the content type served by a given page by setting `Response .ContentType`. The content will be interpreted differently by the browser, depending on the content type. For example, `text/html` content will be rendered, whereas `application/zip` might be downloaded.

4. To extend GeoRSS with Yahoo-specific elements, you need to include the `YMaps` namespace in the document:

```
<?xml version="1.0"?>
<rss version="2.0" xmlns:geo="http://www.w3.org/2003/01/geo/wgs84_pos#"
xmlns:ymaps="http://api.maps.yahoo.com/Maps/V1/AnnotatedMaps.xsd">
<channel>
. . .
```

   By including this namespace, you are free to include Ymaps-specific elements such as `<ymaps:ItemUrl>` and so on.

5. There are many mapping APIs out there that provide various styles and levels of geographical data. Two examples are Google and TerraServer.

Chapter 12 Answers

1. JSON is just a notation, a way of writing down an object's properties and data.

2. Absolutely! Ajax and JSON in no way preclude each other. The term Ajax refers to "Asynchronous JavaScript and XML," but there's nothing to prevent you streaming JSON down the data path in place of XML.

3. Yes, security is of paramount importance in every application. When you refer to a third-party domain as the source of your JavaScript, there's nothing to prevent that third party from sending malicious code in place of a valid response. It's best to only use trusted partner sites such as Amazon in this manner, and validate the results whenever possible.

4. JSON is delivered back to the browser in the form of a string that becomes content for a script tag. That content is actually wrapped with a function call. The function is what actually iterates through the content and processes the data.

5. Dynamic scripting involves writing JavaScript to a page's structure at run-time. The script then executes as if it had been a part of the containing page to begin with.

Chapter 13 Answers

1. To create a delegate you first define a delegate type, which follows the function signature:

```
delegate string myDelegateType(string strMsg);
```

Next, create the function itself. This is the function that will be invoked through the delegate:

```
static string DoSomething(string strMsg)
{
  ...
}
```

Finally, create an instance of the delegate:

```
myDelegateType myDelegate = new myDelegateType(DoSomething);
```

2. Delegates are type safe, whereas function pointers are not. This means the compiler can check your code at compile time for correctness. This is a more object-oriented approach than function pointers.

3. ASP.NET and SOAP provide two main options for asynchronous execution during page generation. The two methods are `MethodAsync` and `PageAsyncTasks`.

4. OpenSearch is an XML-based specification designed on top of RSS. OpenSearch lets you expose search results as RSS XML, and syndicate these results to other applications such as `A9.com`.

5. OpenSearch uses the OpenSearch Manifest file to interrogate the actual search application. This file is publicly accessible and stored with the search application. A typical OpenSearch manifest looks like this:

```
<?xml version="1.0" encoding="UTF-8"?>
<OpenSearchDescription xmlns="http://a9.com/-/spec/opensearch/1.1/">
  <ShortName>Mashups Search</ShortName>
  <LongName>Amazon and Google combined search</LongName>
  <Description>Search Amazon and Google in a single shot</Description>
  <Tags>amazon mashup google content rss</Tags>
  <Contact>email@address.com</Contact>
  <Url type="application/rss+xml"
      template="http://[YOUR SITE
HERE]/default.aspx?Keywords={searchTerms}&amp;SearchIndex=Music&amp;ResultsPage={st
artPage}"/>
</OpenSearchDescription>
```

6. To add eBay or another source to the results, simply add a new `PageAsyncTask` as follows:

```
PageAsyncTask ebayTask = new PageAsyncTask(
        new BeginEventHandler(BeginEbaySearch),
        new EndEventHandler(EndEbaySearch),
        new EndEventHandler(TimeoutEbaySearch),
        null);
    RegisterAsyncTask(ebayTask);
```

Implement the `Begin`, `End` and `Timeout` functions just as you did for Amazon. Lastly, consolidate the results in the `Page_PreRenderComplete` event and translate into RSS by modifying the XSLT sheet.

Chapter 14 Answers

1. WAP is the wireless equivalent of HTTP. WAP stands for "Wireless Access Protocol" and is built on top of TCP/IP.

2. Mobile devices are generally extremely limited in their available resources. HTML has evolved over time, and brings with it a number of inefficiencies that make it unsuitable for consumption from a mobile device. WML is a stricter markup implementation that makes better use of the device's resources; this is particularly pertinent when the device in question is a cell phone.

3. In that case, a data proxy on the Web server could be used. The code provided for `getdata.aspx` in earlier chapters would suffice. All that is necessary is that the proxy can execute an XSL transformation and set the `ContentType` of the response stream before sending back the results.

   Although this does introduce a slight inefficiency in terms of the path the data has to travel for sites that do not perform XSL transformation for you, this is the only option.

4. WML uses a notion of cards and decks instead of pages. Cards are analogous to pages, and a deck can contain multiple cards.

5. Depending on your requirements, it may be possible to support multiple devices by designing an XSL sheet to produce the appropriate markup for each device. For example, you might have one XSL sheet that produces WML, another that produces a reduced set of HTML for Palm or Pocket PC devices, and so on.

6. Double dollar signs ($$) will produce a single dollar sign in WML.

Chapter 15 Answers

1. The S3 is Amazon's Simple Storage Service. The purpose is to provide secure, easily scalable storage needs at a low cost through a Web service platform.

2. SHA1 is a hashing algorithm that computes a unique code or hash for a given piece of content. If even a single byte of the original content is modified, it will result in an entirely different hash value being generated by the algorithm. SHA1 is used as part of the Amazon S3 authentication scheme.

3. Any type! The S3 does not differentiate between the types of file stored. All files types are accepted.

4. No. As of this writing, billing information is not available via Web services. This is a feature under consideration for a future release of the platform.

5. S3 Pros are as follows:

   ❑ It's cheaper than purchasing dedicated hardware.

   ❑ Scales as you need it.

   ❑ Only pay for what you use.

   ❑ Lets you be more "agile" as a business.

   ❑ The procurement time for new storage is instantaneous (versus the weeks you might wait for dedicated storage).

   ❑ Files are accessible from anywhere with an Internet connection.

The cons are as follows:

❏ It costs money (in other words, it's not free).

❏ Requires an Internet connection, so you need to go out to the Internet to access your data. This is going to provide slower performance than if the data were stored on the local network.

Index